- obsession - life & its own overthrow balance & ch.
- intolerance of time
- hurry on
- Impatience of time can hardly be separated from the obsession which grows w/ & feeds it.

JAMES JOYCE:

THE POETRY OF CONSCIENCE

Figure One: *Chaplin in Bloom*

JAMES JOYCE:

The Poetry of Conscience

A STUDY of *ULYSSES*

By

MARY PARR

with Figures by KARL PRIEBE

INLAND PRESS

Milwaukee • 1961

Library of Congress Catalogue Card No. 61-18825.
Printed in the United States of America.

FOR ROGER

Pars Magna Totius

CONTENTS

FIGURES

Karl Priebe shares a major perception with Joyce: the artists see the transparency of things. In Joyce this is the diaphane of which Stephen Dedalus speaks when he says, "Signatures of all things I am here to read", (U 38). He reads the names of things through the "ineluctable modality of the visible" and "the ineluctable modality of the audible". Objective then, and as an instrument of creation, Joyce lets objects in the landscape speak to him through their signatures. The signature of anything is its mode of existence; the signature of any person is his name and what it stands for. A stone's mode of existence is through stone being stone; a man's mode of existence is through human act. The sign that stone is stone is read in the transparency of hard matter being hard matter. The sign that man is man is read through the sensate matter of his flesh to the spiritual substance of his being. Joyce is fully conscious of object as object; in the act of existing, the diaphane leaps forth from its vestment of appearance. Things are born anew through the medium of words.

A Priebe painting is diaphanous. What we perceive in the translucent objects of Mr. Priebe's art is illuminated substance bursting forth from the vestment of its appearance to announce that it is an existant in an ascending order of being. The origin of light upon substance is from within the object itself. He shares the diaphane with Joyce in a liberated objectivity, and his joy in the spectacle of creation like Joyce's issues forth in a sane fidelity to morning knowledge of reality.

Joyce's manshape of the mythical Leopold Bloom is a space-time Chaplin clown. Across the centuries from Odysseus to Charlie his signature is a tumbling act of the Flesh. Bloom's sign is mute yearning: "Perfume of embraces all him assailed. With hungered flesh obscurely, he mutely craved to adore." Mr. Priebe's "Chaplin in Bloom" (Frontispiece) is the Chaplin figure in its new office: the mind and heart of the flesh in an agony of yearning for union with Intellect; in a moment of desire for the creative act of life: judgment. "Chaplin in Bloom" is the master image from which Figures Two and Three emerge.

In intellectual cinema the images on the screen of the mind rise up from dream to wed reality respacing the diaphane of time. "Clown Flesh" (p. 3) by Mr. Priebe transferred from the screen of the mind gives new position to Charlie's tattered clown suit. Rather than the costume of a fallen aristocrat whose Flesh causes his downfall, the Chaplin figure in Bloom wears torn clown flesh. He confronts the real world unaware of his nakedness intent only on surviving through a cheeky self-esteem. Odysseus' self esteem as he grieved out his heart in Calypso's cave is cheek on the grand scale. Mediating within the space-time arc of the flesh, Mr. Priebe has delivered Mr. Bloom's primary signature.

"The Condition of Poetry" (p. 97), Bloom's innermost signature, is the diaphane of the apparent good. Rising in mute adoration toward the tremulous Narcissus, Mr. Bloom as Henry Flowers enters his most secret room, and in the sensuous light of the carnation chandelier, even the kidney he eats tastes narcissus. Auto-eroticism as billy club, Burgundy as distilled narcissus, a roc's auk's egg as defining remnant of the species of vanished good create Mr. Bloom's face. The muted trouser button alone in the dim regions of a realm within Henry Flower foreshadows the poetry of conscience to which Bloom ascends. The signs behind Mr. Bloom's rolled newspaper baton with which he saunters through Thursday, June 6, 1904, are arrested in Mr. Priebe's painting in ascent. They interiorize "Chaplin in Bloom."

Preface

What I see in this book I owe to James Joyce. In ten years I have perhaps been through the canon of his works a number of times, and on all the days of those years his art took seed in my thought life and grew toward an awareness of being. Being in itself and being in particular is the primary good of Joyce's art because it is his primary concern as an artist: to grasp the truth of the being of the visible universe.

Being, the very act of a thing's existence, cannot, of course, err. An artist who grasps *esse* and for whom *esse* is the *raison d'etre* of his art confers the gift of certitude upon the century to whom he speaks. My own study of Joyce has evolved from uninformed consternation at the paradox of his art to informed awareness of the poetry of his art. I was conducted to the poetry through interconnecting channels of human and divine being with which his works are endued, and through Joyce's comedic view.

I have not, of course, traveled alone. My companions, all those who have used their critical gift on the phenomenon of Joyce, are many. The diversity of their studies attests to the profundity of modern art, but conflict in judgment among them attests to its arduous novelty. Had I not met with contrariety in Joyce criticism, I am sure I should have rested with satisfaction in the realized beauty of the Joyce works. The contraries within the criticism led me back and back to the Joyce works to see what he himself had to say about the Critic's pronouncement. I began work on a study of *A Portrait of the Artist as a Young Man.* However, while I was writing it, I made the discovery about *Ulysses* which this book contains. The discovery arranged Joyce's exemplar for both *A Portrait* and *Ulysses,* making the early work obsolete and this one generally permanent. I am grateful therefore for the confusion and conflict I found in Joyce studies, for they served as disciplines. This book extends the work of scholars who have pioneered in the metaphysical comprehension of Joyce's art: Mr. Harry Levin, Mr. York Tyndall, Mr. Francis Fergusson, Mr. Marshall McLuhan, Mr. O. A. Silverman, Mr. Richard Kain. It extends too, years of Joyce conversation with a cherished friend, Mr. Patrick Casey, Professor of Anglo-Irish Literature, Loyola University, Chicago.

I am grateful to the Society of Authors for mediation with the Joyce Estate to use unpublished material in the Cornell Collection, and for agreement on the Buffalo privilege, and to Miss Anne Munro-Kerr of the London office for her intelligent guidance and efficient communication. The Buffalo privilege is an honor conferred through the grace and wisdom of Mr. O. A. Silverman, Director of Libraries, University of Buffalo, who sponsored my appeal for the Sylvia Beach schema. For enlightened direction through the Lockwood Collection I add my praise to that of many Joyce scholars for Miss Anna Russell, Librarian of the Poetry Room in Buffalo, and thank her for the tone and quality of her interest. The richness of the Mennen Collection at Cornell University is enhanced not only by the beauty of its surroundings, but also by the human goodness and intelligence of its Administrative Secretaries, formerly Mrs. Pamela Rogers and now Mrs. Susan Warner. I thank Mr. M. Janenas, Curator, for consideration extended me during my Joyce studies in the Cornell Rare Book Room, and Mr. William McCarthy, Curator of the Rosenbach Foundation, Philadelphia, for his courtesy during my study of the original handwritten manuscript of *Ulysses.* I am indebted to Miss Cecelia Hauk of Marquette University, not only for her service to me in arranging research trips, but also for her extended help over the years in the location of materials, understanding long term use of books and genuine interest in my work.

Acknowledgments for permission to quote materials from copyrighted works are due: Random House for quotations from James Joyce's *Ulysses* (1934); The Society of Authors and The Viking Press, Inc., New York, for quotations from *A Portrait of the Artist as a Young Man* (1925); *Exiles* (1951); *Letters of James Joyce* (1957); *Finnegans Wake* (1939); New Directions for quotations from *Stephen Hero* by James Joyce, edited by Theodore Spencer, John J. Slocum and Herbert Cahoon, Copyright 1944; c1955 by New Directions and reprinted by permission of New Directions, Publishers, and from *James Joyce* by Harry Levin, Copyright 1941; The Macmillan Company, New York, for quotation from *The Odyssey of Homer* tr. by S. H. Butcher and A Lang (1917), and Arthur Knight's *The Liveliest Art* (1957); Harper & Brothers, New York, for quotation from Ernst Cassirer's *Language and Myth,* tr. Susanne K. Langer; Yale University Press for quotations from Volume II of Ernst Cassirer's *Philosophy of Symbolic Forms* (1955); The Yale Review for quotation from *The Obstacles to Odysseus' Return: Identity and Consciousness in "The Odyssey"* by Charles H. Taylor, Jr. (Summer, 1961); from *James Joyce* by Richard Ellmann, c1959 by Richard Ellmann and reprinted by permission of Oxford University Press, Inc.; Harcourt, Brace & World, Inc., for quotations from Sergi Eisenstein's *Film Form* (1949); The Bollingen Foundation for quotations from Jacques Maritain's *Creative Intuition in Art and Poetry* (1953) and from Erich Neumann's *The Origins and History of Consciousness* (1954); Benziger Brothers, Inc., New York, for quotation from St. Thomas Aquinas' *Summa Theologica,* tr. by Fathers of the English Dominican Province; Little Brown & Company for quotation from Edith Hamilton's *Mythology* (1940); The Bruce Publishing Company, Milwaukee, for quotation from Vernon Bourke's *Augustine's Quest of Wisdom;* Frank Budgen for quotation from *James Joyce and the Making of Ulysses* (1934).

Milwaukee, Wis., 1961 M. P.

Welcome, O Life! I go to encounter for the millionth time the reality of experience and to forge in the smithy of my soul the uncreated conscience of my race.

— *Portrait of the Artist as a Young Man*

The theme of Joyce's *Ulysses* is the human ascent to consciousness through the co-action of intellect and feeling which generates the creative act of life. His general artistic mode is to concretize with scrupulous accuracy the nearest verisimilitude to the theme of his vision; therefore, a creative artist and a gifted clown compose the hero, a vast indifferent *Weib* is the heroine, and as a vital trinity they perform the ascent to consciousness.

Part I:

BLOOM AS CLOWN

Figure Two: *Clown Flesh*

Introduction

Seeing Joyce's art through his views of reality is not an invitation to tyranny; it is a liberation towards the freedom we all seek in our own interpretation of that which is. A lesser artist might deprive us of the truth of the spectacle of creation through which we achieve personal identity, but not Joyce. Like every great artist he sees through to the truth of the being of the visible universe. This insight brings him the knowledge of what things and people are; in the perception of essences, he sees analogies; with analogies come similarities, and out of similarities metaphor is born.* In his artistic vision Joyce stands firmly within the classic tradition.

On page 21 of *James Joyce and the Making of Ulysses*, Frank Budgen, Joyce's friend, the English artist, relates this conversation with him:

> Among other things my book is the epic of the human body. The only man I know who has attempted the same thing is Phineas Fletcher. But then his *Purple Island* is purely descriptive, a kind of coloured anatomical chart of the human body. In my book the body lives in and moves through space and is the home of a full human personality. The words I write are adapted to express first one of its functions then another. In *Lestrygonians* the stomach dominates and the rhythm of the episode is that of the peristaltic movement.
>
> "But the minds, the thoughts of the characters," I began.
>
> "If they had no body they would have no mind," Joyce said.

Ulysses creates many things, but its object is to create that living total conscience in man not before created: therefore, the poetry of conscience. The poetry of conscience is located in the human judgment process and its condition is human consciousness in its ascent from the unconscious. Joyce makes his art by imitating the action of complexity in the consciousness process. No approach to the being of human personality is more difficult, and no one has achieved the art of that being more successfully than Joyce.

But where did he begin? He began with logical method by making a chart or scheme. On paper the scheme has nine columns with headings. Across the page the headings are: Title, Scene, Hour, Organ, Art, Colour, Symbol, Technic and Correspondences. The title column is numbered and contains the eighteen episodes of Homer's *Odyssey* chosen for *Ulysses*; the scene column, eighteen places in Dublin which transfer Odysseus' adventures to the plane of every day reality; the hour column, the exact time each episode takes place beginning at eight in the morning and ending at two the next morning; the organ column, the organ of the body symbolizing the scene and dictating its rhythm; the art column, the chief liberalizing arts, the fine arts and the mechanical arts which fit with that part of man which performs the art. Theology, History and Philology, for instance, are the matter of the intellect. They are therefore aligned with the organ of consciousness or intellect. Religion is linked to the Heart, Rhetoric to the Lungs. In this manner Joyce's human being emerges. Fifteen of the episodes materialize through the organs of the body. The shape of *Ulysses* is the shape of the human body whose central consciousness is in the act of ascent as the work progresses. This is why Joyce says, "Among other things, my book is an epic of the human body," for it is not only that. Color, Symbol, Technic and Correspondences columns relate to each other and to the whole as a draftsman's plan for a house. Joyce has a structure to erect: the home of a full human personality; these are his ground plans.

Animating the ground plan is the rich, supple, flexible, realistic esthetic order which precedes the *Ulysses* chart and gives it being. Joyce's creative plan is a carefully conceived set of principles which he follows with scrupulous integrity. An extension of Thomas Aquinas' theory of the beautiful, Joyce's esthetic principles place him in the Realist position in the tradition of Scholastic philosophy and a Realist position in the tradition of art.

The techniques through which Joyce employed his artistic principles were, as we know, the product of keen intelligence cooperating with a quick sensibility to beget a first rate original mode of expression. Employment of his principles animates the definition of epiphany recorded in *Stephen Hero*:

> By an epiphany he meant a sudden spiritual manifestation, whether in vulgarity of speech or of gesture or in a memorable phase of the mind itself. He believed that it was for the man of letters to record these epiphanies with extreme care, seeing that they themselves are the most delicate and evanescent of moments. (211)

Defining the poet's way makes Joyce understand his own function as artist, again recorded in *Stephen Hero*:

> The poet is the intense center of the life of his age to which he stands in a relation than which none can be more vital. He alone is capable of absorbing in himself the life that surrounds him and of flinging it abroad again amid planetary music. (80)

Poetry in the comprehensive sense as that which animates all art is Joyce's meaning here; he happened to be a writer. Absorbing in himself the life that surrounds him is a total experience for the poet: he creates a world in miniature like the world in which he lives. Joyce lived in the dying years of the nineteenth and the formative years of the twentieth century (1882-1941). The death of the one was a slow paralysis; the birth of the other was a new complexity of human consciousness. What is now the atomic and the space age began in a simultaneous manifestation of the technological energy beneath the late nineteenth century paralysis. Among the many twentieth century technics, one stamps the age with a new mode of awareness: the motion picture camera. The motion picture illuminates form, the scholastic term for soul. In 1902 as a college student, Joyce voiced his first esthetic principles; this was seven years after Edison in America, Lumière in France and Paul in England produced their cameras, but three years before Joyce himself had any cinema experience. His views of reality and how to reproduce them in works of art have a close affinity to film technique. Joyce distills experience by disentangling the subtle soul of the image. Then he gives it new flesh. To do so illuminates form. Joyce's aim and the cinema technique have a special identity. It should come as no great surprise to find him employing an "intellectual cinema" technique in *Ulysses* which this book traces in Part Two.

What is a surprise in *Ulysses* is Joyce's use of the hero of early cinema. Leopold Bloom was born into the world of letters when screen comedy was king (1914-1922). He is modelled on the supreme clown of them all: Charlie Chaplin.

Only Chaplin with his world acclaim could fit the condition of Joyce's own burning flesh out of which he had to make the hero of *Ulysses.* Joyce's Ulysses is a clown. Is there a better analogy for the flesh as wanderer? Is there a more accurate anagoge for the flesh abandoned by the spirit? Is there any figure more flexible than the clown to portray those irreversible sadly comic human conditions in which man seeks and finds self-knowledge?

> She had been three times to the pantomime and asked Stephen what he liked best in pantomime. Stephen said he liked a good clown . . . .
> (S. H. 67)

Joyce is that Stephen who liked Chaplin so well that he invited him and his myth to stand for modern times.

When *Ulysses* was published in 1922 what mythic expectancy could Joyce count on in his reader? In Ireland Homer may not have been popular but Chaplin was. Sean O'Casey in *Juno and the Paycock,* whose time is 1922, lets Captain Jack Boyle put English to it:

> Take the real Dublin people, f'instance: they know more about Charlie Chaplin an' Tommy Mix than they do about SS. Peter and Paul!

By 1922 Charlie Chaplin had passed into the collective consciousness of the civilized world. The main reason Chaplin in Bloom has not been discovered until this writing is that Joyce's early critics did not perceive the

Chaplin myth of modern times nor did they work from Joyce's esthetic in *A Portrait of the Artist as a Young Man.*

Once the Chaplin figure is seen in *Ulysses,* Joyce is released from captivity in the academic world to live among those men and women of all ages who seek a life line to the times in which they live. Chaplin is that life line to *Ulysses* that opens the book to public view. Like television now, Chaplin was in every home. He enters the public life again through the greatest book of the twentieth century, Joyce's *Ulysses,* on the silent screen of the mind, in the essence of pantomime, the interior monologue. All that his art has meant flowers in Leopold Bloom. Joyce invites him to symbolize the everlasting apprehension: man has clown flesh.

*Cf. Aristotle's *Poetics,* XXII, 9 and *passim* concerning metaphor and poetic genius.

Chapter 1

MYTHICAL THOUGHT: TWENTIETH CENTURY POETIC

James Joyce contemplated the mystery of art and the artist for more than thirty years before he created a major work. His poetry and the fifteen short stories called *Dubliners* are a liberating process of the essential, twentieth century power of his art, the power of mythical thought. In *A Portrait of the Artist as a Young Man* and its sequel, *Ulysses*, Joyce was destined to create this century's space-time image of man, but to create these works his mythical consciousness had not only to apprehend being as it so superbly does in *Dubliners* but itself be disengaged from the nature of his poetic knowledge by Joyce, the maker. Only by this new and proper use of the creative power of mythical thought does he become mediator between the two worlds that make up poetry: the world of dream and the world of objective reality.[1] It is significant that Joyce does not write the esthetic principle governing the artist's use of mythical consciousness until after his best poetry and the intense early *Dubliners* are finished and before the creation of the great two-part composition of *A Portrait* and *Ulysses.*

> The artist, he imagined, standing in the position of mediator between the world of his experience and the world of his dreams — a mediator, consequently gifted with twin faculties, a selective faculty and a reproductive faculty. To equate these faculties was the secret of artistic success: the artist who could disentangle the subtle soul of the image from its mesh of defining circumstances most exactly and re-embody it in artistic circumstances chosen as the most exact for it in its new office, he was the supreme artist. (S.H. 77)

Mythical thought is complex, intuitive thinking that hovers between the world of dream and the world of objective reality. It gives being to the human power of disengaging intelligibility from existence, apprehends pure form (soul), generates the accurate phantasm, becomes the object perceived and names the unknown. Myth-making in the history of civilization shows man in his ascent to truth, for the myth made is the attempt to understand the larger significance of phenomena. No one escapes the effect the myths of mankind have wrought upon the collective consciousness of society, for society is always the product of the mental activity of the species.

Mythical thought is a quality of consciousness; no normal person is totally lacking in it, for all perceive through the senses and understand through the cooperative union of thought and feeling, but the poet's potential is his mythical consciousness. It enables him to see with terrible clarity the being of things. Terror lasts only as long as the twin power of human consciousness, empirical or discursive reasoning, is delayed in its development. When primitive man evolves to Greek sensibility, terror vanishes because reason pervades, and the first great dramatists put mythical consciousness and its race content in the service of truth. Sophocles uses the Oedipus myth to order experience and assign its artistic meaning. When the Greek sensibility evolves to the Christian writer of Sacred Scripture, myth orders the experience of Revelation and assigns theological meaning to the Christion human condition.

James Joyce's mythical consciousness, comprehensive and comprehending in scope and vitality, seeks mankind's being in history, seeks to disengage the intelligibility of man's highest faculty, judgment, that he might accomplish the artist's highest achievement: the uncreated conscience of the race. The poetry of conscience did not yield until logical thought employed mythical consciousness in the service of poetic truth. Joyce does not become a supreme artist until he mediates between the world of his experience and the world of his dreams without anger and disillusion and in the spirit of tolerance and congenial detachment. But he is an artist in *Dubliners* for whom everything perceived has the character of reality; the image like the word is endowed with real forces. The spiritual paralysis of the Dublin of 1904 provokes his first lyric cry. He names what he sees in a series of Dublin portraits. They are, as he admits, done with scrupulous accuracy and meanness, and to Molyneux Palmer he writes about *Dubliners:* "I don't think you will recognize me in it at first glance as it is somewhat bitter and sordid."[2] All that existed in the Dublin of his youth was by no means sordid, but Joyce's artistic perception is concerned with being. He saw the imbedded, unconscious, immoral character of society with terrible clarity, and he wrote a chapter in the moral history of his country. "I have taken the first step towards the spiritual liberation of my country," he wrote to Grant Richards in 1906.[3] Love's longing commands the lover to release the beloved from disease, sickness, dissolution and death.

Joyce's mythical consciousness pursued the spiritual paralysis of his people with relentless fury in *Stephen Hero,* the first draft of *A Portrait of the Artist,* endowing his own artistic consciousness with permanent reality in the person and sensibility of Stephen Dedalus, its central figure. Several hardships accompanying its completion and acceptance for publication attest to that point in his own development at which Joyce elevates his station of practicing artist to supreme artist. He revised the total book, *Stephen Hero,* into *A Portrait of the Artist as a Young Man. A Portrait* is great art; *Stephen Hero* is the material of art assembled and in formation; *A Portrait* achieves that form. It is enlightening to see just why this is so.

Stephen Hero lacked perspective precisely because mythical thought dominated both the hero and his creator, yet language as science carried him to the logical formulation of an esthetic philosophy. The work lacked the *claritas* of the beautiful.

Joyce's revision of *Stephen Hero* places the mythic mind of the hero in its proper context, revealing it to be central to his struggle for artistic expression and the fundamental reason for his rejection of all organized modes of existence: family, nationality, religion. At the end of *A Portrait,* Stephen Dedalus, through the power of language forming discursive thought, does what no young artist in an artistic creation has done before him: he evolves a theory of esthetic. With language in the service of the logic of the beautiful he makes a plan for creating, a way to see reality, a manner of procedure for the artist, a working notion of the good, a way to reveal the beautiful, an epiphany; a method of beholding the moment of the beautiful in the rhythm of the work made, a stasis. Stephen defines, marks off, evaluates and tests the phenomenon of art and its effects with irrefutable accuracy. He is for a number of years fully prepared to create, but he cannot release the preconscious, complex, intuitive realities which are the substrata of his vision until such time that feeling rejoins thought. As artist he has to become the mediator between the world of his dreams and the world of his experience. At the end of *A Portrait,* Joyce shows us the young man intellectualizing his existence off the human plane into a god realm. The god is pagan and his stick is an ashplant. But the hope at the end of *A Portrait* is through the kind of god he becomes: a waning, pagan god who knows in the beginning he will one day be forced to recant to a human conqueror. That conqueror in Stephen is the use of and not the servitude to an imagination nourished by a regenerated flesh. As god he is conquered by the light.

Stephen enters *Ulysses,* the sequel to *A Portrait of the Artist as a Young Man,* as a grieving, falling god who knows the battle is lost but also with a fierce will to fight the adversary. His descent to reality — to being human — is his difficult birth as an artist and the release of his genius.

Joyce is his own model for Stephen Dedalus. *A Portrait* is not an autobiography which is a man's report of his own life; it is a work of art which imitates the spiritual action of Joyce's first twenty years, but the poetic truth of those years is assessed by Joyce, the mature artist. Biographical facts in abundance show Joyce's own youth to be the parallel from which he creates his Dedalus. The unique nature of his artistic vision and his artistic mode could only evolve from a contemplation and distillation of his own spiritual existence. We have an old biography,[4] a new biography,[5] a volume of letters,[6] rich materials at many European and American libraries and universities all of which converge with evidence that Joyce made no secret of his identity with the fictional Stephen Dedalus. Joyce's brother, Stanislaus,[7] even in his contumely for his artist-brother, attests to Stephen's identity, for Stanie is revolted by the imperial James whose imperiality is one of the psychic bonds that exist between Joyce and the image of himself in *A Portrait.*

There are over six hundred letters and hundreds of other documents at Cornell University: Joyce's artistic process records, manuscripts, notebooks; any which deal with the period of creation up to 1914 help to establish Joyce as Stephen. In a notebook he kept from 1904-1914, for instance, there is this description of Stephen Dedalus, fictional character:

> He was a dispossessed son.
>
> He disliked to be seen in the company of any woman.
>
> At times as he walked through the streets of Dublin he felt that he was really invisible.
>
> Dreaded the sea that would drown his body and the crowd that would drown his soul.
>
> He came to the knowledge of innocence through sin.
>
> He hoped that by sinning whole-heartedly his race might come in him to the knowledge of herself.
>
> He felt the growing pains of his soul in the painful process of life.
>
> He shrank from limning the features of his soul for he feared that no everlasting image of beauty could shine through an immature being.
>
> The applause following the fall of the curtain fired his blood more than the scene on the stage.
>
> He felt the quaking of the earth.
>
> Having left the city of the Church by the fall of sin he might enter it again by the wicket of repentence if repentence were possible.
>
> He desired to be not a man of letters but a spirit expressing itself through language because shut off from the visible acts by an inheritance of servitude and from music by a fever of the mind.[8]

Unpublished letters in the Cornell collection[9] leave no doubt of the young Joyce's identity with the young artist, Stephen Dedalus. One dated August 29, 1904, sent to Nora Barnacle a few months before Joyce's elopement with her to Trieste bears particular witness, for it is biographical and estimative. It echoes the proud, bitter, Irish voice of Stephen in *A Portrait* on family and religion.

He tells Nora that he rejects the social order and Christianity; home is a hollow concept, for his own was a squalid affair where he knew nothing but misery and learned nothing but extravagance. His mother's death is due to the perverse and bestial behavior of both father and son and to a piety toward the Church's ideal of large families. The Joyces had seventeen children of which he, James, is the oldest, and he bore nothing but contempt for his brothers and sisters. Only one brother shows promise of understanding him. He tells Nora he has been out of the Catholic Church six years (he is twenty-two as he writes this letter, the age of Stephen in *Ulysses*), and that when he left, he hated it bitterly. He could not stay in the Church because it repressed his nature. When he was a student, he made hidden war on the Church of his birth and refused an offer to become one of her priests. He became an outcast, but he saved his identity. At the present writing, his war upon the Church is no longer hidden but overt: he writes, speaks and acts against it. He concludes this section of the letter with a proud lament: the social order is possible for him in one way only: he must enter it as a vagabond.

This, of course, is the same proud sovereignty of which Stephen Dedalus boasts when he is in servitude to mythic thought: he is a moral vagabond conscious of his privation but impotent to change it. The works of art, *A Portrait* and *Ulysses,* have among other things a fictional time and a space-time which rearrange the sequence of events and spiritual evolution of Joyce as hero. There is no disparity between what we find in the works and Joyce's actual life if we remember constantly that he is thirty-three when the last chapter of *A Portrait* is sent to the *Egoist* to be published.[10] At this stage he has changed his mind about his family: he brings his brothers and several sisters to Trieste; he makes good his vow to create by means of the nets of nationality, religion and language; and he has another attitude toward the paralysis of Irish life and institutions. He is no longer the lonely, brooding, falling god who holds humanity his enemy, but the human being Stephen Dedalus foreshadows in *Ulysses* and the creator of great comic literature. His attitude towards Catholicism undergoes a metamorphosis, and while Joyce was to remain apostate in real life, both the fictional outcome of *Ulysses* and Joyce's statements over the years reveal the poetic truth of his position towards the Church. Once the pagan god in Stephen vanishes into the darkness (*Ulysses,* p. 567), the artist appears. In 1915 before Joyce wrote the battle-with-the-light scene in *Ulysses,* he says in his notes for his play, *Exiles:*

> Why the title *Exiles*? A nation exacts a penance from those who dared to leave her payable on their return. The elder brother in the fable of the Prodigal Son is Robert Hand. The father took the side of

> the prodigal. This is probably not the way of the world — certainly not Ireland: but Jesus' Kingdom was not of this world nor was or is his wisdom.[11]

During the creation of *Ulysses*, Joyce's conversation about religion was anything but the bitter rejection of young Dedalus in the works of art. This is what he said to Georges Borach, one of his language students in Zurich, November, 1917:

> In my works there is a good deal of talk about religion. Many people think I am a spoiled priest. I profess no religion at all. Of the two religions, Protestantism and Catholicism, I prefer the latter. Both are false. The former is cold and colorless. The second-named is constantly associated with art; it is a "beautiful lie".[12]

Nothing could be more revealing than this for the poetic truth of Joyce's position on Catholicism. We certainly know Joyce's serious struggle to accept his high destiny as artist, and we know his belief in art as a testament of reality, and the *sine qua non* of society. We know the ardor with which he sought to reveal the "truth of the being of the visible world." We know that he knew Plato; Plato reasons conceptually and in an ironic vein that art is a beautiful lie.[13] The poetic truth of Catholicism like the poetic truth of art whose subject is the whole of creation, Joyce continued to see. After the tension between religion and mythical thought disappeared in Joyce's consciousness, it is possible he became, in Ernst Cassirer's words, "appeased" by his direct contemplation of being, and his religious consciousness as such suffered a negation.[14] But his personal, worldly consciousness transformed to poetic truth in his works is Joyce's achievement in art and this is what we look at: from a spiritual abundance, he sings.

Stephen Dedalus' action in *A Portrait* is not an attack on Catholicism; he is apostate as the most important part of the larger action of mythical thought and its effect upon the artist, separating him from the very liberation he seeks. Stephen's imagination is paralyzed for many complex reasons (with which Chapter X in this book deals in detail), but he is not aware of any personal privation; he is convinced that the intellectual imagination is mankind's highest achievement. His mythic awareness is, however, a subject which Joyce pursues relentlessly and often times in a comic vein.

> This morning walk was pleasant for him and there was no face that passed him on its way to its commercial prison but he strove to pierce to the motive centre of its ugliness. (S.H. 30)[15]

This, of course, is the tendency to take a part for the whole; the whole has no parts in mythical thinking. Reason is right to say not every face had a centre of ugliness; right to say ugliness was not the only existent quality on the streets of Dublin in 1900; reason is right to say that not every worker is in prison; that not all commerce is servitude. But, then, reason has no avenue to poetic truth. Stephen does behold a spiritual paralysis in his people, an intuitive knowledge of their deprived humanity. Poetic knowledge is not conceptual knowledge. It visits the artist during periods of receptivity; he is incapable of tracing its entrance into his being, but he alone is capable of forming its exit which is through the cooperative function of intellect and imagination; thought and feeling; mind and senses; soul and body. When mythical thinking serves Joyce as an artistic power, Stephen Dedalus seeks and gains understanding. He regains the power not only to tolerate the human beings to whom he is linked but to love them; not to chafe against the condition of his nature as man and artist but to accept and ennoble it.

There is in *A Portrait* a monster side to Stephen's nature. He is afflicted with the mark of the beast. He is given to uncleanness, bestiality and dream fornication. The Cornell documents leave no doubt that this, too, is transformed in *A Portrait* from the biographical facts of Joyce's own burning flesh.

A lonely, confessional letter to his wife, Nora, written from Dublin during his *Volta* Cinematograph venture hints at the troubled flesh of both Stephen Dedalus and Leopold Bloom.[16] While he does not consider himself a bad man, he admits to the agonizing polarity in his nature between virtue and vice. The good and the bad assail him on every side. He begs her to help him in his struggle against temptation and his frequent falls by sheltering him from the occasion of sin. Then in an exuberant impulse toward what Nora's protection might contain, he tells her a wild desire drives him. He wants her to whip him; he wants the excitement of her anger.[17] We remember Bloom's masochism in the *Circe* episode of *Ulysses* where he begs to be flogged. But the lover lapses into the former lyric melancholy and tells Nora that to others he gave his high spirits; to her he will give his besetting sin and his grief concerning it.

In a previous letter he had given her a name, the name Bloom gives to Molly, "beautiful wild flower of the hedges . . . . dark blue, rain-drenched flower," but after the apostrophe to Nora comes the bestiary. Nothing in

Boccacio equals the animal image of coition Joyce presents to his wife. In a Bacchanalian dream of desire, they are both swine practicing a circean, orgiastic co-habitation whose confounding animality alone the lover craves.[18] It echoes "like some baffled, prowling beast" in *A Portrait* (112) where Stephen Dedalus' flesh suffers the agony of demonic penetration in kind, but in nature the desire Joyce writes to Nora is closer to the comic savagery of the Boylan-Molly Bloom sex act in *Circe of Ulysses.* (552)

The 1909 letters to Nora in the Cornell collection produce a chain of Joyce's identity with the Stephen who longed "to sin with another of his kind" (*Por.* 112). Whispers in Dublin that Georgio was not his son provoked wild demands from Nora of guilt, and one of the letters ends with a recall of that first time Nora embraced him and made him a man.[19] The scene later becomes the dream fornication scene in *A Portrait* where a young woman dressed in a long pink gown "embraced him gaily and gravely" . . . . "and between them he felt an unknown and timid pressure, darker than the swoon of sin, softer than sound or odour." (*Por.* 113, 114)

But the artist was still five years away from the perspective he was to achieve concerning mythical thought and still too close to the terror of his youth concerning his strange biological necessities. As he said of Stephen Dedalus, "shut off from the visible acts by an inheritance of servitude." By this he means a mistaken sense of shame concerning the shape and function of his body. Stephen makes a vow at the end of *A Portrait* "to forge in the smithy of my soul the uncreated conscience of my race."[20] *Ulysses* creates the poetry of conscience.

The use of his own act of existence by any artist is meaningless unless he beholds the universal condition in his own particular attempt at being human. All artists write, paint or compose themselves, but great artists contemplate art and the artist as a way to self-knowledge; they model from authentic material; they model themselves. Creating with personal being, however, has certain self-containing laws. Joyce is able to detach himself from himself which demands courage and honesty and to use those aspects of his personality and character which have universal validity in humanity's act of existence. Nor is the detachment itself of any special value without Joyce's mythic intuition, intellectual understanding and artistic rendering of his soul's very substance and his body's proper act through that substance. Few artists have experienced God's act of creation so intensely that they strive to imitate His Act *qua* act. An amazing dimension in Joyce — often not understood — is his practice of omniscience in an image of God's all knowing. Not only did he achieve a vast store of intellectual knowledge, but he desired to behold "all the ways of glory and error" and in this way "to create life from life."

Mediation then in *A Portrait* consists in disengaging mythical consciousness from Stephen Dedalus, the artist; at the end of the book, the *verbum verum* is that logical thought has fought its way to an esthetic plan and the artist takes a vow, "to forge in the smithy of my soul the uncreated conscience of my race." *Ulysses* is the keeping of that vow. What are the ways of artistic mediation Joyce follows in his vow's execution? The first to locate is the method in his central character, Ulysses, who as we know is Leopold Bloom.

Leopold Bloom in *Ulysses* is a Jewish citizen of Dublin whose act of existence is like the Odysseus of old. He has left home to fight a war over beauty; now that the battle is over, he cannot get on the right course to Ithaca. Home, Ithaca, beauty, the very Dublin he moves through during one day of his existence, all have multiple significances. Properly our first question should be, "Is this Joyce too?" The answer is that of course Joyce's bodily consciousness is in this man, but Bloom doesn't look like Joyce; he isn't Stephen Dedalus; he is too definitely and expertly drawn to be only an aggregate of several Dubliners;[21] he is reminiscent of a time remembered, an experience enjoyed, a face and act the world has known.

There is no great mystery about Bloom's being a Jew. Joyce desires to create the poetry of conscience; since he places his vision in the Christian era, it is logical that he would start with the race which denied myth and its rites and preached consciousness and morality to make way the coming of the Lord. Like the ancient Hebrews, Mr. Bloom doesn't recognize the Messiah, but somehow he takes to St. Paul. Matthew Arnold's Hebraicism[22] had no little effect on Joyce's world view, for we get in Bloom an incapacity for light but a sweetness; an inability to order his existence either with or without the moral law. He is not "mechanical" in Arnold's sense, but the opposite, examining every belief, but the fallacy is he does so in pitch dark. The comedy in *Ulysses* is evidence of Bloom's identity. Who of the critics so far actually believes he is analyzing a comedy when he writes about *Ulysses?* When Harry Levin said so many years ago, "We are not told how the characters behave; we are confronted with the *stimuli* that affect their behavior, and are expected to respond sympathetically,"[23] he could not have investigated the linear picture Joyce gives of the hero. Here are his clothes, his body, a few telling actions:

Mr. Bloom wears a black suit with five button jacket (695), braces with one button eventually missing (539, 695), boots whose shape and angle of flap the newsboys imitate (128), and a black bowler hat (79). "And he always takes off his hat when he comes up in the street like that" (729). In "his pale, intellectual face" (351), or "his dunducket mudcolored mug" (325), or his "olive complexion" (712), the eyes are dark thinking (100), plum eyes (325), large rolling, (the central sadness); he has a splendid set of teeth (731), which are very white against his dark moustache (351). He is five feet nine and one half inches tall, weighs eleven stone and four or one hundred and fifty-eight pounds (652); his chest is 20½ inches; biceps, 10 inches; forearm, 9 inches; thigh, 12 inches; calf, 12 inches (706). He has an enormous, squat neck, size 17 (695).

So, he is a slight man in a black suit with sagging pants, a bowler hat above a squat neck, a moustache, great dark eyes, flashing white teeth. He more than once "steps nimbly aside", and he walks stiff-legged (428). His feet are "listed" (653). He carries a rolled newspaper baton in the beginning (71) and a cane toward the end (570). Who is he? HE IS THE CHAPLIN FIGURE, the world famous comic Odysseus of American film from 1914 to 1952!

Chaplin was a master of pantomime. It is highly probable Joyce conceived the interior monologue as much from Chaplin's gifted pantomime as from Dujardin.[24] Magalaner and Kain report that Dujardin felt like Lazarus in the sudden recognition he began to enjoy for his long forgotten novel of 1887.[25] There has been general distrust of the Dujardin imitation even though Joyce did claim it. Joyce never writes with his tongue in his cheek,[26] but he often speaks this way deliberately. Pantomime as interior monologue is highly logical. Ten minutes with Chaplin transcends dialogue, for the mental word is the poetry of acting.

Ulysses, as we know, takes place on one day, June 16, 1904. Chaplin's silhouette in front of movie houses bore one little sign: "I am here today!" There was no title, just a cut-out of the little man tipping his hat and flourishing his cane.

Chaplin was an immediate success. From the release of his first picture, *Kids Auto Races At Venice*, February, 1914, he was noticed in Europe as well as in America. Within two years his name became a household word. "There were Chaplin dolls, Chaplin toys, Chaplin contests. People danced the 'Chaplin walk', children used his name in their counting-out rhymes. There were Chaplin imitators on and off the screen; Chaplin cartoons in newspapers and magazines."[27] He was a gifted young Englishman who left Fred Karno's music hall troupe while they were touring the East to join Mack Sennett's Keystone Comedies in Hollywood. In *Kids Auto Races,* he put on what was to be the world famous "Charlie" costume: Arbuckle's pants and hat, Ford Sterling's shoes on the wrong feet, a tight fitting five-button cut-away, Mack Swain's Boer War moustache cut to tooth brush size, and a slender bamboo cane. His walk in that first film was to become the famous Chaplin "stiff walk": it was jaunty, jauncy, stork-like with out-facing knees and flopping out-toed feet. He wore a flower in his button hole, and on his face whose "central sadness" is the great rolling eyes was the comic mask of *l'homme moyen sensuel.*[28] He addressed a new myth to the screen.

If we imagine Joyce was unaware of this myth, we have only to examine his interest in motion pictures as a twentieth century art form. Always ideally hoping Ireland would respond to his redemptive vision, Joyce tried to establish a cinematograph, *The Volta,* in Dublin in 1909. He with Guiseppe Caris, Giovanni Rebez and Caterina Machinick formed a partnership for the purpose of establishing movie houses and the showing of films in Dublin, Belfast and Cork. Joyce brought experience and knowledge to the enterprise and the other three the capital.[29] *The Volta* opened in late December of 1909, but the Dublin response was poor and Joyce missed Nora desperately, so he withdrew from the partnership which was soon dissolved. But much earlier in 1904 we hear of Joyce and Nora at the Bioscope in Pola, Austria. In a letter to Stanislaus, December 28, 1904, Joyce tells him that they went to a bioscope of a series of pictures about betrayed Gretchen. In one of the last the hero, Lothario, throws her in the river after which comes the chase by rabble and the police. Joyce writes that Nora cried out to the policeman to catch the vile cad.[30]

Esthetically, Joyce meditated the cinema as an art form. Under the subject heading of "Esthetic" in the 1904-1914 Notebook we find this notation:

> An enchantment of the heart
>
> Phonographic and cinematographic images act like those stimuli which produce a reflex action of the nerves through channels which are independent of esthetic perception.

It relieves us to hear or see our own distress expressed by another person.

The instant of inspiration is a spark so brief as to be invisible. The reflection of it on many sides at once from a multitude of cloudy circumstances with no one of which it is united save by the bond of nerves and possibility veils its afterglow in an instant in a first confusion of form. This is the instant in which the word is made flesh.[31]

The family interest in Chaplin is revealed in this anecdote about Joyce's daughter, Lucia, related by Richard Ellmann:

> Some of Joyce's friends, such as Valery Larbaud, had always thought Lucia strange; others dismissed her somewhat unusual behavior as the effect of her extraordinary father. At parties she was gay and talkative, and sometimes did an impersonation of Charlie Chaplin with baggy trousers and cane. Chaplin alternated with Napoleon as her favorite hero, and was the subject of a brief article she wrote in 1924 for a Belgian review, *Le Disque Vert,* which Larbaud prefaced and slightly revised for her. The combination of heroes was reminiscent of her father's joining Dedalus and Bloom, and was taken as an amusing foible.[32]

Lucia's performance for the guests was in 1929, seven years after the publication of *Ulysses.* Who had really read the book carefully by that time? And with detachment? It was Pound's view, for instance, that the Homeric parallels were edifices around the work that had very little relation to the work itself.[33] This view is still current.[34] A passage in *Finnegans Wake,* containing quite a "throwaway" for Joyce, seems also to be bypassed in the light it throws on *Ulysses* and, I believe, the use of the Chaplin figure in Bloom.

> Then, pious Eneas, conformant to the fulminant firman which enjoins on the tremylose terrian that, when the call comes, he shall produce nichthemerically from his unheavenly body a no uncertain quantity of obscene matter not protected by copriright in the United Stars of Ourania or bedeed and bedood and bedang and bedung to him, with this double dye, brought to blood heat, gallic acid on iron ore, through the bowels of his misery, flashly, faithly, nastily, appropriately, this Esuan Menschavik and the first till last alshemist wrote over every square inch of the only foolscap available, his own body, till by its corrosive sublimation one continuous present tense integument slowly unfolded all marryvoising moodmoulded cyclewheeling history (thereby, he said, reflecting from his own individual person life unlivable, transaccidentated through the slow fires of consciousness into a dividual chaos, peri-

> lous, potent, common to allflesh, human only, mortal) but with each word that would not pass away the squidself which he had squirtscreened from the crystalline world waned chagreenold and doriangrayer in its dudhud. This exists that isits after having been said we know.[35]

The passage is about Shem, the penman, who is Joyce and his finished works. Shem and the "matter not protected by copriright in the United Stars of Ourania" is, among other things, primarily a pun on the motion pictures in the United States and of the boob cops in the Keystone and Chaplin comedies; the "double dye" is the way in which the Chaplin material was disguised; "this Esuan Menschavik" is who is brought to blood heat, "gallic acid and iron ore", Joyce's wit on the earthy vein of Chaplin's art; and by Shem in the ways described, "through the bowels of his misery, flashly, faithly, nastily, appropriately." Who is this Esuan Menschavik? Chaplin went to Essanay in his second year of pictures. The studio name was made up of George Spoor and Bronko Billy Anderson. The "S" of Spoor's name became "Ess", the "A" of Anderson's name became "ay", the word "an" joined the two syllables. Joyce is punning on the coined name in his one word Es-u-ay-n to make an adjective of Chaplin's firm and also to further disguise it by passing it for a first name. Menschavik is "Mens", the Latin for "mind" which is also the derivation of "man", the one that thinks, plus "cha", the Gaelic for "not", plus "vik" or "ic", meaning having the nature of. Combined, Esuan Menschavik seems to mean the one at Essanay whose nature was not to think but to feel, which of course, was the "Charlie" of the Chaplin canon. Towards the end of the passage, "the squidself which he had squirtscreened from the crystalline world waned chagreenold and doriangrayer in its dudhud"; the squidself is Shem or Joyce and Leopold Bloom in *Ulysses* who was taken from the crystalline world — Chaplin's — and squirted on the screen of the reader's mind. It was not the halcyon, brilliant moment of comedy Chaplin gave us. Nor was it meant to be. For Joyce wishes us to understand that his picture of the squidself in *Ulysses* is "doriangrayer" than Wilde's.

Joyce's interest in Chaplin no doubt began as early as the first sketch, *Kids Auto Races,* but his whole admiration probably came during the year at Essanay when Chaplin's first great classic, *The Tramp,* was made and released, April 11, 1915. He had the courage to give this a sad ending. "I dislike tragedy," he said. "Life is sad enough. I only use pathos as a means of effecting beauty. For so much of the tragic is in all beauty."[36]

If we had to assign any other reason, however, for Joyce's use of the superb Chaplin to play his own flesh, we might say he was attracted by the same qualities of greatness that James Agee saw in Charlie:

> Of all comedians he worked most deeply and most shrewdly within a realization of what a human being is, and is up against. *The Tramp* is as centrally representative of humanity, as manysided and as mysterious as Hamlet and it seems unlikely that any dancer or actor can ever have excelled him in eloquence, variety or poignancy of motion. As for pure motion, even if he had never gone on to make his magnificent feature-length comedies, Chaplin would have made his period in movies a great one singlehanded even if he had made nothing except *The Cure* or *One A.M.*[37]

Joyce's early adult mythic conception of the Church in Ireland is in a letter to Lady Gregory when he was twenty years old, "I want to achieve myself — little or great as I may be — for I know that there is no heresy or no philosophy which is so abhorrent to my church as a human being, and accordingly I am going to Paris."[38]

At thirty-two he is determined to account for the human quality of the race: its act and its potential. He is no longer that same young man of the letter to Lady Gregory, but a man free now to put his superior mythical consciousness in the service of the more total truth of the being of the visible human world.

Chaplin's first film was released in February, 1914. Joyce began the earnest composition of *Ulysses* in March of 1914. The notebook in which we find sketches of persons and scenes in *A Portrait* and *Ulysses* and in which he records such notes as cited earlier in this chapter on cinematographic images bears no individual dates, but the entries reveal Joyce's analytical approach to his own creative receptivity. "It relieves us to hear or see our own distress expressed by another person." This note found among the cinema references certainly applies to Chaplin's possible effect on Joyce's condition of burning flesh or the memory of that agony as the young Stephen Dedalus. Chaplin and Joyce may have co-incidentally entered on great careers at the same time, but what is not co-incidental is the evidence in the text of *Ulysses* that Joyce uses the Chaplin figure to illuminate the meaning and economize the significance of his slight man of many devices, Leopold Bloom. Through the collective memory of Chaplin when he was in bloom and the created poetry of conscience as it exists in Leopold Bloom, bi-hero of *Ulysses*, the total work is an enchantment of the heart.

Chapter II

HOMER AND THE CHRISTIAN ACCRETION

Homer's divinities are travesties, but his men and women in the *Odyssey* do not parody existence. They parody the Greek ideal, "Nothing in excess". Even though he conquers the results of excess through wit, cunning, craft and skill, Odysseus' wanderings imitate the action of intemperance. Everyone but Odysseus, the intelligent one, knew his way home from the Trojan war. He was not ignorant of navigation, law, order; he was not innocent of the danger in visiting chthonic personalities such as the non-Olympians, Poseidon's son, the Cyclops, Calypso and Circe. Odysseus' excess is a sensuous passion of the flesh which Homer assesses through a particular knowledge of man's nature. That knowledge is poetic in substance. Poetic knowledge is not moral knowledge, but the wisdom it supplies to the poet cannot be unethical, for it is a knowledge of being: its essence, act and existence. Such was Homer's insight. The effect of the epic may be parody, but the soul of its creation is poetry.

Odysseus in the tradition of literature appears always as a real human being. In Dante, Homer's highly moral tale receives its first Christian estimate, for Dante places Ulysses, the other name for Odysseus, in the eighth chasm of the eighth circle of hell where Fraud is punished.

> . . . it cast
> A voice forth from the strength of its desire,
> Saying: "When I from Circe broke at last,
> Who more than a year by Gaeta (before
> Aeneas had so named it) held me fast,
> Not sweet son, nor revered old father, nor
> The long-due love which was to have made glad
> Penelope for all the pain she bore,
> Could conquer the inward hunger that I had
> To master earth's experience, and to attain
> Knowledge of man's mind, both the good and bad.
> But I put out on the deep, open main
> With one ship only, and with that little band
> Which chose not to desert me; far as Spain,
> Far as Morocco, either shore I scanned.
> Sardinia's isle I coasted, steering true,
> And the isles of which that water bathes the strand.
> I and my crew were old and stiff of thew
> When, at the narrow pass, we could discern
> The marks that Hercules set far in view
> That none should dare beyond, or further learn.[1]

After tempting his men beyond this forbidden point, Ulysses and his crew perish in a collision with

> a mountain in the sea,
> Dimmed by the distance: loftier than aught
> That ever I beheld, it seemed to be.[2]

His spiritual fraud is a persuasion of his men to imprudence under the guise of fortitude and justice. Tennyson, on the other hand, writes a Victorian hymn of praise to the adventuring Ulysses who boasts, "I am a part of all that I have met," and although no longer of that strength which moved earth and heaven, but

> Made weak by time and fate, but strong in will
> To strive, to seek, to find, and not to yield.[3]

Joyce complained to Georges Borach that "Dante tires one quickly; it is as if one were to look at the sun."[4] Since he made the remark during the making of *Ulysses*, we can perhaps see the comic basis for Bloom's action with the sun:

> He faced about and, standing between the awnings, held out his right hand at arm's length towards the sun. Wanted to try that often. Yes: completely. The tip of his little finger blotted out the sun's disk. Must be the focus where the rays cross. (164)

Joyce may have agreed with Dante's judgment of Ulysses, but he prefers a more natural method of beholding being than through a steady gaze at the sun. He was not, however, free from personal concern over his own search for omniscience. He analyzes many of his dreams for fictional material. In one of them, he dreamed that he and his daughter, Lucia, were attending a performance of a newly discovered Shakespeare play and that Shakespeare himself was in the audience near them. Lucia appears overwrought and terrified in the dream as she looks at Shakespeare and her father and almost unable to view the play on stage, and Joyce is deeply disturbed for Lucia. As the dream ends, he is about to carry her in his arms out of the theater. Joyce's interpretation:

> The fear for Lucia (herself in little) is fear that either subsequent honours or the future development of my mind or out of its extravagant excursions into forbidden territory may bring unrest into her life.[5]

Joyce's *Ulysses* deals with neither a doomed hero nor a praiseworthy modern adventurer of the intellect. It deals with a man of the flesh who through the Christian accretion surrounding Homer's highly moral epic can be nothing other than a clown, and a man of the intellect who can be nothing other than a waning pagan god. The two beings are the contraries out of which grow the metaphor for twentieth century consciousness. Their unity in *Ulysses* is effected through that ancient Homeric journey rearranged by Joyce for a new office — a twentieth century epic.

Like all great artists, Joyce distills experience for his art, but few have left so accurate a record of self-knowledge in the method of distillation. All experience received by the artist imprints an image on the mind. The artist disengages the soul of that image.

> The artist, he imagined, standing in the position of mediator between the world of his experience and the world of his dreams — a mediator, consequently gifted with twin faculties, a selective faculty and a reproductive faculty. To equate these faculties was the secret of artistic success: the artist who could disentangle the subtle soul of the image from its mesh of defining circumstances most exactly and re-embody it in artistic circumstances chosen as the most exact for it in its new office, he was the supreme artist. This perfect coincidence of the two artistic faculties Stephen called poetry. . . .[6]

Distilled, the essence of Homer's myth as Joyce sees it is this: Odysseus is a noble man and a soldier who through foolhardiness and a love of cunning delays his homecoming from the war ten years. For his folly he loses favor with "the old man of the Sea," Poseidon, the image of evil, who commits him to a sleep of the intellective powers and to a turbulent, destructive unrest of the sensitive appetite. His torture is keen because his imprisonment in concupiscence makes him grieve for his lost state of husband, father and ruler. His indignity, ignobility, perversion and blindness during the time of enchantment bring him to the verge of complete corruption, but intercession to a goddess breaks the enchantment, brings a return of prudence and fortitude and the manhood to undergo the last ordeals rationally and to arrive home. He regains his lost status by demonstrating in one last stratagem that he is the lawful ruler, the legal husband and the blood father of his son. A further illumination: Ulysses in the full glory of his manhood, goes out from his home against his reason and his heart, wins the war — a conflict between two peoples over beauty — and in the attempt to re-instate himself in the first glory, falls prey to evil days and nights the journey through which is not orgiastic dream but a day to day sleep of the intellectual powers and an almost imperceptible submission to corruption and decay. Odysseus' passage through the enchantment of the spirit to an heroic reclamation of his manhood are the soul of the Homeric myth as Joyce sees it. The myth was, of course, the artistic expression of the stories of many peoples and as such revealed the conscience not only of Greek human beings but antiquity in general. Tales and legends gravitated orally into the Troy cycle for centuries and finally in Homer's (or some poet's) vision became a work of art. Homer's *Odyssey* is the classic conscience of ancient peoples. Joyce to create the uncreated conscience of the race was not artistically free to choose any other but the Homeric myth.

In its new office for Joyce's *Ulysses* the Homer myth is the unifying fiber of man's hominisation, a functional space-time device through which Joyce evokes in us a collective consciousness, a memory of the intelligence of the human biota. And it is the perfect link from the past to illuminate modern man's disquiet, his "malady of space-time." As Pierre Teilhard de Chardin tells us in *The Phenomenon of Man,* "In the first and most wide-spread degree, the 'malady of space-time' manifests itself as a rule by a feeling of futility, of being crushed by the enormities of the cosmos."[7] The enormities of the cosmos include the vast socialization of reflection as evidenced in men's institutions, inventions, and government. In its new office the myth generates a cosmic dimension without which total significance or full creation of the conscience of the race is possible.

A brief analogical relation established between Homer's *Odyssey* and Joyce's *Ulysses* by episodes will demonstrate the necessary use Joyce makes of the ancient epic to illuminate his comedy. Essentially Mr. Bloom is no more a mock hero than the Odysseus of old: Joyce dissects the psychic similarity between the two conscience archetypes, Odysseus and Chaplin, into psychic similarity between Odysseus and Stephen Dedalus, strategists. We are not surprised to see Joyce name the first three episodes in his work *Telemachia,* and then deliberately fashion Stephen not as the wanderer's son, but the wanderer's intellect seeking a father which intellect is clothed with full being and which Father is not alone his lost Flesh, but the Supreme Being through a proper function of intellect with sense. A distillation of the opening books of the *Odyssey* presents Joyce with the soul of Telemachus' action: a youthful spirit seeks the security and certitude only the Father can furnish. For Homer this is of necessity the person of Odysseus, the lost father-king. For Joyce, since man has been redeemed, this is the eternally youthful intellect of the creature seeking the Father he lost, Christ the King.

Part Two in Joyce's schema is called *The Odyssey.* It is like Homer the longest action in the epic and contains the esthetic moment of the work. Odysseus is the narrator in Homer: Ulysses is in act in Joyce. The first episode is *Calypso.* In Homer the Greek hero consumed his own heart in the anguish of his plight which was to be imprisoned on the island paradise of the nymph, Calypso, who held him under a sexual spell which he could not break. In Joyce, the island paradise is the hero's own home; the nymph is his wife, Molly Bloom, who has blocked his ascent to consciousness beyond the limits of physical passion. Abortively he has tried to develop at least a semblance of intellect, but the nymph pulls him back to the earth levels of her existence through memory and romance. The result is he eats his own heart out in an anguish of frustrate attempts to exercise his act of existence in work, love and co-existence all of which fare in varying degrees. Almost solely through the power of a cheeky self-esteem he is able to defeat "the powers of enchantment" which assail him on every level; solely through the power of a nourished perversion is he able to tolerate the act of daily existence. He has for ten years been away from all normal relationships. "The old man of the sea", Poseidon, who punishes the hero in Homer becomes in Joyce "the old man" in Bloom in St. Paul's sense. Withal, Mr. Bloom is heroic because he endures; comic, because he is a clown; clown, because he has no conscience. He has a roiling, tempest-tossed, image-crowded unconscious. His action is often the real pathos of man, the eternal clown.

The Lotus-eaters in Homer is a land of sweet forgetfulness, a *tabula rasa* where men exist not by food but for the food and its false liberty. In its new office the episode reveals man's need to forget that his manhood has eluded him: In *Ulysses,* Mr. Bloom substitutes for his impotence: the clandestine affair with a mysterious little typist, logicising religious faith, a warm and scented bath — "This is my body." He offers himself to himself.

Hades finds the Greek hero visiting Teiresias, the underworld hermaphroditic prophet, who possesses the secret of his release from Calypso and his safe return home. In its new office the underworld becomes a graveyard; the caretaker, Hades; Sisyphus in strong torment with his stone becomes a Dubliner, Martin Cunningham, who rolls his heavy cronies to the funeral in pseudo control of the stone of their sentimentality and prejudice; Cerberus, the three-headed hound of hell, a toadbellied priest, Father Coffey, who performs the services at the graveside; the dead warriors and greats such as Hercules, Agamemnon and Ajax, the dead Irishmen, O'Connell and Parnell, who met their deaths by the hand of Irish treachery. Elpenor, who dies in a plunge from Circe's roof, becomes Paddy Dignam who dies of drink. A mysterious M'Intosh who must be identified to understand *Ulysses* attends Paddy's funeral. Ulysses' new function is to listen to the living and the dead at the eleven o'clock funeral and from it gain the secret knowledge of how to get home. He stumbles out of the cemetery "chap-fallen". The second sequence of *Hades* follows the *Circe* scene.

Aeolus for the Greek hero was the pinnacle of irony. He was in sight of Ithaca when his companions loosed the bag of winds planted by the god, Aeolus, blowing the whole company into the swine obsessed land of

Circe. In its new office Aeolus is a newspaper editor, his scenes a movie scenario. Ulysses' new office is to work as an ad man for the press. Communications in general and his job in particular drive Joyce's Ulysses straight into the arms of Circe, for he does not sell ads, he cannot communicate, he feeds upon the root of frustration, failure and effort to win personal prestige. He cannot come home, his ship (body and soul) is tempest tossed in the unknown sea of communication; he will be not swine but swinish. His members (wits) will become swine.

Lestrygonians lands the Greek hero in the city of the cannibals who destroy all his fleet save one ship by which he makes his escape only to land on the isle of Circe. The ships of Joyce's Ulysses' fleet (the hero's diverse powers of soul) are destroyed except in one sense: he saves face and soothes his senses by a mission at the museum. He goes there expressly to discover if the nude statues have mesial grooves. Mr. Bloom seeks Circe.

Scylla and Charybdis are perils skillfully avoided by Homer's Odysseus on his homeward journey. One false steering would have landed him in the multiple arms of the octopus, the *pieuvre* of antiquity, which dwelt in the homeward waters. In Joyce the octopus is the human mind; his Ulysses is in the climate of the tentacles, but he avoids intersection by doing what he came to do: see the copy of an ad he has hopes to copy. Joyce makes him invisible and in his place, his fated counterpart, Stephen Dedalus, intellect, speaks with the "intellectul imagination".

The Clashing Rocks, another peril avoided by Odysseus, is a hazard where rocks close on ships. Its new office is the streets, the rocks are the multifold citizens known personally by Ulysses; their action and existence haunt his consciousness and threaten his destiny. He guides his bark carefully through this labyrinth of torment by buying *Sweets of Sin*, a book which lifts him magically to a daydream and delivers him from the perils of reality.

The *Sirens* in Homer are so powerful in their love song, Odysseus to avoid seduction must lash himself to the mast of his ship. The Sirens in Joyce are barmaids who work their art on the hero, but he lashes himself to the mast of what by now has become his full ship: the letter to Martha, the nymph, the symbol, the substitute, the soother. This is his unseen love with whom he corresponds under a fictive name. He survives.

The Cyclops wherein Odysseus falls prey to evil days and nights is the pivotal action in Homer. In foolhardiness and enamoured of cunning and device, he has stolen into the land of the lawless giants, lost some of his members to the being who was greater than Zeus, duped him with wine and the device of "Noman", blinded him and escaped successfully with his remaining crew on the underside of the special ram. His ringing and proud shout, "say that it was Odysseus that blinded it, the waster of cities, son of Laertes, whose dwelling is in Ithaca,"[8] even as it echoes in the lawless country begets an evil enchantment that is to last ten years.

The episode in Joyce has, of course, a new Cyclops, an Irish Fenian, a self-styled giant of brutish dimension, "From shoulder to shoulder he measured severel ells and his rocklike mountainous knees were covered. . . with a strong growth of tawny prickly hair in hue and toughness similar to the mountain gorse (Ulex Europeus)" (291). His lair is Kiernan's Public House; Joyce's Ulysses is aware that the true Irish giant rules here a law unto himself; apprehensively he draws near the public house to meet his pretended appointment outside, but finally the Cyclops badgers him to come in and he does. Bloom's fearful curiosity of the Irish citizen, his drink and his talk is fairly balanced by a cheeky self-esteem which gets him through the ordeal of the Irish Cyclops with a bravura and cunning illuminating Odysseus' escape on the ram, space-timing man's evolutionary casuistry, highlighting man's increasing comedic behavior. Polyphemus' meal of the men becomes the Fenian's destruction of Bloom's wits: the device of the wine is Bloom's humanism; the cigar, throw-away, masonry, nationality combine to make a blinding stake of anger by which the Fenian is roused against Ulysses. The escape device Mr. Bloom concocts, however, is the underside of the Lamb of God. His ship is a tramcar. As he swerves off down the street, the Fenian in blind fury hurls the stone of a biscuit box after him. Ben Bloom Elijah has come and gone to Old Father Poseidon, St. Paul's "old man".

The overall "Noman" intelligibility of the scene culminates in Bloom's concept of love,

> But its no use, says he. Force, hatred, history, all that. That's not life for men and women, insult and hatred. And everybody knows that its the very opposite of that that is really life.
>
> Love, says Bloom. I mean the opposite of hatred. (327)

Joyce's inference that Bloom is no-man but boy and small one is in the *Portrait* parody that follows:

> Love loves to love love . . . . You love a certain person because everybody loves somebody but God loves everybody. (327)

Poseidon is clearly Satan: Polyphemus and the Fenian, Satan's sons. Joyce's Ulysses flees the Fenian, but he is now in the power of the "old man of the sea" and bound for a long separation from home (harmony of flesh and spirit).

Nausicaa, the Phaeacian maiden who discovered Odysseus naked in the golden sun, helps him to reach home. Joyce's Ulysses fully clothed commits the sin of Onan at the spectacle of a young, love sick girl flirting with him on the twilight beach. She is the granddaughter of the Fenian Cyclops, and she is as romantically sentimental as he is romantically brutish; her view of reality is as veiled as his was curtained. The land Phaeacia in its new office is transformed to the Star of the Sea Church from whose open windows there floats the voice of prayer to Mary, the Mother of God.

The Oxen of the Sun with the calamity of the men eating the oxen drove Ulysses alone and desolate to the Isle of Calypso. In Joyce deliberate rearrangement of the Homeric myth's chronology is illuminating. For his Ulysses lands on this island (now a hospital) as a waster of seed, as a slayer of fertility. His Calypso is, among other things, a living separation from his wife. This is one of the reasons he is an auto-erotic and by the same token why he cannot live in one flesh with his wife. He is too far from home in his own frail bark which he has abused and shamed, from which he has drowned his manhood. The hell of Circe awaits him after he has been witness to the Purefoy child's birth and after he has kept the jovial company of many medical students. He meets up with the other side of the coin here, Stephen Dedalus, a man with paralyzed flesh. Stephen's vivisective pursuit of reality brings him the rich treasure of gold intellectual ornaments whose essences can be disengaged but not reborn in new flesh. Mr. Dedalus cannot create; Mr. Bloom cannot think; Mr. Dedalus thinks; Mr. Bloom feels. Each has exercised his act of existence in the arid climate of the half-man. Their emergence into the flesh pungency of a June night in Dublin after rain begets the high comedy of nemesis through death and regeneration through birth.

Circe turned Odysseus' men into swine and kept him for a year as her lover. She promised him release and direction for his homeward journey after she had her way. The new office for Circe in Joyce is the prolonged esthetic moment of the work. The scene is a brothel in Dublin's Nighttown; Circe becomes Bella Cohen, well known house mistress; Stephen and his reptile-faced companion, Lynch, and Mr. Bloom re-enact the drama of their disunion through a comprehensive portrayal of their separation and its causes; their fraudulent act of existence as separate entities within one and the same being; their roles as transgressors against the principle of existence, and their comedic agons as area by area the matter of conscience is delivered through their co-active revelations. *Circe* is intellectual cinema divided into the three areas of knowledge upon which conscience acts and the three aspects of judgment which determine self-knowledge: (1) witness, (2) incite or bind, (3) accuse, torment or rebuke.[9] Survival for both is in terms of consciousness which is a matter of intellect and feeling. Each experiences a birth and regeneration. Circe's delivery of them into Hades for homeward direction becomes a scene outside the brothel where for the first time in Stephen Dedalus' existence he has sought understanding through the cooperative action of both the masculine and feminine principle in his nature. His Tieresias is an interior power of judgment through imagination presented to the intellect. He is knocked out. Mr. Bloom revives his lost intellect through a zany attempt at feeling presenting itself to thought. Homer's suspense after Hades is distilled in Joyce to create the life-like, eventual process by which human nature achieves itself through conscience. Joyce creates the poetry of conscience in the intellectual cinema of *Circe.*

Eumaeus, an old retainer in Odysseus' household, aids the hero and his son, Telemachus, in the overthrow of his wife's wooers. But Odysseus has to disguise himself as a beggar to get the information he seeks. In its new office Bloom and Stephen beg what they can from each other for information about suitors to their common affliction, the flesh and the intellectual imagination. Their plight is dramatized by an old tar in a cab-shelter who romanticizes his existence which is the *reductio ad absurdum* of the bi-heroes' act of existence. After a spirited, overwrought, "colossal," off the reel rendition of his larger purpose, Mr. Bloom, delicate always in his taste for cleanliness and wholesomeness, entices Stephen Dedalus to Ithaca, Bloom's home on Eccles Street, for cocoa and a chat. "You'll feel a different man," he tells the emerging poet who has just lived through "Bella poetria" in *Circe,* and with some skedaddling they take their low-backed car over the way to home.

Ithaca, the household of Odysseus, is his final battleground where with his mighty bow he slays the suitors and reclaims his manhood, his position as husband, father and ruler. The soul of the image in Homer's Ithaca is the birth of judgment, so Joyce disentangles this subtle soul to fit his space-time mosaic of a giant, single hero composed of two men and a woman. The intellectual soul of the hero has body and soul in Stephen Dedalus, paralyzed poet achieving locomotor apparatus or the power of movement through his poetic knowledge; the sensitive soul of the hero has body and soul in Leopold Bloom, lyric clown whose locomotor apparatus has all the accidents, some of the incidents and an abundance of the complements of Charlie Chaplin, silent movie clown. But the sensitive soul of the hero is wedded to the Flesh as feminine unconscious. He must come to terms with her not by separation but in adjusted marriage wherein her intractable energy ministers not to his destruction but his needs; not to his perversion, but to his rectitude. He orders her to serve him his breakfast in bed.

Penelope is the Greek archetype of feminine *ambiance.* She is wife to Odysseus, faithful to one husband even though he might live on in her consciousness as a memory only. She is beset by wooers who demand her hand in marriage, for they vow Odysseus is dead, but rather than renounce hope or break faith, she weaves a web by day and unravels it at night to prolong the completion of a tapestry which will mark the death of her belief in Odysseus' power to endure.

Joyce's habit of apprehending the being of a thing illuminates the conundrum of the Penelope episode in *Ulysses.* Molly's forty page, unpunctuated interior monologue given at the level of the conscious unconscious has a simultaneity of meaning which does not distinguish it from the other episodes in nature but in kind. The kind of consciousness Bloom has is sensitive, for he is the clown and exists on the level of feeling. Stephen Dedalus' consciousness is an intellectualized imagination and memory. But Molly Bloom, wife to Leopold, has the kind of consciousness that the unconscious realm of personality possesses: a natural confusion of past images weaving webs of present meaning through complex strands of past experience. It is a rich reservoir of the total residue of all that life has conferred on each individual containing all the aspects of love, faith, hope, pity and terror that the days and nights have wrought in a human life. This is the bottomless well of dream; the potential pit of evil; the generative source of ideal and good. No creating artist can account for his work done without the rich complexity of the unconscious as penetrable flesh nourishing the sensitive soul and body of his image. Bloom's wife, normally the mate who administers to any man's needs, has all but destroyed his very existence by her thematic sexual obsession, her animal attraction and her plump abandon. Joyce has made Molly Catholic, for Irish Catholicism had delivered him first to the power of the unconscious: the body was shameful, sex was a sin; urges of the flesh were in themselves corrupt; any man's desire for any woman was evidence of lust. The fact of birth itself was only to be tolerated for the act by which the new being joined humanity was the work of Satan. In Molly Bloom Joyce exorcises the paralyzing demon in Irish Catholicism. Molly is created in the full measure of what sex must be if Irish Catholicism of the nineteenth and twentieth century is right. Molly Bloom is the history of a repression, the art of a maimed personality whose gaucherie is comic because she is created in good humor and with infinite wit. Penelope weaves a web by day and unravels it at night; Molly Bloom is *weib* by day and unravels her *weib* at night releasing the earthy womanicity which she has woven over Bloom by day. Who are her suitors? Blazes Boylan at present and innumerable gents in the past. She cannot be faithful to Bloom because fidelity is the power of the intellect not the flesh. The power of the flesh is nutritive supplying corporeality to new being and individuating matter to that being within whose confines consciousness dwells in the action of ascent. The potential of the unconscious is separation from the matter of flesh to the substance of consciousness.[10] Joyce creates in Molly Bloom the knowledge that conscience acts upon, for she is the embodiment of an individual unconscious that is rife with complex, contrary images begotten of past experience; rebirth into the imagination creates the climate of judgment for the intellect. Molly Bloom is the third person in the trinity of being in Joyce's *Ulysses* whose unity is a full human personality.

Homer's Odyssey and its Christian accretion is essential to the intelligibility of Joyce's *Ulysses.* Without the arc of space-time created by the ancient and the modern myth there is no avenue to Joyce's essential gift to the twentieth century: the poetry of conscience.

Chapter III

TWENTIETH CENTURY MYTH

The Greek myth shows man at the mercy of fate. He is powerless to avoid long sensual imprisonment, and he is to be pitied not because his own intellect and will have caused him to lose his manhood, but rather because the gods have taken it away from him. Behind the meaning which is still unuttered in Homer, Joyce beholds the Greek mind perceiving mankind's voluntary submission to his lower nature through misuse of his powers. Odysseus did not have to visit the Cyclops nor use his cunning at the cost of peril. Odysseus knowing the power and influence of the giants could have been prudent and avoided them. But Odysseus is human, a man, a hero, an adventurer. At times he compromises his fortitude with foolhardiness, but he is bound to pay the consequences. In conscience Odysseus rebukes his foolhardiness with the Cyclops. On the island of Circe, in the jaws of Calypso, in the descent into Hades, Odysseus is tempted by sleep suicide; he longs to submit totally to his unconscious. Throughout the whole of his "enchantment" he pines for his lost state, and his constant aim is to get home. Finally he accomplishes it but only after indignity, privation, surfeit of lust, gluttony, sloth. The conscience of man pervades the Homer myth not because Homer is didactic, but because Homer is an artist-seer: he sees that conscience is a human act, an act which bears witness, binds and incites a man to the good, accuses, torments or rebukes him. Man's nature is to judge what he does, apply knowledge to his acts. He will know he has or has not done something required to maintain his identity or forbidden to him because the evil act destroys his wholeness. Odysseus knew he was playing with extraordinary fire when he visited the Cyclops; for ten years this foolish act is a witness to his imprudence. During his enchantment self-torment and rebuke are his recurring states of mind. Homer's art reveals a law of man's nature — that the act of conscience informs the acts of men. If an artist omits the act of conscience from the actions of man, he has in mind something even more revealing than sublimity alone: he has in mind high comedy.

Greek theology is eloquent on man's response to his universe: he feared it. How else an Aeolus, Poseidon, a Wandering Rocks, a Scylla or Charybdis? It is eloquent too in its expression of the unalterable laws of society: birth, life, death. How else the genealogy of the gods, the invention of Hades? It was this very eloquence, however, that saved the Greek mind from looking upon the stars as impersonal, the universe as cold, existence as futile. Greek theology made personal every element of the universe just as it made intimate the multiple gods to whom man appealed for life, good fortune and a happy death. We remember Odysseus' trials ended only after his intercession to Pallas Athena, goddess of wisdom; not only is his prayer answered, but under the deity's protection, he is harbored, disguised, given strength to shoot his bow, and finally to be victorious in his homecoming. Joyce's use of the Greek myth in *Ulysses* illuminates not only Homer but historical truth: man's psychic motion is toward redemption through temptation and fall.

From his twentieth century position Joyce has the advantage of space in the long history of humanity which shows him what time has wrought in man. Time has dispelled Greek theology and brought Christianity. Time has brought knowledge of the universe and dispelled superstition. Time has brought invention, organization, increased consciousness. The organized complexity of mens' minds over the space of time has been a process of thought reflecting upon itself, a process of reflection that has revealed as Teilhard de Chardin says, "the irreversible coherence of all that exists."[1] Joyce's work exists in the reality of space-time.

Humanity's jolt, however, in finding itself in space-time has confounded, confused and paralyzed it. It is this state of human consciousness and especially its conscience Joyce transforms in his art. In the history of the world had any artist a more suitable model than Charlie Chaplin and a more suitable *techne* than the cinema? Stand the myth of Odysseus beside the Chaplin cinema myth, and you have at once an arc of space-time to illuminate the conscience of the race.

Charlie Chaplin, screen hero, began in 1914 as a basically unsympathetic though engaging character — a sharper, a heel, an annoying blunderer, a thief, an obnoxious drunk, who was cruel, sometimes sadistic. Mr. Theodore Huff,[2] biographer and critic of Chaplin's art, states that the real Charlie does not emerge until Chaplin's second year in films with Essanay.

The real Charlie's emergence was not without shucking the matter of the Keystone style of Mack Sennett. Chaplin played one year for Sennett, and the style of those comedies, while Chaplin was to retain many of its best features and refine them, was briefly this:

> . . . a blend of lunatic fantasy, preposterous physical types, exaggerated costumes and make-up, whirlwind pace, violent action, zany gags. His films were improvisations: "shot on the cuff," and on the spot — a laundry, a restaurant, the park, anywhere.
>
> After a violent action, a comedy would be resolved by and culminate in a wild chase. This often resembled a ballet in its movement and staging, though, of course, a cinematic chase had qualities impossible to any other medium.[3]

To fool the public Chaplin's Keystone comedies were issued under new names and spliced into a composite thirty-reel serial called *Perils of Patrick.* Another pirate trick was a rehash of Chaplin clips called *Charlie Chaplin — A Son of the Gods.* These tricks were lucrative and safe in the international film market. We can imagine European audiences seeing a new title for many old Chaplins. But the very matter Chaplin passed through and departed from gave to the "Charlie" he was to develop a perspective amazing to view in restrospect. All of Charlie's being is in the thirty-five comedies made for Sennett, 1914-1915. Refinement and depth were possible only through the evolutionary process of experience, and at Essanay, Chaplin's second studio, this process was effective because he was in complete command of every phase of his show. At Essanay the Chaplin myth became the narrative linked to the daily ritual of twentieth century existence with its enormous socialization of reflection made concrete in twentieth century industry, levels of society, politics, invention, science, and chaotic psychic profile.

The action in the Chaplin narrative is analogous to the Prodigal Son in Scripture with this distinction: the twentieth century son intends permanent exile from his father's house. The moral meaning of Charlie is that *l'homme moyen sensuel* has cast his intellectual powers into a deep sleep; he must therefore live a pseudo-existence and achieve a pseudo-consciousness until such time as the intellect is disenchanted. This offense against nature brings a host of perversions in its wake. But the sobriety of the philosopher is cancelled by the lyric greatness of the clown. Charlie is simply a marvelous little man without a conscience. Anything goes; everyone makes the identity; all views of Charlie are pure joy, for they furnish the vicarious experience of human nature before it needed conscience. The comedy comes in the tension between the dream and the reality. Here is the narrative.

The Chaplin myth: Charlie is a fallen aristocrat who has renounced his birthright and his heritage in the human family so that he can live a *natural* life. He is of the noble family of man whose deeds are eloquent in the institutions, inventions, arts and sciences of humanity. Charlie renounces his birthright voluntarily that he may indulge his natural curiosities, employ his natural cunning, live a day to day existence without the continuum of thinking that belonging to his family demanded. To him the heritage was peanuts compared to freedom from all restraint, indulgence in all desire. What was the heritage? Mankind, his family, at its best could teach him patient endurance of his human condition, show him the way to unite intellect with flesh. Mankind at his best could teach him the way of his full nature: incarnate spirit. But Charlie has no appetite for such wonders. He knows what he knows; he is what he is, and he wants to be what he knows and what he is. He wants, for instance, to live without judging or being judged. He just wants to be left alone to follow the star of the day (usually a pretty girl), to laugh at what amuses him, to cry if he's touched, to fight if he feels like it. Conscience is *ad nauseam;* he has heard of it since birth and it chokes him. Far better to wander the earth without the cumbersome human luggage. Far better to be *l'homme moyen sensuel.*

In spite of Charlie's compulsion to exist outside the human family, strong evidence of his lineage manifests itself in what he wears and what he does, whom he sees, the places he goes, whom he outwits, whom he fears. He wears the clothes of a fallen aristocrat: tight little five-button cut-away, baggy trousers, a jaunty derby hat that he tips grandly, "the salutation with the hat takes seriously a social convention and carries it as far as it can go."[4] He wears worn-out gloves and carries a cane. The suit itself is an over-used and ill-fitting morning suit, but the boutonniere in his lapel is vibrant and ever fresh. He knows where the flowers grow and he respects them. But the most revealing evidence of our fallen aristocrat is his enormous feet. They fasten him to the earth from which he sprang; they make him shuffle, plodge and splay. They bind him to the loamy sentience of his family; they keep him on the hunt for earthy, natural satisfaction; they direct him to alleys, garbage cans, doss houses, second rate hotels; they direct him to hidden, out of the way places where he can in secret satisfy unfulfilled desires, dreams and fantasies.

Charlie is a wanderer who rejects his father's house because hypocrites dwell there and proud pampered women: because financiers gaff there and scheme for empires; because the princes of commerce plot in his father's halls how to manipulate sister and brother; because decadent priests, sly missionaries, false prophets preach an empty word, because all that he sees and hears defiles the glory of the visible and the power of the audible. Where does he wander and how does he spend his time? Who does he encounter and whom does he fear?

Charlie wanders through the great cities of the world denying his birthright but revealing his lineage. He wants to live as other men; he makes a real effort to work, to love, to found a family, to find a home. But interior questions go unanswered: why, if the Father redeemed man, does not the human family show its redemption? Why is there not spontaneous love among "these Christians"? Why, if mankind has a new sonship with God does he still lie, cheat, swindle, steal? Why does he still betray and kill? Ah, but these are remote disturbances of Charlie, fallen aristocrat. After all, he was not born for philosophy, theology, psychology; he was not meant to live by bookish learning; the history of the race is no concern of his. He was meant to live freely, instinctively and follow the law of his nature. He has, in spite of his enormous earth bound feet, a gift for ebullience, a sense of song, dance and gaiety. He will wander forever escaping if he can the remembrance of who he is, from whence he sprang, where he is going. He will create his own world, peopled with his own creatures who live an ideal natural existence. Charlie is the twentieth century clownman for whom the supernatural is a lost myth, the cosmos an unintelligible enormity, the waste hordes of the living and the dead mute evidence of the futility of any human endeavor.

But as already observed, the clown cannot escape his humanity. He will try as every one does for glory; he will attempt all that challenges his cunning, his sense of decency, all that arouses his curiosity, all that challenges his sense of fair play. Charlie is a hero. He will fight the bruiser time and again; he will outwit the criminal; he will save the widow and orphan; he will mock the pompous, undress the proud, capture the enemy, rescue the drowning, convert the suicide, make glad the blind girl. He is a hero amidst slapstick pie throwing, break away vase, trick shot, super imposed image. Charlie, fallen aristocrat, voluntary outcast, dispossessed son, everlasting wanderer is the hero in the cities of men. During the First World War "people everywhere cried out for a hero; now they had one, and there had never been a hero less demanding. There was nothing swashbuckling about him. He asked for nothing, only to be left alone. . . ."[5]

In *Shoulder Arms* (released October 20, 1918) Charlie disguised as a tree captures a flock of Germans, and then disguised as a German captures the Kaiser and the Crown Prince. At a testimonial dinner, the King of England asks for a button off his uniform, but he refuses elegantly to be souvenired; he just wants to be left alone. This is one comic aspect of Charlie the world cherished in 1918; today's audiences find it a rich human amusing antic. But he was never left alone. The challenge presented itself in every film. Charlie is explicitly hero in *The Vagabond, One A.M., The Pawnshop, The Rink, The Cure, The Adventurer, Easy Street, The Immigrant*; these films were made for Mutual 1916-17.

But Charlie is not only a wandering hero who rejects the human family while he is defending it, he is a tramp, a vagrant. He operates under the illusion that he is looking for a home, a beautiful wife, lovely children and a position of respect and esteem in the community. This is so much marvelous make-believe because we know he detests work, cannot possibly be attractive to women who judge men by clothes and money; he cannot abide children because he is too much the child; he cannot gain prestige because he doesn't earn it. As tramp Charlie is hand to mouth, straw pallet to farmer's chickens, a companion of bums, a free and easy spirit who scorns sanitation but whose sanity often leads to a sacramentalizing of the beauty of the earth and the goodness of the human spirit. But a tramp is always suspect in the cities of men. Vagrancy is a-societal and, therefore, a case for the police. As tramp and vagrant Charlie is under suspicion, and the Keystone cops are his bone, his constant fear.

It is perfectly logical. The Keystone cops do not know that beneath that shabby exterior Charlie yearns to come back to the human family and be a man. They will not admit he has a right to steal food when he's hungry or break windows so he can work as a window setter or pose as an ambassador from Greece to make love to a pretty girl, or put a horseshoe in his boxing glove to keep the bully from killing him first. They book him for breaking the law. No wonder Charlie lives in fear of the cops, and no wonder the cops are mindless boobs whom he usually dupes. The law as the human family practices it, Charlie sees as a travesty of justice. Anarchy, then, and poetry; rebellion and profundity; rejection and reform motivate the tramp in search of imperishable beauty.

This is because Charlie is a lover. He loves himself but not enough to know himself; he loves others if they are beautiful. The perfect reflection of his own self-love is his romantic hunger for the beautiful woman. For himself he wants what for him is good; this way all his desires become his goods; he has no conscience about his appetites; he has no conscience in his search for beauty. He loves blindly without knowledge; his sacrifice is to Aphrodite of the young and lovely limb, the soft innocent eyes, the fresh beautiful face, the radiant dark hair (Chaplin's heroines, Mable Normand, Edna Purviance, Lita Grey, Georgia Hale, Paulette Goddard were all brunettes). He longs to possess the high and ideal goddess, but he is clumsy, ineffectual, inconfident. He blunders his love; "He wants to love," Chaplin said of him, "but his big feet won't let him." Partly he has too much common sense to fall for his own goddess cult; partly he is happy in failure for there are always other goddesses; mainly he cannot know without the heritage of his race that possessing the sensuous beauty of self is an intellectual matter. The perfect wedding of the intellect to the senses is not only a necessary human fusion, but it is the union that begets the child of creation; the mating that begets one mind, one flesh. Charlie never pities himself; he goes over the horizon after a moment's despondency in a caper of hopeful tomorrows. But he is chafed, he does walk stiff-legged. He must work off his aroused emotion in lonely ecstasy yet keep his secret from mankind.

In the whole Chaplin myth, Charlie's interest in women increases in consciousness. He evolves from the clown's lechery in the Keystone films where he hooks skirts, peeks at women's unmentionables, grabs at bloomers, chases socialites, puts his foot in the laps of great ladies to look at their bosoms, to the clown's unrequited love for the beautiful, unattainable girl who is unaware he exists. Charlie's romantic hunger is consistent with his existence outside reality. This is a great clown's way of seeing through to the heart of humanity, to human privation, degradation, illusion.

The counterpoint of Charlie's romantic hunger is the dream. A blow on the head never fells him; it transports him to ideal existence wherein he is the re-instated aristocrat, his Father's son, the hero with matchless strength and cunning, the free and integrated spirit who welcomes all responsibility, the lover for whom women compete, the ethereal dreamer and the great reformer. The special appeal of the dream is Chaplin's grace and agility as a dancer, his gifted pantomime, his perfect inflection towards the gag, and finally, the supreme incongruity of the little fellow achieving worldly perfection. The fantasy sequences of the films marked by Chaplin's gifted imagination and brilliant execution are the lyrical profundity existing side by side with the big feet and the stiff walk. Always the clown dreams of himself as the good man.

Everything points to the clown as reformer. If Charlie had his way, many things would be different. He would release humanity from war, pestilence and disease *(Shoulder Arms, The Cure)*; he would have humanity remember its origins and revel in its natural appetites *(His Prehistoric Past)*; he would establish the order of the sensuous and let the intellect go hang; he would be Lord Mayor of No Restraint, and every day would be a holiday. He would be brother to the ass and draw in all his human brothers as brothers to the ass. This way is Paradise; this way is fulfillment. Down with capitalism, man is history, forget religion. Build the new cities of man with new organization. Live! "I am here today." The clown certainly asks twentieth century man to consider species of sickness in the world's soul. "Life is so sad he has to make a comedy of it," Chaplin said of Charlie.[6] No wonder the world took Charlie to its heart and went away cleansed. They saw with Charlie their own malady of space-time, their own serious loss of the supernatural. They loved the spectacle of their own thousand day dreams wrecking havoc before them on the screen. Charlie tickled them by eye, by ear (although he rarely moved his lips), by unspoken thought, by absolute and genuine lack of conscience. All men would like to do as Charlie does. He does not plead as Siegfried[7] for an ideal humanity who will do the right thing with or without Christianity nor for human passion as the highest good, but he pleads at the bar of folly and wandering for the poetry of conscience. Like Joyce, Chaplin has an appetite for contraries: Charlie has no conscience precisely because conscience is a potential act pervading existence: the poetry of conscience is judgment through thought and feeling. Charlie's thought is mythical and his feeling richly human. Joyce's good fortune in Charlie Chaplin is like Shakespeare's in the five foot poetic line and like J. D. Salinger's contemporaneity with Joyce in this century. The evolutionary character of the world has complexified man's consciousness. Great artists of the twentieth century create out of psychic similarities.

Chaplin's last film made in America was *Monsieur Verdoux* (1952). Shortly after this film he sailed with his wife, Oona O'Neill, for a European holiday. While he was on the high seas, the State Department cabled him not to return. Over a period of years Chaplin was in serious trouble with the government over income taxes, and his last films were thought to have a treasonous tone. The final irony in the Charlie legend is that the people who begged him to show them further the image of themselves as natural, now turned on him because he obliged them. Chaplin's case in its fundamental irony is not unlike Joyce's predicament in Ireland and later the Supreme Court case of *Ulysses'* publication in America.[8] Chaplin needed a Judge Woolsey, but since his offense was not really an artistic one — eventually intelligent critics like James Agee could have convinced the moralists that Chaplin's film intention was right.[9] He was at fault with the law. Why he fought paying his share of income tax is difficult to understand.

On February 26, 1916 Chaplin signed with Mutual for ten thousand dollars a week with a bonus of one hundred and fifty thousand dollars. At First National in 1917, he leaped from six hundred and seventy thousand to one million dollars a year.

> The contract received world wide publicity. It gave him a million dollars, plus a fifteen thousand dollar bonus for signing for eight pictures to be made within eighteen months. They were not to run under 1600 feet. If they ran over 2300 feet he was to receive a proportionate increase and other financial inducements.[10]

The greatest significance Chaplin's off the reel behavior has is to make clear again that a man's art is separate from his private life. Charlie is immortal. Long after America has forgotten the grievance against Chaplin, Charlie will reawaken the first joy audiences felt in the little hero. The Chaplin films, controlled by a Moroccan distribution company, are played all over Europe not as silent screen antiquaries but as modern entertainment, and the museum of Modern Art in New York has a complete Chaplin library.

Gilbert Seldes, one of many Chaplin admirers, says of him:

> . . . he achieved a fame which passed entirely by word of mouth into the category of common myths and legends of America.[11]

By 1915 people were singing "O, the moon shines bright on Charlie Chaplin." T. S. Eliot's use of the parody appears in *The Wasteland,* "O, the moon shines bright on Mrs. Porter." The men sang it in the trenches as a marching song. Children in London made rhymes about the current films. Here is one on *Easy Street* (released January 22, 1917):

> Love backed by force
> Forgiveness sweet
> Brings Hope and Peace
> To Easy Street.[12]

"But there were a hundred other songs about Chaplin who had captured the public imagination as it has rarely been captured before; and long before *Shoulder Arms,* street arabs played hopskotch as they sang the Chaplin songs."[13]

"I am here today: Charlie Chaplin." Robert Payne describes the sign and gives it a meaning:

> . . . a *papier mache* tramp the size of a cigar store Indian, waving his jaunty cane with the hat a little on one side was like an invitation to license.[14]

Gilbert Seldes is inclined more toward sublimity, "**I am here to-day** was his legend."[15] It is enough to know that over the full world, the cardboard figure announced not what he would play but that he would play.

Theater people from all countries admired and respected Chaplin's Charlie. When *Easy Street* (1917) was being filmed, Nijinski playing Los Angeles suddenly spotted Chaplin in the audience with Dorothy Gish. He stopped the show to invite Charlie backstage, and the audience waited a half hour while each member of the company embraced him.[16]

Minnie Maddern Fiske was one of the first theater people to write about Chaplin's art. In an article in Harper's Weekly, May 6, 1916, she compared Chaplin to Aristophanes, Plautus, Shakespeare and Rabelais. Carl Van Vechten, avante-garde leader in the twenties, pronounced for the American intelligentia the absolutely newest thing of the century: Charlie Chaplin.

Max Eastman wrote of him, "His life is filled to the brim with what most lives consist of yearning after — wealth and fame and creative play and beautiful women — but he does not know how to enjoy anyone of the four . . . and is in the depths of his heart humble, a poor boy who had no opportunities and is eager to learn."[17] Eastman also feels that Chaplin had fallen short of his potentialities: he would have gone much farther could he have let himself go intellectually, poetically, and financially.

Woolcott named Chaplin "the foremost artist of the world;" Winston Churchill wrote of the silent film as "everybody's language" and analyzed Chaplin's pantomime art; George Bernard Shaw says Chaplin is "the only genius developed in motion pictures."[18]

Chaplin was born April 16, 1889 in London. His father, Charles Chaplin, was from an Anglicized French Jewish family, and his mother was said to be of Spanish and Irish origin. They both performed in the English Music Halls, Chaplin under his own name and Mrs. Chaplin under the stage name of Lily Harley. Chaplin senior was famous in the eighties for his baritone voice while his wife sang and danced in various troupes including Gilbert and Sullivan companies. Mrs. Chaplin had been married before to Sydney Hawkes, a Jewish bookmaker, by whom she had four sons. The eldest, Sydney, came to live with his mother and took the Chaplin name.

Chaplin senior died an alcoholic when Charlie was five, reducing the Chaplin boys and their mother to a sad hand-to-mouth existence in London's Kennington slum. Mrs. Chaplin's health failed and during her convalescence the boys were placed in Hanwell Residential School, a kind of orphanage where both suffered loneliness, privation and shoddy treatment. Sydney got out to go to sea, but Charlie was too young to do anything but creep off by himself and dream of grandeur and riches.

Charles was seven when he joined a music hall act, "The Eight Lancaster Lads". His dog pantomime singled him out as a clever young lad. He toured a year and a half and then his mother placed him in Hern Boy's College near London for two years. This was his schooling. His mother taught him everything else he knew: her powers of observation were uncanny; she could tell by a man's gait, the condition of his shoes, the expression of his face, and the fact that he entered a bake shop, that he had a fight with his wife and left without breakfast. Often Charlie checked her observations and often they were right. She studied people with him; he showed early the transference of her intuitive gift. His mother's mind collapsed when he was almost nine years old: she was taken to an asylum. He was alone, a waif on the London streets. He was hired as a chore boy at Covent Gardens market; he danced in the street; he made and sold paper boats, he was lather boy in a barber shop. He slept in the park.

Sydney came back from the navy. He was forlorn to learn of his mother's illness, but he saw to Charlie. Sydney made the rounds of theatrical agencies with Charlie and some of his shows are on record. At ten Charlie played *Giddy Ostend* at the London Hippodrome in January, 1900. He toured the provinces as the boy hero in *From Rags to Riches,* received fine notices and saved some money. He placed his mother in a convalescent home, dressed nattily and sported a cane.

Between the ages of ten and fifteen Charlie had many acting jobs, and in 1905 at the Duke of York's Theater, when he was playing Billy in *The Painful Predicament of Sherlock Holmes* for the Gillette Company, King Edward saw the performance with Queen Alexandra and the King of Greece. The actors were ordered not to look at the royal box, but Charlie looked, and the King chuckled. He was scolded for his boldness, but it exulted him to make the King laugh.

His next luck was with *Casey's Court Circus,* a skit wherein youngsters impersonated public favorites. Charlie had to do Dr. Walford Bodie, a patent medicine faker and "electrical wizard", then a London sensation. His satire of Dr. Bodie involved several funny turns with a silk hat. He was a comic success in large or small assignments. So far, lines were as important as pantomime. He scored in a burlesque of Fred Sisnette's *Turpin's Ride to York.* When *Casey's Court Circus* played in the Channel Islands, Charlie found that his jokes were not getting over because, as he soon discovered, the natives knew little English. He pantomimed all his jokes and brought down the native house. Pantomime is the major element of his art; he learned it as the first entelechy.

Sydney got Charlie into the Fred Karno Company when the boy was seventeen. Karno's was a famous pantomime troup with whom Chaplin acted both in Europe and America until during an American tour, Mack Sennett signed him to make Keystone comedies for the then unbelievable salary of one hundred and fifty dollars a week.

Chaplin was twenty-three when he went to work for Mack Sennett. In one year he made thirty-five comedies at the end of which time much of the civilized globe knew he "was here to-day". There is no question about his acquisitive nature or his almost psychotic fear of insecurity, for his childhood haunted him. He had anxieties over the capital investment in a picture; he feared that he might lose his gift and that his audience might suddenly desert him.

These complex reactions to his films kept him deeply dissatisfied with each picture, tensely creative in the new work and always searching for new dimensions in the strange Charlie of whom he said: "He is chasing folly and he knows it. He is trying to meet the world bravely, to put up a bluff, and he knows that too."[19]

In 1921 when *The Kid*, Chaplin's autobiographical film, was released he went to England for the European première. His reception in England was beyond anything he could have imagined in the far off days of Hanwell Residential School where as a lonely boy of seven he dreamed of pomp and grandeur.

News releases of *The Kid* preceded its formal opening in theaters all over the world (February, 1921), and no doubt the film was advertised as Chaplin's autobiography. Joyce's letter to Budgen December 10, 1920 has in it (until now) a mysterious bit of cockney:

> A point about Ulysses (Bloom). He romances about Ithaca (Oi want teh go back teh the Mawl Enn Road, s' elp me!) and when he gets back it gives him the pip. I mention this because you in your absence from England seemed to have forgotten the human atmosphere and I the atmospheric conditions of these zones.[20]

The pip, slang for a person or thing much admired, is exactly what Chaplin got. The Maul End Road could be any grand exit from the Kennington slum area.

Chapter IV

CLOWN FLESH

Joyce's black crayon drawing of Mr. Bloom done in 1926 shows him in clown suit and small derby.[1] The suit has a touch of ruff, two large front buttons and a medieval sleeve. He is in the tradition of clowns, not as a performer, but as the basis for the tradition: man, the sad funny fellow; life, the sorrowful hilarity; existence, the comic impossibility; destiny, the ridiculous height.

Mr. Bloom is man, the living clown — not the fool, jester or wit we see in Shakespeare nor tumbler in the circus, but man who inspired the fool and tumbler to shake the solid ground underfoot that he might roar at his own folly. The difference between Bloom as clown and Deburau as clown (French 1796-1846) is the distinction Stephen Dedalus makes between "poetry and the chaos of unremembered writing."[2] A man playing clown puts on the manner of a clown and does what is customary for a clown to do: defy logic, time, space, convention, and often the law of gravity. His humor is robust, broad, physical. He creates havoc and disorder for man's delight; he releases man from himself.

A living clown, on the other hand, is the performing clown's model. He is a contradiction and a paradox; a denial and an affirmation of his nature and his destiny. The best example, however, is the man unaware that his antics are antics. This affords immediate fun for others, and he becomes a "character." The living clown never knows his behavior is ridiculous and this is the comedy: the sober ridiculous act. He has, of course, no moral position: he is usually kind and sympathetic, but he has no charity. Such a man masks successfully an interior monolog of actual contumely for others, yet he is outwardly sweet and kind. His love for others or for the created universe is a fiction even he believes in. He is peace-loving but without fortitude; self victory is unknown to him. The comedy, then, of a man who above all cherishes good will, smiles and total acceptance from everyone, yet lives a life of self indulgence, secret gratification, moral perversion is the tension between the two very human forms of egotism. The living clown is rarely a food glutton, but he often is a pederast, pimp, adulterer, lecher. He might show no pride at all, yet he could with sufficient romantic impetus be a two toed sloth always hoping for professional success. The living clown can be fastidious and sanitary yet he can habituate the red light district. The living clown is neither a man nor a clown; he is man as clown, man wondering about much; knowing about little; curious about everything, certain about nothing, beholding everything, understanding nothing. This man is funny because he gathers into himself the fragments of all human failure. He measures by his lacks the extent of human potential. He is a real clown because he has no conscience. He is the height of the ridiculous because the law of conscience is an unalterable law of society.

Stephen Daedalus rejected the term "literature" because to him "the realm of its princes was the realm of manners and customs of societies — a spacious realm." He was interested in something far more basic than manners and customs of society in his art. He was interested in the realm of the poet.

> But society is itself, he conceived, the complex body in which certain laws are involved and overwrapped and he therefore proclaimed as the realm of the poet the realm of these unalterable laws.[3]

This realm of its nature is a labyrinth rather than one of linear space. Its microcosm is the human soul. Many souls are a society; each is governed by the unalterable biological laws of birth and death, growth and maturity, survival; each is governed by the unalterable law of his nature: the habit of first principles, *synderesis;* each is governed by the unalterable law of evolution, organized complexity, *consciousness;* each is governed by the unalterable law of consciousness: *reflection*; each is governed by the unalterable law of reflection, *conscience.*

Mr. Bloom in *Ulysses* does not wear a baggy clown suit or a ruff. He wears a black funeral suit cut in the style of 1904 which includes a waist coat and a black derby hat. He carries a newspaper rolled as a baton; the newspaper is the *Freeman's Journal,* the paper for which he canvasses ads. This is his sign. Charlie of the Chaplin cannon wears a black cut-away, a waistcoat, baggy pants, big shoes on the wrong feet, a small derby and he carries a bamboo cane. The cane is his sign. As Mr. Bloom unfolds in *Ulysses,* his costume converges toward Charlie's total get-up. Eventually his pants sag, eventually in *Circe* he is to use almost every aspect of Charlie's absurd get-up and as he does, not only is Charlie, the model, illuminated, but Bloom is explained and analyzed through the costume; man the universal clown is delivered through the medium of Chaplin as clown who becomes Bloom, the extension of man, the living clown.

I think we have to take a close look at Mr. Bloom's body and how he uses it to appreciate how clearly he is built on Chaplin's lines. The complexity of *Ulysses* does not obscure Joyce's insistence on "the ineluctable modality of the visible" (38). His primary matter is always the "diaphane", the thing with its transparency. The whole object, its appearance and its essence commands his power. Bloom has to be object as well as subject (which he mainly is), but we will never see the act of Bloom's life in *Ulysses* unless we behold him with our eyes. The Chaplin figure in Bloom is the key to his actuality, his mode of existence, his habit of mind, his presence. See him through the being and the technique of the silent cinema hero, and all Mr. Bloom does, fits and is proper to him. He is a clown.

The first thing to look at is the tone, texture, size and weight of Mr. Bloom's famous body. It bears a most careful likeness to Charlie. Stephen Dedalus in the Eumaeus episode, when Mr. Bloom took his arm, "thought he felt a strange flesh of a different man approach him, *sinewless and wobbly and all that* (644). He did feel a different man as Bloom just told him he would, and this is the different man we have to look at.

Mr. Bloom has a clown's body. It is soft like his heart which, when he meets Blazes Boylan, Joyce tells us "quopped". He is not muscular, strong or physically forceful. While a performing clown is in reality athletic and sinewy, Bloom acts as though he had neither bones nor muscle. Mr. Bloom's body is wobbly; he tumbles easily. The traditional clown tumbles actually; portrays wobbliness. What is Chaplin's flesh? Is he this "different" man? His comedies always have a bruiser who even with a light shove puts Charlie in a wobbly heap. Attracted by beauty everywhere, Charlie dances with grace ignoring the big shoes, forgetting contumely, hardship and hunger. Charlie stylizes his walk, stance, run, but he is a wobbly little man without sinew; his forte is grace. His victory, if he wins, is by the sword of wit; his courage, if he maintains it, is the courage of a cheeky self-esteem. Bloom's central hope lies in his private estimate of himself and others. His victory over "the old man" is by his wits, but Bloom is more inclined to *coups* of various kinds rather than victories. He accomplishes no self victory — nor does Charlie — but Bloom's *coup* at Kiernan's might be described as an ironic self-identity. The irony of the *coup* is that it should suffer a "one night stand" as it were. The God of which Bloom speaks is a fiction for him.

The tone and texture of Bloom's and Charlie's bodies are similar. How do they compare in size? Bloom is five feet nine and one half inches tall; he weighs eleven stone and four, 158 pounds (652), and his neck is size 17 (695). His chest is the size of a 13 year old boy or small woman: size 29½ (706). He gained some chest girth by using his Sandow Exercisor, an early moving picture novelty; that is why his chest is now bigger. Bloom has an arm muscle expansion of ten inches and a twelve inch thigh (706). This is the comparatively small man who wanders through Dublin, Thursday, June 16, 1904.

Chaplin is five feet, four inches tall, and when he played Charlie, especially during the years Joyce saw him as model (1914-1921), he weighed 130 lbs. Chaplin told Theodore Huff if he were three inches taller, he could not have played Charlie.[4] He is probably right, but the observation is question begging since the chance of his being taller did not exist. For Bloom, however, it does exist. Charlie as so many of his critics have said is a small man who acts taller than he is. Much of Bloom's comedy depends on his being comparatively small, slight, skimpy of limb, thick necked, withal graceful — in spite of his feet and his walk.

Bloom's feet and his walk are in the novel from his entrance on page 55, but the first deliberate use of Chaplin in Bloom is in the scenario, *Aeolus*, where two Bloom scenes confirm the feeling all along: that Bloom is a legendary someone we have seen and experienced.

The scenes are called "Exit Bloom" and "A Street Cortege" (128). They have the ethos of a Chaplin comedy and what is more, a direct description of Bloom's feet and his walk. Here is the Scene: Bloom from the door of the editor's office says with dash and bravura,

> —I'm just running round Bachelor's walk . . . about this ad of Keyes's. Want to fix it up. They tell me he's round there in Dillon's.

The company in the office: Myles Crawford, the great cock editor of the *Evening Telegraph;* MacHugh, Professor of Classics; Lenehan, writer for *Sporting Magazine* never heard of Keyes, and Bloom for them is a daily joke. The editor flushes Bloom off with,

> —Begone! The world is before you!

From the window, however, Professor MacHugh gives Bloom an afterthought. He watches him on the street:

> —He'll get that advertisement . . . . Look at the young scamps after him.

Both Lenehan and the Professor are then seen to smile over the crossblind at the file of capering newsboys in Mr. Bloom's wake, the last zigzagging white on the breeze a mocking kite, a tail of white bowknots.

> —Look at the young guttersnipes behind him, hue and cry, Lenehan said, and you'll kick. O, my rib risible! *Taking off his flat spaugs and the walk.* (italics mine)
>
> He began to mazurka in swift caricature cross the floor on sliding feet . . . .

The word "spaug" is from the Gaelic noun, "spag" meaning large and misshapen foot which in turn is the root word for the noun, "spagach" meaning a splayfooted person. As an adjective "spagach" means splay-footed and out-toed.[5] These several connotations cluster in the image "flat spaugs". Bloom's feet are large and misshapen on the most literal level and in the light of evidence before and after the above passage, we can believe Bloom is out-toed. The newsboys imitate the flat spaugs and the walk. The walk in this scene is a comic mazurka — a hop with three short steps which Lenehan does with "sliding" feet. *Kid Auto Races at Venice* created a dominant Chaplin image: a zigzag of ragged urchins following the clown, delighting in his antics, often imitating him, vying for his favor, claiming him, as it were, their lawless King of Laughter. The scene is as familiar as "I am here to-day: Charlie Chaplin." Joyce's use of it is (a) to let his model for Bloom epiphanize, (b) to thrust a sabre at the conscience of Ireland's Wexford Boys "who fought with heart and hand."[6]

Chaplin's big shoes on the wrong feet become Bloom's big feet in real shoes; Chaplin's walk, an artificial out-toeing by virtue of the shoes becomes a real misshapen foot on Bloom; Chaplin's stiff-legged, jutting-kneed shuffle becomes in Bloom a verified chafing.

There are any number of Chaplin touches in Bloom before page 128. Specifically his legs and feet are pointed as early as Molly's breakfast in bed scene. When she smells the kidney burning, she stops stirring tea, arches her nostrils, inhales and says,

> —There's a smell of burn, she said. Did you leave anything on the fire?
>
> The kidney, he cried suddenly. He fitted the book roughly into his inner pocket and, *stubbing his toes* against the broken commode, hurried out towards the smell, *stepping hastily down the stairs with a flurried stork's legs.* (65, italics mine)

This image of stiff stork legs should convey the notion of the knees and the out-toeing, but it would be easy to mistake it for the length of Bloom's legs rather than their quality of movement. Fitting it with the rest of the bundle, however, is the necessity to see Bloom. As soon as "flurried stork's legs" is fitted to flat spaugs and the walk there is no longer any doubt. That Bloom stubs his toes against Molly's commode is a possible misreading too, until Bloom has "spaugs". The word is used in *Ulysses* just once. Molly's description of Bloom ascending the stairs is illuminating and fits by way of full circle:

> —I love to hear him falling up the stairs of a morning with the cups rattling on the tray. (749)

Anyone who has seen Charlie use a stairs knows the accuracy of "falling up the stairs" with a tray in his hands and on innumerable exciting occasions "stepping hastily down the stairs with a flurried stork's legs."

In *Lestrygonians* we get another look at Bloom's walk before the direct evidence of *Aeolus*. To dodge his rival, Blazes Boylan, Bloom must duck somewhere. So,

> Making for the museum gate *with long windy strides* he lifted his eyes. (180, italics mine)

The stride in the later light of "flat spaugs and the walk" is the typical Chaplin strut. He could, though a little fellow, give the effect of taking "long, windy strides." They were long for his short legs; they were windy because he willed them to be windy. Bloom, too, under the pressure of social fear affects a nonchalance and a busyness about the museum building to avoid a self-made catastrophe. How often has Charlie given the aggressor the slip by just such comic nonchalance.

Joyce's concentration, however, on the Chaplin movement in Bloom comes much later in the novel. He saves Bloom's stiffleggedness until it can be a stasis: a moment of total apprehension. Joyce's apprehension of Bloom comes to us in act; therefore, experiencing Bloom's nature is a progressive process. The progress gathers to a greatness — a stasis, an arresting of the total sensibility on Bloom in *Nausicaa*. This is a scene on the strand at dusk where, through brooding on a pretty lame girl a few yards away from him, he exposes the tragic spectacle of his comedy of existence. The girl, true to her Greek-myth prototype, finds Ulysses cast up on the shore. She finds him tired and hungry. She gives him nourishment although in her romantic innocence, she is unaware of her deeds. Joyce's Ulysses suffers from a romantic hunger; he is tired from his fight with the Cyclops and from his fatiguing swim in that day's sea of existence. So, Gerty spins dreams (to herself) and flirts with Mr. Bloom. He takes from Nausicaa-Gerty much nourishment for his romantic hunger. Looking upon Gerty and thinking of Molly: lusting after Gerty and yearning for Molly; possessing Gerty vicariously and himself actually, through the belief in Molly's adultery, Mr. Bloom commits the sin of Onan. His romantic hunger, momentarily appeased, he silently thanks the maiden for "making him feel young again." Supposedly Nausicaa arranges Ulysses' homeward journey and decks him for the occasion. Gerty shows Mr. Bloom the way to go home. But to get there is indeed not only a stiff proposition on stiff legs, but it is through a prolonged birth of conscience. Joyce uses Circe's enchantment as Ulysses' real homecoming which is interior. When he goes home to Molly it is as a man of potentially purified flesh.

Bloom's romantic hunger is symbolized by sex but made manifest in a multiplicity of false views of reality. The one we are concerned with here, however, is what produces the stiff walk. Bloom leaves the strand wet and uncomfortable. This makes him walk with legs apart. Add to this the out-toed misshapen feet, and follow him to the hospital where ironically enough he goes to contemplate and await the birth of the Purefoy child. During his vigil with the medical students and Stephen, he is seated, of course, and his discomfort is lessened. But the moment the birth is announced, it is celebrated by a riot of pubbing into Nighttown, and Bella Cohen's brothel. Bloom, having wasted his own generative seed (slain the Oxen of the Sun) celebrates life through orgy. In the "Circe" scenario he is specifically described as walking stiff-legged, and it is here he becomes the Chaplin figure of fantasy and the dream. Life has clobbered Bloom as so often Chaplin gets an actual blow on the head. Chaplin's blow is the bridge to another world where distortion becomes reality and the little fellow comes into his own. Mr. Bloom's blow — gathered in Gerty — is his bridge to the distorted world of fine frenzied pleasure at Bella's. This is a sample of his mein and what is said of it. He seems to be crossing the street in the path of a sandstrewer. Joyce says of him:

> (The brake cracks violently. Bloom, raising a policeman's white gloved hand, blunders *stifflegged,* out of the track. The motor man thrown forward, pugnosed, on the guide wheel, yells as he slides past over chains and keys.) (italics mine)
>
> **THE MOTORMAN**
>
> Hey, shitbreeches are you doing the hattrick?
>
> **BLOOM**
>
> (Bloom trickleaps to the curbstone and halts again. He brushes a mud flake from his cheek with a parcelled hand.)

And in Bloom's comment on the motorman's remark:

> The stiff walk. True word spoken in jest (428).

The speech ends with "ow". A moment later, Bloom's action is described:

> (He swerves, sidles, stepsaside, slips past and on.)

The Nighttown scenario employs Chaplin business, Keystone techniques, gathers to itself wild characters from within the novel and outside it, presents Bloom in dream relief and does one more thing. Two times Bloom is addressed as "Charlie".

Bloom is about to enter Bella Cohen's. His escort is Zoe Higgins, a young whore in a sapphire slip (466). At the door "he trips awkwardly" (491) under the sinister gaze of two sister whores, but Zoe saves him with Molly's line, "Hoopsa! Don't fall upstairs." Joyce says of their entrance into Bella's:

> (She crosses the threshold. He hesitates. She turns, and holding out her hands, draws him over. He hops . . . .) (491)

As soon as they enter the musicroom where Stephen and the medical students are, Zoe says this to Bloom:

> More limelight, Charley. (She goes to the chandelier and turns the gas full cock) (492)

As if to light his entrance as well as the person for his identity, Zoe calls Bloom, "Charley". His name is spelled with an "ey", not "ie" as is Chaplin's; Joyce's distinction is not finer in the whole novel.

Buck Mulligan's improvisation at the end of the "*Oxen of the Sun*" episode prepares us for Zoe's limelight speech. He says when Bloom comes out of the maternity hospital, "Jay, look at the drunken minister coming out of the maternity hospital?" Bloom joins them and Mulligan says, "Righto, Issacs, shove 'em out of the bleeding limelight. Yous join us, dear sir?" Even though the medical crowd needs to keep on the darker parts of the street as they hoot along to Burke's pub, to avoid identification, Mulligan's primary meaning here is "Now that you're here, you'll take over the limelight." Mulligan's speech to Bloom is, of course, ironic; Joyce's meaning behind Mulligan is not ironic. Zoe turns on more actual light: Joyce behind Zoe means "the hero is here, let's light the set; Charlie is the model; let's call him Charley."

Bloom's Bella Cohen experiences dramatize his nature and sensibility. The line a man descends from is actively involved in any visit he might make to a brothel. Fittingly Virag, Bloom's grandfather, pays him a spiritual visit, and the visit is externalized in *Circe* (504). After an analogy insinuating Bloom's behavior is like the insects, Virag throws him the challenge, "Chase me, Charley! Buzz!" (504)

To address Bloom as "Charley" in *Circe* couldn't be more appropriate, for this is an enriched Keystone scenario from one view. In the round *Circe* is the total Chaplin myth 1914-1921, from *Kid Auto Races* where Charlie's flesh is born to *The Kid* where he reclaims his spiritual innocence through a spiritual son.

Bloom's derby[7] is one of the first clothing props he handles. We learn it is a derby, however, fourteen pages later. On the second page of his opening scene,

> His hand took his hat from the peg over his initialled overcoat . . . . Plasto's high grade hat. He peeped quickly inside the leather headband. White slip of paper. Quite safe. (56)

We see at once the hat contains his romance. Chaplin's use of the hat in the beginning was, again, to attempt the dandy. On Bloom it is not different, but it is more. In a thousand ways he "talks through his hat" — not least among these ways in his secret correspondence with Martha. In his eloquent pantomime, Charlie spoke volumes through his hat. He was never outdone, he could always bluff, he could and did save face.

Joyce employs cinema to show Bloom in the act. Bloom has no secrets. Mulligan sees him peeking at the nude statues; the butcher Dluzac sees his male interest over the counter; the sandstrewer driver sees his stiff walk; the unnamed one in Kiernan's pub sees his latent artistry; Stephen feels a different man when he leans on him for support. The other side of the coin in Charlie is manifest through running off the picture frames in psychological time.

Bloom's business with the hat as he nears the post office in Westland Row (70) is uniquely Chaplinesque. Chaplin's eyelids over his large, dark, expressive eyes are as memorable as those eyes. Photographed so often in a gesture of sudden innocence, one of his most characteristic motions was to drop his lids. Here Bloom, too, is affecting a casual innocence. He pretends to remove his hat because of the heat.

> . . . he took off his hat quietly inhaling his hairoil and sent his right hand with slow grace over his brow and hair. Under their dropped lids his eyes found the tiny bow of the leather headband inside his highgrade hat. Just there. His right hand came down into the bowl of his hat. His fingers found quickly a card behind the headband and transferred it to his waistcoat pocket.

The fun in this scene is the accuracy of the pantomime, the picture of Bloom's casualness, the beauty of the bluff. The action continues,

> His right hand once more more slowly went over again:. . .

Then after a long image on the tea window displays,

> He turned away and *sauntered* across the road. (italics mine)

This is rich, careful comedy. The literary art is imperishable whereas already many of the early Chaplin's are disintegrating. Bloom including Chaplin as he does stands witness. Science may have to reconstruct its spectacle from literature.

In the Mass scene at All Hallows, Bloom comments on his derby,

> These pots we have to wear. (79)

and again the costume epiphanizes. Bloom's little Henry Flower card so carefully stowed away in the headband makes of the hat a figurative pot: he has to find a Martha to pour off his poison grief of Molly. This is human, of course, but wry; natural but compromising; understandable but ignoble; credible but insubstantial and foolish. Bloom talks through his hat when he bows his head piously at the cemetery and says to himself "Once you are dead you are dead." The hat is described as "black" for the first time at the cemetery. (102)

Chaplin's bamboo cane usually tucked under his armpit as he sauntered or strolled went into action as a naughty hand, a mysterious arm, a hook, a club, a baton. He had a thousand uses for it over and above the stick of a vagabond dandy. Bloom has just such a magic prop in his baton made of the *Freeman's Journal.*

> As he walked he took the folded *Freeman* from his side pocket, unfolded it rolled it lengthwise in a baton and tapped it at each sauntering step against his trouserleg. (71)

He tells us himself why he creates a hand prop: "Careless air: just drop in to see." He sets the post office scene with such skillful comedy touches whose naturalness under the circumstances fit and are, if you like, artistic necessities. Bloom doesn't give one damm about his transgression: he does care what people would think were they to discover he resorted to a pen name and that the name was "Henry Flower" and that his unseen ladylove is a little typist and that one of his prime adventures of the day is to call incognito at the postoffice to claim her letters. Of course, loss of prestige to the Irish is a calamity more grave than a secret sin. Bloom's correspondence with the girl, Martha, is stimulation more than anything. He loves to dwell on the mystery of her looks, the image of her love making, the image of himself as master lover.

Bloom reads Martha's letter protected by his baton, purchases his soap and carries it unseen in his baton, gets into the hearse conversation at last because he has the newspaper (baton), kneels on his baton at the cemetery; it keeps his "suit" clean: The newspaper baton is Bloom's protection from multiple harms. When at last he is the "Ad Canvasser" at work, the baton loses its magical properties and his *bête noir* is how to make the perfect advertisement. Charlie's major pathos is no less: I have my stick, why am I not considered a gentleman of breeding, a tycoon even? In spite of the stick Charlie has to forage for food, shelter, respect, handyman jobs. The magic properties of the stick last as long as Bloom's protective baton and disappear as soon as he enters the real world of his job, Canvasser for Ads. But he keeps the baton nevertheless. He has it with him in *Sirens.* (274)

Chaplin's face is a face with dark thinking eyes. The height of his merriment depended on the thought quality of his eyes. He says in "What People Laugh At,"

> . . . all my pictures are built around the idea of getting me into trouble and so giving me a chance to be desperately serious in my attempt to appear as a normal little gentleman. That is why no matter how desperate

> the predicament is, I am always very much in earnest about clutching my cane, straightening my derby hat, and fixing my tie, even though I have just landed on my head.[8]

The "thinking eyes" are the focal point of any Chaplin film. The little fellow plays it "dead pan" because a gentleman is "dead pan", but his eyes perform the miracle of his interior monolog. His "thinking" eyes move with his mind through the orbit of jest in the path of tragedy; often his lids become as expressive as his eyes. He uses the dropped eyelids to express a thousand secrecies, to betray a private universe in creation. Joyce establishes Bloom's expressive eyelids before he says the eyes are dark thinking. This is Bloom *in act,* however, and in his nature. In the first seventeen pages of Bloom's activity in *Ulysses,* five references to Bloom's eyes, some by means of his lids, relate him solidly to Chaplin in filmic metaphor,

> His eyelids sank quietly often as he walked in happy warmth. (57)

> His eyes rested on her vigorous hips. (59)

> He held the page aslant patiently, bending his senses and his will, his soft subject gaze at rest. (59)

> . . . under their dropped lids his eyes found the tiny bow (70)

> Drawing back his head and gazing far from beneath his veiled eyelids he saw the bright fawn skin shine in the glare, the braided drums. (73)

Offstage, Chaplin in his youth resembled Keats.[9] It was often said of him he was too beautiful for a man, and surely he does have beautiful screen teeth at least. As Charlie, no one can deny the intellectual quality of his face. That it came off in comedy is what Joyce is saying, of course, and having Gerty in all her romantizing say Bloom is like Martin Harvey, the matinee idol, is a rich inference. Charlie's moustache we know. He wanted a Boer War effect; Bloom is only two years after the Boer War. He is reminded of the fracas by the squad of constables in *Lestrygonions* who no doubt had Boer moustaches. The Keystone Cops often had Charlie's moustache.

Bloom's face, Joyce tells us, "is a face with dark thinking eyes" (100). The darkness of the eyes with their prominent lids and their "soft subject gaze" (59) create an immediate image of Bloom's general physiognomy.

Molly tells us in her long perusal that he was "too beautiful for a man" and that he was "trying to look like Lord Byron" (728), "splendid set of teeth he had made me hungry to look at them" (731). Gerty McDowell tells us "wonderful eyes they were, superbly expressible, but could you trust them? . . . She could see at once by his dark eyes and his pale intellectual face that he was a foreigner the image of the photo she had of Martin Harvey, the matinee idol, only for the moustache which she preferred because she wasn't stagestruck . . . but she could not see whether he had an aquiline nose or a slightly *retrousse* from where he was sitting. . . . The story of a haunting sorrow was written on his face." (351)

The story of a haunting sorrow was never written on Charlie's face. His sorrows did not haunt; they inhabited. Life was so sad he had to make a joke of it. We know "a haunting sorrow" was not written on Bloom's face. He was so busy *in the act* he had scarcely any time to let a sorrow haunt him. His sorrows like Charlie's are an encompassing sense of loss whose levels are many, and whose total meaning is the "esthetic moment" of the novel.

Does Bloom have Chaplin's face and head? We know Bloom's collar size is 17 inches, (695) and Chaplin's neck too is very large and thick set. There is no pedestal for his head nor is there for Bloom's. Joyce has enormous fun with this, of course, but the comedy goes from the overt to the interior, and it is only after we have seen Bloom's head operate in myriad ways that we can easily see why collar size No. 17 was just the right measurement.

The Chaplin figure in Bloom has visual concreteness in *Ulysses:* Joyce's symbolic and analytic use of Charlie's costume, dark suit with pants that eventually sag; derby, flat spaugs — big misshapen, out-toed feet, and the rolled baton of the *Freeman's Journal* is the old comedy with the new effect. This establishes that Chaplin is the model from the outside. An analysis of Chaplin's comic behavior in Bloom is now in order to see what degree of likeness the two living clowns bear each other.

Joyce is his own model for Stephen Dedalus; the men and women he knew best are his models for everyone who surrounds Bloom in *Ulysses.* Bloom himself, however, must come from as fabled a world as Odysseus and so he does — from the modern twentieth century fable of the silent cinema created by Charlie Chaplin.

Chapter V

BLOOM ON LOCATION

Joyce's non-linear Bloom spaces the Chaplin signs in psychological time: they appear in conjunction with significant acts and events in *Ulysses* for the purpose of a larger revelation. Joyce separates "The flat spaugs and the walk" from Bloom's open admission of "the stiff walk" by 300 pages; Bloom's Chaplin face in *Calypso* from Bloom's Chaplin body in *Eumaeus* by twelve episodes; Bloom's "flurried stork's legs" from his "listed feet" by 588 pages; Bloom's stage business with his derby in the early episodes from Molly's statement of how he "always takes off his hat when he comes up in the street like that" by over 600 pages. The convergent rays of the comedy unite in *Circe,* to communicate Bloom's life and times in terms of Odysseus-Chaplin-Keystone-twentieth century consciousness. *Circe* is treated in a separate chapter. The externals of the Chaplin figure are not Joyce's chief interest; he is interested in what Chaplin signifies for

Bloom. To imagine he was eager to hide his use of Chaplin is to forget Joyce's esthetic. The Chaplin figure to go forth as Bloom has a personal history, specific profession, a name, lineage, wife and children. Details for these inventions spring from the world Joyce absorbed; it is perfectly fitting that he use McCoy's ad canvassing, Mrs. Charlie Chance's singing, Leopold Poppert's first name, a Dublin Bloom's murder of a young girl in a photograph shop for Milly's job.[1] These are not the hero's nature; they are his accidents. Joyce said to Sylvia Beach, "If you want to know what Leopold Bloom looked like, here is someone who resembles him. . . . The photo is not a good likeness. He doesn't look as much like Bloom in it."[2] It was a picture of Holbrook Jackson, editor of *Today*, a London little review of the twenties. The picture of Jackson is not unlike Chaplin.

Essentially what interests Joyce in Chaplin for Bloom is the Charlie Chaplin pattern: (1) food, (2) lechery, (3) dream fantasy, (4) bully sequence, (5) the chase. The last is fully discussed in the "Circe" chapters in Part Two of this book. Charlie is a vagabond gentleman gourmet; his taste is flawless, the menu might be stolen beans; he dines in his barn drawing-room with delicate grace, might dip his elegant fingers carefully in a milk bucket and dry them on a flour sack, but *he dines.* Digestive noises follow rapidly: the belch of the silent screen is louder than sound — so are the hiccups, the stomach growls. Bloom as we know is fastidious at table; taken in the privy, he is heard releasing rectal gas after food and drink. Joyce's design for this man of many devices is not simple indigestion.

Bloom opens with a food scene. The high comedy of his grilling and savouring of the kidney, burned but succulent, eaten with such restrained relish in the gelid light of the kitchen might have been played in a typical desolate Chaplin shack instead of Bloom's desolate home on Eccles Street. "Then he put a forkful into his mouth, chewing with discernment the toothsome, pliant meat. Done to a turn. A mouthful of tea" (65). But the scene is not paced in simple hunger as it might have been in the vagabond's shack and eaten in imagined elegance or eaten rapidly by a famished gentleman. For Bloom is a psychological vagabond wandering anxiously in the back alleys of his (and the world's) emotions. The pace of Bloom's eating is dictated by Bloom's interior monologue on Milly's letter which whets his kidney appetite; Molly's adultery which increases his nervous intake of food to the point of bolting it: "He sopped other dies of bread in the gravy and ate piece after piece of the kidney" (66). Charlie, too, bursts through his impeccable manners to satisfy a more basic need. He might, for instance, eat the bean can. Mr. Bloom forgets his love of dining and ends up "feeding".

Consider that Bloom is presented to us with what to Joyce is a hilarious introduction, "Mr. Leopold Bloom ate with relish the inner organs of beasts and fowls. He liked thick giblet soup, nutty gizzards, a stuffed roast heart, liver slices fried with crustcrumbs, fried hencod's roes. Most of all he liked grilled mutton kidneys which gave to his palate a fine tang of faintly scented urine" (55). So, Mr. Bloom is of this kidney from the first.

This is where the operation of the two major myths of Homer and Chaplin combine to create a new office for both. The comic refinement of manner derives from Chaplin; the Calypso enchantment of the senses derives from Homer. Bloom is powerless to move in the direction of his daughter's safety or his wife's fidelity precisely because he is himself emmeshed with nymphs like the girl next door of the whacking skirt, "Full gluey woman's lips" (67). His graceful dining and his graceless pining create a comic tension whose tragic energy drives inward and comedy potential drives outward.

The cannibal episode, *Lestrygonians*, wherein the mythical man of many devices lost all but one ship, in Joyce's *Ulysses* becomes the scene of Bloom's lunch. "Perfume of embraces all him assailed. With hungered flesh obscurely, he mutely craved to adore" (166). It is one o'clock. He has a normal bodily hunger, an abnormal sensuous hunger. He shops for a restaurant, is repulsed by the swilling crowd at the Burton, finally settles for Davy Byrne's. The hunger at one p.m. will rout his whole fleet except one, his last ship, auto-eroticism. Later, this propels him to Circe. "Walking by Doran's public house he slid his hand between waistcoat and trousers and, pulling aside his shirt gently, felt a slack fold of his belly." (179)

The outward driving force of the comedy in *Lestrygonians*, however, is Mr. Bloom's constant grace and gentility in the midst of grossness. Chaplin is refined in spite of his surroundings; often refined in contrast to "dirty eaters". *His Trysting Place, His Favorite Pastime, The Star Boarder, Mable's Busy Day, Dough and Dynamite, In the Park, The Jitney Elopement, By the Sea, The Paperhanger, Shanghied,* films 1914-1916, all have food scenes touching on refinement and grossness "at table".

Mr. Bloom, planning to enjoy his food in solitary elegance, is forced to accept Nosey Flynn's invitation to join him "in his nook" (169). Nosey is a snuffler, drinks grog, has an abundance of licey habits; Mr. Bloom is given the Chaplin pantomime here:

> Mr. Bloom cut his sandwich into slender strips.
>
> . . . Nosey Flynn . . . , putting his hand in his pocket to scratch his groin.
>
> He (Bloom) smellsipped the cordial juice and, bidding his throat strongly to speed it, set his wineglass delicately down.
>
> Nosey Flynn snuffled and scratched. (170)

Mr. Bloom's Chaplinesque politeness to his dinner partner contradicts the interior gesture of his mind:

> Flea having a good square meal.
>
> Hope that dewdrop doesn't come down into his glass. No, snuffled up. (170)
>
> Nosey Numbskull . . . . Dewdrop coming down again. Cold nose he'd have kissing a woman. (171)

Mr. Bloom's food scenes use his extraordinary nicety at table to point his ordinary lack of nicety in the moral order. Breakfast is preceded by comic lechery with nymph, acceptance of Molly's adultery not only as *fait accompli* but as normalcy; lunch is preceded by "Henry Flower", Bloom on the hunt for satisfaction. Awakened passion surrounds each of the three food scenes in *Ulysses*, a Chaplin elusive; a Joyce penetration:

> . . . Time going on. Hands moving. Two. Not yet.[3]
>
> His midriff yearned then upward, sank within him, yearned more longly, longingly. (170)
>
> Wine soaked and softened rolled pith of bread mustard a moment mawkish cheese. Nice wine it is. Taste it better because I'm not thirsty. Bath of course does that. Just a bite or two. Then about six o'clock I can. Six, six. Time will be gone then. She . . . (172)
>
> . . . Touched his sense moistened remembered. Hidden under wild ferns on Howth. . . . Hot I tongued her. She kissed me. I was kissed. All yielding she tossed my hair. Kissed, she kissed me.
>
> Me. And me now. (173)

The wan little fellow with the penchant for culture, the romantic hunger, the secret sorrow, the interior insouciance, the exterior congeniality, the obedience to nature's call ends a Bloom food scene in *Ulysses* this way:

> Dribbling a quiet message from his bladder came to go to do not to do there to do. A man and ready he drained his glass to the lees and walked, . . . (174)

Mr. Bloom's evening meal at the Ormond bar a few minutes to four is the confrontation scene with his rival, Blazes Boylan, who arrives at the Ormond Hotel on Hackney car No. 324.[4]

> Between the car and the window, warily walking, went Bloom, unconquered hero. See me he might . . . . Black wary hecat walked toward Richie Goulding's legal bag, lifted aloft saluting. (260)
>
> The bag of Goulding, Collis, Ward led Bloom by ryebloom flowered tables. Aimless he chose with agitated aim, bald Pat attending, a table near the door. Be near. At four. Has he forgotten? Perhaps a trick. Not come: whet appetite. I couldn't do. Wait, wait. Pat, waiter, waited. (261-2)

Mr. Bloom, the hecat in the dark suit and the derby, with the flat spaugs and the walk enters the dining room; his rival goes in the bar. The episode is *Sirens*, the music of which our hero must escape. He must lash himself to the mast of his ship to withstay enchantment through the corn and the contrition of the Cowley-Dollard-Dedalus trio in the bar adjoining, the trio who tantalize his triangle. Mr. Bloom orders cider, liver and onions. And he dines with Richie Goulding who eats steak and kidney pie.

> As said before he ate with relish the inner organs, nutty gizzards, fried cods'roes . . . .
>
> Bloom with Goulding, married in silence, ate. Dinners fit for princes. (265)
>
> In liver gravy Bloom mashed mashed potatoes. (266)

The song is *When love Absorbs my Ardent Soul.*

> Bloom ate liv as said before. Clean here at least. That chap in the Burton, gummy with gristle. No-one here: Goulding and I. Clean tables, flowers, mitres of napkins. (266)

The song is *M'appari Tutt 'amor.*

> Gravy's rather good fit for a. (267)

> Steak, kidney, liver, mashed at meat fit for princes sat princes Bloom and Goulding. Princes at meat they raised and drank Power and cider. (267)

As the music continues, Bloom is tender over "liverless bacon" (268); "askance over liverless" (268), and finally his princely plate clean, he hears Si Dedalus sing, *When first I saw that form endearing.*

> Bloom. Flood of warm jimjam lickitup secretness flowed to flow in music out, in desire, dark to lick flow, invading. Tipping her tepping her tapping her topping her. Tup. Pores to dilate dilating. Tup. The joy the feel the warm the. Tup. To pour o'er sluices pouring gushes. Flood, gush, flow, joygush, tupthrop. Now! Language of love. (270)

Then, he hears an aria from the opera *Martha.* "Coincidence. Just going to write. Lionel's song." We remember as Henry Flower he writes love letters to Martha, a girl he's never seen. The reverie the song produces is, of course, Molly, his wife, who at that moment is about to receive her lover while he-cat is about to write to Martha-love; the last he will use to fasten himself to his mast: auto-eroticism.

> But Bloom sang dumb. Admiring. (272)

He is the while stretching a rubber band over his fingers and as he does, he thinks,

> Leave her: get tired. Suffer then. Snivel. Big Spanishy eyes goggling at nothing. Her wavyavyeavyheavyeavyevyevy hair un comb: 'd.
>
> Yet too much happy bores. He stretched more, more. Are you not happy in your? Twang. It snapped. (273)

And this is the lashing to the mast:

> Better write it here. (273)

> I feel so sad today. La ree. So lonely. Dee. (275)

He sends Martha a money order for two shillings, half a crown. Lashed now, safe, Mr. Bloom at the bardoor is about to escape the siren music when *The Croppy Boy* is announced.

> Must go prince Bloom told Ritchie prince.
>
> But wait. But hear. Chordsdark. Lugugugubrious.
>
> Low. In a cave of the dark middle earth. Embedded ore. Lumpmusic.
>
> The voice of dark age, of unlove, earth's fatigue made grave approach, and painful, come from afar, from hoary mountains, called on good men and true. (278)

> . . . *in nomine Domini,* in God's name. He knelt. He beat his hand upon his breast, confessing: *mea culpa.*
>
> Latin again. That holds them like birdlime. (279)

> He bore no hate.
>
> Hate. Love. Those are names. Rudy. Soon I am old. (280)

> Get out before the end. . . . Waaaaaaalk.

> By rose, by satiny bosom, by the fondling hand, by slops, by empties, by popped corks, greeting in going, past eyes and maidenhair, bronze and faint gold in deepseashadow, went Bloom, soft Bloom, I feel so lonely Bloom. (282)

> Up the quay went Lionelleopold, naughty Henry with letter for Mady, with sweets of sin with frillies for Raoul with met him pike hoses went Poldy on. (283)

Mr. Bloom has suffered the sirens through princely dining on liver and bacon, sipping cider, hearing the music. But his mast (self induced passion) has held him fast. He-cat who yearned and pined and wrote in secret while his wife received her lover now fades out over the quay, a sad man, a secret man, a funny man. Instead of a dead stop and a little hop, jig and shuffle as the scene fades, the Chaplin figure in *Ulysses,* Mr. Bloom, is heard to emit rectal gas often, loudly and long. He will carry on.

The three principal food scenes in *Ulysses* form a Chaplin trilogy patterned on the basic Chaplin comic elegance at table. The new pattern imposed on the old: Bloom is elegant in contrast to his mental state, his dining companion, his sordid "enchantment". In *Calypso* he dines with unpleasant thoughts of his daughter, his wife. He has a "soft qualm regret" (67). In *Lestrygonians,* he dines with anguished thoughts and an unpleasant person. His qualms have vanished, a shadow of sorrow visits him, "Me. And me now" (173). In *Sirens,* he dines with agonizing thoughts and an unpleasant personality, "Callous: all for his own gut" (274). He decides not to leave his wife because she would suffer. The three scenes are a vignette of Bloom who in the total stasis of *Ulysses* is apprehended as moral vagabond crossing the morass of self to his home. This conceived by an artist who has *full insight* into what it means to be a human being must be comic. In the highest reaches of the concept of Bloom's "home", Joyce's symbolic meaning is man not as rational animal but incarnate spirit. The necessity of Joyce's art is sound, clear — once separated from matter — and properly comedic.

The vagabond of Chaplin's canon is forever seeking romance but his feet won't let him. For Mr. Bloom "the feet" are solidly planted among the rhododendrons on Howthhead, but he is forever seeking among the daily "moving hams" of the girl next door, the Marthas of his ficticious love life, the women's breasts at Mass, the Gerty McDowells and even the Mina Purefoys for a rebirth of his romance with Molly. "Yes he said I was a flower of the mountain yes so we are flowers all a womans body yes that was one true thing he said in his life and the sun shines for you today yes that was why I liked him because I saw he understood or felt what a woman is. . ." (767).[5]

Mr. Bloom's romantic hunger is insatiable: no amount of goddess peeking, foetus concentration, secret orgasm bathing, silks, satins, perfumes, onanisms, women's drawers, cattle urine will sate his infinite longing. Mr. Bloom seeks to satisfy infinite longing in finite rooting. If he is ever to be appeased, the rutting of his senses must be anneald by spirit. Whether or not Bloom evolves to incarnate spirit from semi-rational animal is a process which must be demonstrated not claimed, so the answer to this speculation must come later.

Charlie's romantic hunger is Mr. Bloom's comic basis. The little fellow who sped through 35 Mack Sennett comedies in 1914 usually hooked skirts with his bamboo cane, peeked at dainty unmentionables, spied on feminity in private abandon, pinched, rubbed, jostled intentionally women of all shapes and sizes. One early comedy, *Laughing Gas* (released July 9, 1914) has a remarkable bloomer scene. Charlie is a dentist's janitor who pinch-hits for dentist, dental assistant, surgeon and consultant. Finally, after he has set a patient laughing with a gas anaesthetic, he is sent for a prescription to save the man from death. On his way to the drug store, he meets the dentist's wife. To escape the amorous Charlie, she runs up the stairs of a public building, catches her skirt, loses it and is seen frantically clutching her balloony bloomers. The show of drawers in Chaplin's films was a frequent climax. In *His New Job* (released Feb. 1, 1915), Charlie playing a stage Hussar leads the queen up the palatial stairs, steps on her train and leaves her shocking the assembly, again in wonderful bloomers. The bloomer device in itself was not the comedy; Charlie's perfect inflection toward the gag brought the laughs.[6]

Mr. Bloom loves bloomers. His fixation, too, is comic through inflection of the gag. He disrobes no women; his is a far more realistic situation. He loves his wife's drawers, on her, on her bed, on the line, in his pocket, in his mind; Molly on Bloom and his weakness:

> . . . hes mad on the subject of drawers thats plain to be seen always skeezing at those brazenfaced things on the bicycles with their skirts blowing up to their navels . . . (731)

> . . . anything for an excuse to put his hand anear me drawers drawers the whole blessed time till I promised to give him the pair off my doll to carry about in his waistcoat pocket . . . (731)

> . . . that old Bishop that spoke off the altar his long preach about womans higher functions about girls now riding the bicycle and wearing peak caps and the new woman bloomers God send him sense and me more money I suppose theyre called after him I never thought that would be my name Bloom . . . (746)

Molly's assessment of Bloom's delight in drawers is one aspect of his comedy with them; she speaks late, however, and for the groundwork on Bloom and bloomers or Bloom on drawers we have to turn to other than the *Penelope* episode.

In *Nausicaa*, Bloom's twilight affair with new Gerty sets him to reminiscing about Molly's drawers:

> Tell you what it is. It's like a fine veil or web they have all over the skin, fine like what do you call it gossamer and they're always spinning

> it out of them, fine as anything, rainbow colours without knowing. Clings to everything she takes off. Vamp of her stocking. Warm shoe. Stays. Drawers: little kick, taking them off. Byby till next time. (368)

And then about Gerty's drawers:

> . . . showed me her next year in drawers return next in her next her next. (375)

In *Circe* Bloom is seen to lose a button off his trousers, and the transposed chant from his early tune, "O, Mairy lost the pin of her drawers"(77) is "O Leopold lost the pin of his drawers". (539)

Charlie and the drawers is lively bawd; Bloom and the drawers is bawdy thought life: Molly reminisces, Bloom reminisces. The drawers are an aspect which does not make a Bloom scene but rather promotes a healthy evocation of Bloom's model.[7] The drawers remind us we are in the clown's arena of permissive buffoonery. Mrs. Fiske writing in 1916[8] compares Chaplin's vulgar buffoonery with the best in Aristophanes, Plautus, Shakespeare and Rabelais. Joyce has installed much of Bloom's buffoonery on a mental stage. The comedy lies in the tension between Leopold's polite and smiling exterior (no skirt torn off on the street) and Poldy's unabashed, bawdy, often licentious and lecherous interior monolog. This is his perfect inflection toward the bloomer gag.

Charlie began as a comic lecher, moved into the tragic mask and finally played the hero whose gentle pathos lifted his films into high comedy. In 1921 *The Kid* marked Chaplin's departure from caricature and a genuine engagement with realistic comedy. The element he kept in caricature was the bruiser. Charlie's impish behavior in the early comedies becomes Bloom's "slyboots" behavior in *Ulysses.* Perhaps one of Joyce's favorites, a film called *The Paperhanger,* (also called *Work,* released June 21, 1915) has definite Chaplin touches transposed for "slyboots" in *Ulysses.*

In *The Paperhanger,* Charlie, shocked at the sight of a nude statue supporting a lamp, prudishly slips a lamp shade over the bold hussy; then he naughtily lifts the skirt for a peek.[9] By making the statue dance the hootchy-kootchy, he inflects the gag further to suggest to the pretty house maid (Edna Purviance) that they have an affair.

Compare Mr. Bloom's business with the nude statue at the National Library. We were there of course, when fraught with memories of Molly at lunch in Davy Byrne's, Mr. Bloom decides to look at the mesial grooves of Venus, but he is pushed to do this ahead of time by Boylan's sudden appearance on the street. This gives us his wonderfully prudish pretense in order to achieve the right angle:

> His eyes beating looked steadfastly at cream curves of stone. Sir Thomas Deane was the Greek architecture.
>
> Look for something I.
>
> His hasty hand went quick into a pocket, took out, read unfolded Agendath Netaim. Where did I?
>
> Busy looking for.
>
> He thrust back quickly Agendath.
>
> Afternoon she said.
>
> I am looking for that, Yes, that. Try all pockets. Handker. *Freeman.* Where did I? Ah, yes. Trousers. Purse. Potato. Where did I?
>
> Hurry. Walk quietly. Moment more. My heart.
>
> His hand looking for the where did I put found in his hip pocket soap lotion have to call tepid paper stuck. Ah, soap there! Yes. Gate.
>
> Safe! (180-81)

The Chaplin figure here is not the carefree, unmarried paperhanger who tries for an illicit delight with the house maid. He is a married man made cuckold by a bruiser, and his try is for an illicit delight with the statue. The comic flavor is the same, but in rearrangement the unuttered meaning of Bloom's romantic hunger gains many dimensions in the real world Joyce creates.

The Agendath Netaim unfolded is the superior dimension, for this is a bleat of conscience. When Bloom first obtained the pamphlet, he suffered a walk back in the Sodom and Gomorrah conscience of the race. He silenced it. Mr. Bloom aware at the conscious level that his curiosity is a form of lust becomes operative on the sub-conscious level; he likes lust — custom forbids open show of it, but privately? As long as nobody sees? Nobody is scandalized.

Bloom's action covering his purpose at the statue is the Chaplin comic prudery: the extent to which man will go to seem perfectly honorable in all his acts. We do learn later from Bloom he was foiled, that he did not see the mesial groove after all. What is even richer, of course, is that Bloom's elaborate pretense is all the while observed by Buck Mulligan, who says to Stephen:

> O, I fear me, he is Greeker than the Greeks. His pale Galilean eyes were upon her mesial groove. (198)

Charlie's symbol of romantic hunger is the used boutonniere in his lapel; roses for the pretty secretary in *The Bank* (released August 9, 1915); the daisy as the badge of his authority in *Sunnyside* (released June 15, 1919). As Charlie's romantic hunger matures and takes stock of itself, the flower bespeaks tenderness and pathos rather than the earlier attack and rascality.

What use does Joyce make of flower as sign for Bloom? His pseudonym is Henry Flower. As Flower, Bloom loves the unknown, unseen Martha safely, secretly. Her letters stir his senses, make him gallant, give him a conqueror's image:

> Could meet one Sunday after the rosary. Thank you: not having any. Usual love scrimmage. (77)

Martha is his lotus of forgetfulness-temporarily-of-Molly-Penelope at home weaving a youthful image of herself through "songs" with Blazes Boylan. Martha sends Bloom a yellow flower with flattened petals which he places in his heart pocket.

> Language of flowers . . . . Then, walking slowly forward, he read the letter again, murmuring here and there a word. Angry tulips with you darling manflower punish your cactus if you don't please poor forgetmenot how I long violets to dear roses when we soon anemone meet all naughty nightstalk wife Martha's perfume. (77)

Bloom's imposition of the flower image on Martha's actual letter is a sample of Joyce's invention for Bloom as Henry Flower. To have separated this aspect of Bloom through the natural device of a penname is another of many master strokes. Every shade of the model, Charlie, is put to new work in a new office to relate new significances. A comic deflation is Bloom's "Has her roses probably" (77). This is his expression for menstruation.

Henry Flower protects Bloom from assaults on his heart in the *Sirens* episode. Sentimental Irish songs, the sirens who strangle, reach him, but he is safe on his tempest-tossed ship through the Martha rope with which he has lashed himself.

Henry Flower's language and art help him home through Gerty MacDowell, the little lame Nausicaa.

> O sweety all your little girlwhite up I saw dirty bracegirdle made me do love sticky we two naughty Grace darling she him half past the bed met him pike hoses frillies for Raoul to perfume your wife black hair heave under embon *senorita* young eyes Mulvey plump years dreams return tail end Agendath swoony lovey showed me her next year in drawers return next in her next her next. (375)

At this point we wonder what is Bloom's home? Is it Eccles Street, union with Molly, the Jewish tradition? The Agendath pamphlet is recalled at every Bloom transgression. His conscience, awakened and always with the recurring image of the dead, the dead sea, the dead civilization, Sodom, Gommorrah, bears witness, but it makes no judgment. In Bloom there is no *Agenbite* only *Agendath:* prickle-passing tinge. Home then ever in the distance is that long haul to manhood, that potential personal power to regulate life according to the act of conscience. Does Bloom *ever* get home? Again the answer depends on how we find our Chaplin figure, Bloom, at novel's end.

Charlie is "forever seeking romance but his feet won't let him." He becomes as the Chaplin canon unfolds too real for honest romance. Thus, in *The Tramp* (released April 11, 1915) the first sad ending appeared in film comedy. The little fellow does not get the girl, he departs sadly on the long lonely road. Suddenly he stops, shrugs, does a little dance and goes jauntily over the hill. He knows he is chasing folly, but folly is beguiling fun. Why not?

Bloom is forever seeking romance as salvation. He knows it cannot save him. From what? For what? Joyce's sights for the man are as realistic as the man himself. He will let him do out the story *in act.* We are never unaware of Bloom with feet planted firmly on the ground. Why does he run counter to his earthly recognition? Folly is beguiling and in his case an Odyssean attempt to reach home.

Whenever Charlie of the innumerable comedies takes off on the dream, he often gets there by a blow on the head. The blow instead of felling him, inspires him to heroic achievements: in *The Knock-out* (released June 11, 1914), Charlie is an officious referee at a boxing match between Arbuckle and Kennedy. He is hit in the interchange of blows, and the classic scene is his pulling himself along the ropes counting stars. In *Easy Street* (released January 22, 1917), he is rascal turned policeman and hero who finally unites all the warring factions of Easy Street into a great heavenly brood wherein villain, hero, poor and rich all wing their way toward the peace of the distant horizon. In *The Champion,* also known as *A Dream* (released March 11, 1915), Charlie as sparring partner puts a horseshoe in his glove for good luck. The comic results provide an incomparable dream sequence. Sometimes the dream comes through sleep or weary meditation, i.e., *His Prehistoric Past* (released December 7, 1914), wherein the whole film is a dream of the sex life of the race and Charlie is King; in the end he awakes to regret that he is a rootless vagabond, lonely, hungry and poor. In *The Bank* (released August 9, 1915), Charlie, the janitor, takes a little snooze and dreams of conquering bandits; he awakes to capture real bandits escaping with the loot. In *Sunnyside* (released June 15, 1919), the dream epitome of the Chaplin canon, Charlie is bucked from a wildly prancing cow into a stream where he is knocked unconscious. Immediately the dream rescue by a bevy of beautiful wood nymphs bare limbed in Greek costume, casts the scene in a sylvan setting where Charlie dances with lyric mastery. On a bed of flowers he is tended and adored by the lovely nymphs who vie for his favor. As the dream fades, the maidens grow into his fiendish boss and retinue who have tracked him down. They pull him out of the stream with a rope. In every film Charlie is the dreamer; at the end of most of the classic films he shrugs, shuffles and hops as he disappears over the horizon.

Joyce has allowed Bloom much low-keyed bodily farce: he stubs his toes in Molly's bedroom (65); J. J. O'Molloy hits him in the small of the back as he comes in the door (123); Mr. Bloom moved nimbly aside (123); Mr. Bloom bumps against Lenehan (127); Lenehan clutches him (127); the newsboys "taking off his flat spaugs and the walk" (128); he holds out his arm's length toward the sun. The tip of his little finger blotted out the sun's disk (164); he raises two fingers doubtfully to his lips (167); he skips around nimbly when he's taking Stephen home (644).

Mr. Bloom's big blow comes in the *Ithaca* episode after Stephen hurries away from the Eccles Street garden gate and Bloom goes into the house for his final reflection. As he enters the living room, he bumps his head on a timber angle of the walnut sideboard (690). At once everything in the room is translocated, and the central focus of his now heightened attention is on the room's two chairs. Through them he experiences again Stephen's possession of him: the large dull passive and the slender bright active:

> One: a squat stuffed easychair with stout arms extended and back slanted to the rere, . . . The other: a slender splayfoot chair of glossy cane curves, placed directly opposite thc former, . . . (690)

For Bloom the glow of the act with Stephen (under the influence of the dream blow) endows many objects in the room with new meaning. He relives the act in the incense (691), sees it enacted in the belled tree and the owl on the mantle. In this fine glow he faces himself in the mirror. What does he see?

> The image of a solitary (ipsorelative) mutable (aliorelative) man. (692)

Bloom's knock-out blow alerts him to unknown waters surrounding Ithaca. He is close to home in the channel of self-knowledge, but he is plying unfamiliar waters. Does he survive the channel? Is the channel a means of getting home?

The first comic level is a real dream home. Charlie's dream opened often on the rose covered cottage and love's old sweet song. Bloom's dream opens on such a cottage a little more fully realized:

> . . . but to purchase by private treaty in fee simple a thatched bungalow-shaped 2 storey dwellinghouse of southerly aspect, surmounted by vane and lightning conductor, connected with the earth, with porch covered by parasitic plants (ivy or Virginia creeper), . . . lounge hall fitted with linen wallpresses, fumed oak sectional bookcase containing the Encyclopaedia Britannica and New Century Dictionary, . . . (697)

> What might be the name of this erigible or erected residence? Bloom Cottage. Saint Leopold's. Flowerville. (699)

Bloom of Flowerville is like Charlie of *Sunnyside,* costume, farm activities and position. (699)

In this idyllic setting Bloom of Flowerville dreams of becoming resident magistrate of the peace wherein through an "innate love of rectitude" his aims would be the strict maintenance of public order (700), the "upholding of the letter of the law" (701). Charlie is a rascal turned policeman in *Easy Street;* in his films the Keystone Cops provoke many a blow-on-the-head-dream for Charlie. Joyce's perfect weaving of the Chaplin elements and themes hides the identity of his model. Once, however, a reader *sees* Charlie as the model every thread of the vast tapestry of *Ulysses* functions directly from the artist's *necessity*. Bloom's cop connections are numerous; the constables epiphanize Bloom's nature in *Lestrygonians*. The particular fun here is the comic transportation of Bloom to dream profession of magistrate, because *he has loved rectitude*. As we said, self-knowledge is an unfamiliar channel to him. But Joyce has a marvelous time with Bloom's "rectitude". He proves it: (a) Bloom as a high school lad rejected the faith of his father, Rudolph Virag: Irish Protestantism; he converted to Roman Catholicism in 1888 to be married. (He has since faded away from both Catholicism and marriage.) (b) As a youth he advocated colonial expansion and the theories of Darwin; (c) still as a youth he adhered to the great policies of Davitt and Parnell, and to prove it he climbed a tree to see the torchbearers' procession march through Dublin. Surely no one could ask for taller rectitude?

Bloom will pay for this dream cottage on a 20-year plan. But wait! What about the downpayment? Clever scheme? Meditation brings one grand scheme among assorted very grand ones: the use of human excrement for fertilizer. But better even than fertilizer or Poulaphouca is the discovery of a goldseam of inexhaustible ore. Ah well, this kind of meditation for Bloom is excellent,

> It was one of his axioms that similar meditations or the automatic relation to himself of a narrative concerning himself or tranquil recollection of the past when practised habitually before retiring for the night alleviated fatigue and produced as a result sound repose and renovated vitality. (704)

A narrative concerning himself, epical preferred, wherein he sees himself as the man who loves rectitude, who conquers and subdues, as the beloved magistrate: this is as far as Charlie's dreams go. Bloom, remember, is in the channel of self knowledge. His bark responds to the waters. His need to relax before retiring via auto epic is to allay fears. Of what?

> The committal of homicide or suicide during sleep by an aberration of the light of reason, the incommensurable categorical intelligence situated in the cerebral convolutions. (705)

So, finally his last therapy is to meditate on the greatest scheme of all:

> What were habitually his final meditations?
>
> Of some one sole unique advertisement to cause passers to stop in wander, a poster novelty, with all extraneous accretions excluded, reduced to its simplest and most efficient terms not exceeding the span of casual vision and congruous with the velocity of modern life. (705)

Here, events of the day converge to reveal another dimension of Bloom's advertising ability. The subtle suggestion is that while Bloom is an ironic ad for manhood, his search is the irony of his situation. Objectively he would very much like "to stop in wander" and gaze directly at a simple, efficient, casual technique for "modern living". This is because he loves rectitude and because he's a real epic. Dear Bloom is carefully plying these self-knowledge waters. Are they infested?

The past lurks here. Mr. Bloom unlocks his personal drawer — bits of folly, pornographic and adulterous; his Sandow earned measurements — biceps 10″, and a very nice description of the wonderworker, a cure for stomach gas. To this collection he adds Martha's newest letter. This action causes him to reflect pleasantly on the fact that (a) Martha wrote (b) Mrs. Breen enjoyed her visit with him and then (c) Gerty. It made him dream of dining with an elegant courtesan, a lady — in a private apartment. The second drawer, his father's, consoled him partially for sad reminiscences: the endowment policy, the bank passbook, the certificate of the possession of scrip.

The past bites out at the frail bark: suddenly Bloom is examining his conscience,

> Reduce Bloom . . . by elimination of all positive values to a negligible negative irrational unreal quantity.
>
> . . . Poverty: . . . Mendicancy: . . . eccentric public laughingstock seated on bench of public park under discarded perforated umbrella. Destitution: the inmate of Old Man's House. . . . Nadir of misery: the aged impotent disfranchised ratesupported moribund lunatic pauper. (710)

A new and fascinating moral journey ends with the Dead Sea wherein his dead self would be cast. He could die or he could depart from folly. He prefers the latter. Imagine all the places in Ireland and the world he could go! A long European list ends with the Dead Sea. To guide him in his travels at sea: by night the polestar — located geometrically in the figure made by Alpha and Omega;[10] on land: the moon in varying phases of lunation through the posterior interstice of the imperfectly occluded skirt of a carnose negligent perambulating female, *a pillar of cloud by day.*[11]

This is not only what Mr. Bloom would do were he to depart from "the old man", but it is what he did do "on land" regarding the girl next door; if he put off "the old man", the "pillar of cloud by day" would still guide him. He would still be blind. Were he to do this demi-"old man" off, he would have two names: *Everyman; Noman.* Weighing what each would bring him: *Everyman:* honour and gifts of strangers; *Noman:* a nymph immortal, beauty, bride of *Noman.*

If the "old man" in Bloom were to go, would he ever return? Yes, but then as a dark crusader, a sleeper awakened with financial resources (by supposition) surpassing those of Rothchild or the silver king (712). But the interior debate continues: Such a return cannot be accomplished in so little time. Departure of the "old man" now seems undesirable. Why? It is late, the journey is too dark, he doesn't know how to let "the old man go," too perilous: whereas, closeby there is a bed with Molly in it and before him is the statue of Narcissus, sound without echo, desired desire. *How* can the "old man" in Bloom who pervertedly loves his wife and himself go away? Journey to the Dead Sea?

Bloom recapitulates causes of his fatigue: they are the fifteen events that constitute his wandering held up for comparison with religious thought life of ancient peoples (Bloom's roots, Everyman's roots). The powerful parody brings into sharp relief Bloom's knowledge of himself.

Recognition: the "old man" must go; confrontation: hero buckles before "old man" (perverted sense life), (a) tired (b) fearful (c) ignorant of spiritual thoroughfare (d) journey appears cold, desolate, unhuman, (e) decides to linger a while in mute immutable mature animality. Bloom has moved out from *despair* into *realization* of his condition. At least he knows the "old man" should go, but the way is dark and perilous. His impulse to goodness is never a matter of will. He has not willed "to put off the old man;" he has not willed the *melons,* but he submits to them. Joyce's *Ulysses* is not an indictment of modern man; it is a recognition that his soul has an uneasy home in the body.

Joyce's exuberance for his comic character is without duplicity. It is in Bloom's reach for self-knowledge that this is revealed. The esthetic moment of *Ulysses* is *Bloom's self knowledge of his sorry predicament:* "eccentric public laughing stock" bound for the poor house. As entity he is Everyman into whom has been infused the conscience of the race. As nonentity he is Noman. For he is sorely in need of the advice to Job, "Gird up thy loins *like a man*". Bloom as caricature of a hero is without manhood; he is no man and impotent because marked by the beast.

To take the critical position that Mr. Bloom is kind, he is a lover of dogs, he is gentle, fastidious, courteous, thoughtful, of good will and altogether liberated from organized religion and therefore the post Christian man[12] is simply not to catch the spirit, essence or significance of Mr. Bloom, comic Ulysses. Such an inocuous analysis robs him of his stellar role as clown.

An artist's clown is a true medium for his "sane and joyful spirit" (SH 78). This spirit, this appetite for incongruities, maintains sanity by laughter and manifests its joy in a superabundance of absurdity. Beneath the laughter and absurdity, of course, is the ever abiding irony of pathos. As was so often said of Chaplin, "Life is so sad, he makes a comedy of it", can be stated dispassionately of Joyce. His use of Chaplin and the Chaplin pattern is one of the great economies in literary history. Mr. Bloom is the logical extension of the twentieth century legend (Chaplin) to its pathetic proportion and to its highest comic dimension. He is after all the great and mature reversal of the young Stephen Dedalus' soul-sorrow in *A Portrait of the Artist as a Young Man* (109). "He repeated to himself the lines of Shelley's fragment. It's alternation of sad human ineffectiveness with vast inhuman cycles of activity chilled him and he forgot his own human and ineffectual grieving." Joyce, the mature artist, makes of "sad, human ineffectiveness" a comic thing, a thing to be suffered good naturedly and with wisdom and of the "vast inhuman cycles of activity", a self inflicted privation of spiritual cycles of activity. What seemed brutish to the young man and remote is not the *bonum arduum* of society. He is face to face with the unalterable laws of society in *Ulysses.* These laws inescapable and eternal demand first that man when he reaches man's estate be a man.

He is bound by the law of conscience, that act of thought and feeling which bears witness, which binds, which incites; that act of thought and feeling which accuses, torments, rebukes. The human account is laid out for inspection after Ulysses-Bloom gets home, and he reveals with unmistakable clarity the nature of his privation, the *status quo* of his dwarfed spirituality. For this man so concerned with the stars and orbit of the heavens is shut out by his own choice from the reach of the human soul. He says to Stephen after one day of degradation, however comic, ". . . but it's a horse of quite another colour to say you believe in the existence of a supernatural God."

Ulysses is an enchantment of the heart; apprehension is arrested upon the infinite possibilities life affords not by the day in June, 1904 with its typical peregrinations, not alone by the Chaplin figure and his travels, not with the words, not with patterns, but beyond these to the center of the work, the metaphysical realities evoked by Joyce. Joyce has bottomless depth but also its contrary: vast spiritual cycles of activity. His Noman-Everyman-Charlie-Bloom has been with every "Bad" (722). The question is "Where?" (722). After all is said and done, where has Ulysses travelled? The unspoken answer to the last word on Bloom is answered only by the totality of the novel. He will have to pay the price of conscience. About what? His destiny. Which is? Get rid of Darkinbad the Brightdayler. Get rid of daytime conscious human ineffectiveness. Get rid of the manchild. Be a man! The cunning "little fellow" of the Chaplin canon says no less, but his appearance is brief, brilliant, ephemeral beside the elongated, discerned, scrutinized, permanent and imperishable reality of Mr. Leopold Bloom of "the flat spaugs and the walk".

The bruiser in Chaplin's comedy often played by Mack Swain or Eric Campbell, six feet four, two hundred pounds, was a bully Charlie had to combat. He was the visible evidence of a tough, cruel, unscrupulous world where might makes right and the muscular survive. Charlie's mirth and high spirits toward the fact and person of the bruiser are excellent comedy because the little fellow conquers the brute most often by his wits. His outwitting, accompanied by a series of impish gags such as a spoonful of soup in the eye, a kick in the pants, a flowerpot on the head, a trip, were all meant to provoke the bruiser to action. The action was a chase, Charlie outsmarting the bully by dodges, decoys, sudden turns, hidings and finally a climactic delivery of the bruiser into the river or some similar, certain trap. The little fellow enjoyed nothing so much as encountering the bully of life and laying him low. It was one of the many lucid messages of hope in the Chaplin comedies to the common man everywhere: might does not make right; the muscular need not necessarily survive. You, the little man, must wrestle with trouble head on, without fear, and with confidence in your wit and cleverness.

Meeting a superior force and handling it through intelligence and fortitude is Odysseus' problem in Homer.

The protagonist-antagonist order imposed on experience by the artist is the essence of all great literature; Chaplin, however, was the first screen comedian to endow his films with this image of life. Theodore Huff says the Chaplin tramp is "possibly the most significant artistic archetype of this century."[13] The antagonist as evil in the Chaplin films is the cop, the boss, the rival, the thief, the wife, the giant, the tycoon, the social snob, the headwaiter, the tough, the miser, the manager, the floorwalker, the missionary, the Kaiser, the bully. Conquering evil is essential to the Chaplin theme.

Joyce's use of the Chaplin bully pattern in Bloom evokes, extends and heightens the Chaplin myth and in so doing acts to function as the central pivot in the new myth of *Ulysses*. Mr. Bloom is set upon by a variety of superior forces which are evil; he defeats them not by brute force (which is sometimes a Chaplin gag) but always in his mind. He has a cheeky self esteem like Charlie: Bloom's interior monologue is his pantomime. Five such superior forces confronting Bloom illustrates Joyce's unique use of the existing myth. Odysseus' combat was heroically serious; Chaplin's combat was entirely comic. Mr. Bloom's combat is the high seriousness of high comedy.

Formed in Chaplin is Bloom's image of the constable. He's a filcher of nymphs, "for another: a constable off duty cuddled her in Eccles Lane" (59); he's a dirty eater, "Let out to graze. . . . Bound for their troughs (160); he's a bully, "Nasty customers to tackle" (160). "That horse policeman the day Joe Chamberlain was given his degree in Trinity he got a run for his money. . . . His horse's hoofs clattering after us down Abbey Street. Luck I had the presence of mind to dive into Manning's or I was souped. . . . Police whistle in my ears still. Why he fixed on me. . . . Right here it began." (160); he's Bloom's *bête noir*, "Arrest him, Constable," says Mrs. Yelverton Barry in *Circe*: accusation, lechery (457); he's a bribe taker (588); he'd sooner lag you than love you (602).

The Keystone Cops as caricature of authority are gauche in the Mack Sennett mode. Sennett more often than not had Irish cops. Joyce transforms Sennett's cops back into Irishmen. In *Ulysses*, caricature of the cop disappears; Bloom's fear and estimate of them is valid. The constable's nature Bloom abhors; his authority he fears and with good reason. Bloom could have been "lagged" often if he were indiscreet, but so far he's covered his tracks and kept his prints from being made. Bloom conquers the cops in his mind by refined eating, refined "moving-ham" following; refined lechery; refined perversion. In his own mind, the constable's grossness is animality; but he, Bloom, is a gentleman.

Bloom's rival, Blazes Boylan, is a first rate bully. He's a bruiser-dandy, "Straw hat in sunlight. Tan shoes. Turnedup trousers. It is. It is" (180); he's bold, broad shouldered, tough and possessive. When Bloom feels Boylan's form in his bed,[14] he is roused to meditate what he might do to defeat this cad.

> Assassination, never, as two wrongs did not make one right. Duel by combat, no. Divorce, not now. Exposure by mechanical artifice . . . not yet. Suit for damages . . . not impossibly. If any, positively, connivance, introduction of emulation (material, a prosperous rival agency of publicity: moral, a successful rival agent of intimacy), depreciation, alienation, humiliation, separation protecting the one separated from the other, protecting separator from both. (718)

So, if Bloom could be like this virile, forthright bounder: do it and be done — all to the good. This is the tentative solution. Blazes for all his sportiness is not a slave to his senses. But what is rich in the Boylan-Bloom combat is Bloom's unknown blow to his rival. He has inadvertently caused Boylan to lose money on the races by the "Throwaway" gimmick Joyce gives to Bloom. Blazes is supposed to be the expert bookie and bettor on horses. Bloom who knows nothing and cares less about the race track has wounded him commercially. This for Boylan is a more serious blow to his vanity than to be told hands off Molly.

Bloom's decision to emulate Boylan is a healthy solution to his central disproportion. Virility, sexual confidence, manliness if abstracted from

Boylan's transgression are desirable potentials in Bloom. At least the lasting impression we get from Bloom's combat with Boylan is that he intends to learn from the adversary. It may include a share of adultery on his part. On this we can only surmise. We're safer in the light of his request to Molly that *she serve* him to conclude he will strive to make his senses serve him in a virile, forthright and comparatively free manner. The little fellow of the Chaplin canon more than once slipped away from his lady love and her lover because he knew the world was full of freshness and bloom. He'd love again.

The overpowering social forces that surround Mr. Bloom on his way to Paddy Dignam's funeral at Glasnevin contain an important and deliberate clue to the Chaplin Figure.

The ride to the cemetery is heavy with the overtone of contumely for Bloom. The three Dublin men who treat Mr. Bloom so shabbily constitute a full scale Irish reaction to a man who has not through drink, boastfulness, athletic power or oratory won a place in their hearts. What they know about Mr. Bloom they dislike; what they don't know, they suspect. The secret connections with his wife, Molly, they enjoy, but he is of no consequence. They tolerate his company. This makes Bloom stammer, articulate too eagerly, play up to their patronizing and in general behave freakishly. In his mind he has each of them sized up. He suffers no interior wounds during the ride or the funeral service because of their detraction. In fact, he is so free from brooding on what the immediate others think about him at the cemetery that at one point when the coffin is wheelbarrowed to the grave, he feels like dancing:

> The ree the ra the ree the ra the roo. Lord, I musn't lilt here. (103)

This, while highly Chaplinesque, is not the central revelation of the Chaplin figure in Bloom. A descent into Hades for Mr. Bloom (a) on the social level of scorn and contumely (b) on the theological level of his response to Dignam's Catholic burial service:

> Once you are dead you are dead. That last day idea. Knocking them all up out of their graves. Come forth, Lazarus! And he came fifth and lost the job. Get up! Last Day! Then every fellow mousing around for his liver and his lights and the rest of his traps. Find damn all of himself that morning. Pennyweight of powder in a skull. Twelve grammes one pennyweight. Troy measure. (104)

On the level of charity:

> Got a dinge in the side of his hat. Carriage probably.
>
> —Excuse me, sir, Mr. Bloom said beside them.
>
> They stopped.
>
> —Your hat is a little crushed, Mr. Bloom said, pointing.
>
> John Henry Menton stared at him for an instant without moving.
>
> —There, Martin Cunningham helped, pointing also.
>
> John Henry Menton took off his hat, bulged out the dinge and smoothed the nap with care on his coatsleeve. He clapped the hat on his head again.
>
> —It's all right now, Martin Cunningham said.
>
> John Henry Menton jerked his head down in acknowledgement.
>
> —Thank you, he said shortly.
>
> They walked on towards the gates. Mr. Bloom, *chapfallen,* drew behind a few paces so as not to overhear. (114, italics mine)

Joyce creates by means of the perfect word. In the reach and dimension of the English language is it possible he could have selected a more natural or revealing word than "chapfallen" to describe Mr. Bloom here?[15] Gaze at the fullness of its meaning, its spatial function in *Ulysses.* Joyce puts Chaplin in Bloom's act with "chapfallen". Examine the cluster image:

(1) Bloom would be long faced or drooped-jawed over the Menton slight. He tried to heal their old wound (Bloom beat Menton at bowls ten years ago) with simple courtesy; he put his foot in it.

(2) Bloom is distilled from Chaplin high flung and riotous farce comedy to dimensions of real comedy; descent to reality.

(3) Bloom is saddened as Charlie is often saddened by the bully's glare, his ingratitude, his intransigence.

(4) Bloom is immediately cheered by the thought that Menton will "be sorry after, perhaps when it dawns on him." He'll get the "pull" over him that way.

This is Chaplin action, mentality, energy of pantomime converted to interior monologue.

Odysseus' encounter with the Cyclops, Homer's anarchy symbol, causes him to live for ten years in a state of personal anarchy. He is committed by a superior force (Poseidon) to a life of decadent enchantment whose thongs he endeavors to cut, but release from one lurid adventure plunges him into the next and the next. He gets home only after prayer and supplication.

Charlie's encounter with his cyclopian Swains and Campbells is deliberate like Odysseus' exhilarating conquest of the mythical giant, and often "Noman" is the pun that lets Charlie escape. In *Easy Street* (released January 22, 1917), Charlie joins the police force. (Odysseus had decided to investigate the lawless giants.) He asphyxiates the bully. For this courage he is put through a series of ordeals by the gang, and finally through a happy accident he gets home to Edna. He is often "Noman" as he encounters the Cyclops of Easy Street.

Mr. Bloom's bully scenario redolent of the Keystone Chaplin freaks, characters and costumes, has a Homeric flavor with a New Myth essence. If Joyce was to be true to Homer's allegory in Odysseus, the *Cyclops* adventure had to be pivotal to Bloom's wandering. The *Cyclops* episode in Joyce's *Ulysses* is placed midway in Bloom's scenes. He is in the novel for 667 pages. The pivotal action comes on page 336, three pages from the literal center of Bloom's print. This accurate shot makes of *Cyclops*, the wheel around which *Ulysses* revolves. It is the central stasis at which we apprehend the hero as Odysseus, Charlie and Mr. Bloom. The following chart demonstrates Joyce's fusion of three myths.

THE HOMER - CHAPLIN - JOYCE MYTHS FUSED

HOMER	CHAPLIN	BLOOM
Odysseus visits lawless Cyclops.	Charlie (in *Easy Street,* released Jan., 1917) provokes big bully.	Bloom goes to Kiernan's where Citizen (brute voice of Irish) hangs out.
Cyclops imprisons Odysseus; plans to eat men.	Charlie is cornered by big bully who is about to kill him.	Citizen corners Bloom on politics, Home Rule, Royal Navy, HRM, King of England; finally catches him on his nationality.
Odysseus presses grapes; Cyclops gets drunk on wine.	Charlie plays the "receiver of the alarm box" like a musical instrument and looks through it like an eye glass. The bully is intrigued.	Bloom soothes the citizen with talk of love. "A new apostle to the gentiles", says the citizen. Universal love.
Odysseus blinds the Cyclops as he sleeps.	When the bully picks the receiver up to take a look, Charlie clubs him. Sneering, the bully bends the gas lamp post as a show of strength before killing Charlie; Charlie leaps on his back, clamps lamp over bully's head to asphyxiate him.	Gossip about Bloom blinds the Citizen (a) Throwaway (b) Sinn Fein (c) Virag's usury in Ireland.
Odysseus escapes by lashing himself to underside of a ram and using "Noman" as password.	Charlie falls on a dope fiend's hypodermic needle, becomes a superman by the accidental injection and subdues the bully and his mob — comic twist to make "Noman" become "Superman".	Bloom escapes by lashing himself to the Lamb of God "Christ was a Jew like me" (336). Through the arrest of apprehension at this point, Bloom is *Noman* in deceiving himself and others about his relation to the deity.
Cyclops hurls a boulder on Odysseus' fleet. Odysseus escapes but Poseidon's curse is on him via Cyclops.	Brickbats, pies, tables, chairs, windows, stairways, boards are hurled at Charlie. He escapes with Edna. Poseidon's curse inferred in canon of film. He is doomed to wander ceaselessly as *l'homme moyen sensuel.*	Bloom escapes on jarvey; Citizen hurls biscuit box after flying car; it misses Bloom. Rift in the nature of man (Poseidon) — senses serve intellect; *l'homme moyen sensuel* is Bloom's doom until final *stasis.*

— And I belong to a race too, says Bloom, that is hated and persecuted. Also now. This very moment. This very instant.

Gob, he near burnt his fingers with the butt of his old cigar.

— Robbed, says he. Plundered. Insulted. Persecuted. Taking what belongs to us by right. At this very moment, says he, putting up his fist, sold by auction off in Morocco like slaves or cattles.

— Are you talking about the new Jerusalem? says the citizen.

— I'm talking about injustice, says Bloom.

— Right, says John Wyse. Stand up to it then with force like men.

That's an almanac picture for you. Mark for a softnosed bullet. Old lardyface standing up to the business end of a gun. Gob, he'd *adorn a sweepingbrush, so he would, if he only had a nurse's apron on him.* And then he collapses all of a sudden, twisting around all the opposite, as limp as a wet rag.

— But it's no use, says he. Force, hatred, history, all that. That's not life for men and women, insult and hatred. And everybody knows that it's the very opposite of that that is really life. (326-7, italics mine)

Charlie's jobs are janitor, waiter, farm hand, stage doorman; menial assistant; this covers his shifting and short-lived employment. Mainly, however, he is remembered in the first few years of films as a janitor. In *The Bank* he has a sweeping brush, wears an apron, and wields a mop by which he produces some of his funniest business. His gags taken seriously, his nature explored fully, the little tramp transforms Bloom's action into the figure of Charlie. Other Chaplin bits: the fist, the wet rag, the weak defense, the quick ideal. The major Chaplin tone: Charlie was in each and every film fighting prejudice, hatred, force, and a loveless world.

The lyric passages evoked by Homer are humanized by the sudden facetious parody after every utterance. The drunken voice of Ireland is the superstructure of the Chaplin caricature of names, places, topics of the day. Count Chloride de Lime, Count Broho, Miss Moneybags, Mr. Stout, Mrs. Stout; "I'll put kinks in your auto-suggestion." Chaplin was always enamored of puns. The many punning sallies Joyce offers us in Cyclops is not a device inspired by Chaplin; it is a tendency they have in common.

Circe contains more direct and continuous evidence than *Cyclops* of the Chaplin figure for this is the place of poetry. It is a scenario, of course, like *Aeolus.* Converting the balance of *Ulysses* to a full screen scenario should be attractive with two such fully realized models.

The poignancy and pathos of what lies behind the walk does not contradict a world that loved its Charlie. Joyce is behind the little fellow's romantic hunger; the way he feeds it is Bloom's way.

The full page black letters facing pages 5, 55 and 597 of the Random House *Ulysses* did not appear in the first edition. Joyce withheld them for the popular printing. The letters are three different views of the trinity who compose the full personality of Ulysses: Stephen's "S" is an aerial view of his comic flesh; Mr. Bloom's "M" is a front view with dragging rere of Bloom's flesh, and Poldy's "P" is a profile view of Bloom's preparatory period to unity. Molly is the absent flesh which causes these letters to move across the screen of the mind. "M" is an essential line drawing of Bloom's lower body with the "flurried stork's legs", the chafed stiff walk, and the large, misshapen out-toed feet. If it were to walk off the page toward you, how would it move? The downward slanting rere at the center of the letter is the whole story of Bloom's body prostitution.

Does this grim reality destroy the comedy of the man and his walk? This is the truth of the being of the visible world of Leopold Bloom. Truth as comedy has a quick healing agent, because comedy promises salvation. Tragedy to be logical must portray man's destruction through folly. Joyce sought not death but life in the human condition.

Part II:

POETRY OF CONSCIENCE

Figure Three: *Condition of Poetry*

Introduction

Joyce's basic definition for the act of conscience comes from the *Summa Theologica* of Thomas Aquinas whose esthetic philosophy he extended to make a philosophy of creating:

> So far as this side of esthetic philosophy extends, Aquinas will carry me all along the line. (*Por.* 245)

Definitive esthetic positions as Joyce sought them have inherent morality. The beautiful in conscience must be seen in its moral truth within the larger context of poetry.

Circe is organized in the three-fold Thomistic analysis of conscience as set forth in the *Summa Theologica, I,* 79, 13.

A. That conscience is not a power but an act:

> For conscience, according to the very nature of the word, implies the relation of knowledge to something, for conscience may be resolved into *cum alio scientia*, i.e., knowledge applied to an individual case.

B. That certain things are attributed to conscience:

> For conscience is said to witness, to bind, or incite, and also to accuse, torment, or rebuke.

C. That the application of knowledge or science to what we do is made in three ways:

> a. We recognize that we have done or not done something. Conscience is said to *witness.*
>
> b. We judge that something should be done or not done. Conscience is said to *incite* or *bind.*
>
> c. We judge that something done is well done or ill done. Conscience is said to *excuse, accuse,* or *torment.*

D. Conscience denominates an act:

> Since habit is a principle of act sometimes the name conscience is given to the first natural habit — synderesis.
>
> a. Jerome calls synderesis conscience.
>
> b. Basil, *the natural power of judgment.*
>
> c. Damacene says that it is the *law of our intellect.*

Chaplin's stiff walk is a witness to Bloom's lonely autoeroticism; Bloom's real father, Virag, grows horns and a tail before our very eyes; he incites Leopold toward licence, but he also binds him to a primitive good, self-preservation. Bloom gives "the old man" the boot and has his first experience of self-knowledge. With self-knowledge Bloom accuses, excuses and torments himself as he judges his act of existence present and past.

> When we come to the phenomena of artistic conception, artistic gestation and artistic reproduction, I require a new terminology and a new personal experience. (Por. 245)

The extension of St. Thomas' outline of conscience is most evident in Joyce in the matter of artistic reproduction. *Circe* is pyrotechnics of the unconscious, the feminine principle in any human personality; beings swing up from "the great mother" to objectivize latent images, and they duel with the real people in the episode in the manner but not the mode of conscience. All planes of consciousness are masculine. It is only by the penetration of the masculine principle into the passive receptacle of the unconscious, that creative judgment is begotten. Thus Bloom who is flesh and whose major reality is imagination and therefore conscious unconscious, becomes the feminine principle for Stephen who is conscious intellect and intellectual imagination. Their co-active existence initiates in the Musicroom, the place of poetry, and their individual identities are rescued in the climax of the Musicroom scene by the condition of poetry.

Joyce's new personal experience has an affinity with Carl Jung and his disciple, Erich Neumann, but identity with the historical mythopoetic nature of Holy Scripture. In Scripture gender is a poetic constant. The Song of Solomon foreshadows Christ's relation to the Church. In the New Testament doctrine of the Mystical Body wherein Christ is the head and all of the members of His Church are his limbs, organs and flesh, Joyce found his masculine-feminine principle. His awareness of modern psychology, however, which develops the historical position of the gender symbol archeologically is manifest especially in *Circe.*

Joyce agrees with Jung in characterizing the organ of consciousness, the intellect, as masculine, and the organ of the unconscious, the sensorium, as feminine. He disputes Jung and his disciple Erich Neumann, however, in their view of conscience:

> The development of the persona is the outcome of a process of adaptation that suppresses all individually significant features and potentialities, disguising and repressing them in favor of collective factors, or those deemed desirable by the collective. Here again, wholeness is exchanged for a workable and successful sham personality. The "inner voice" is stifled by the growth of a superego, of conscience, the representative of collective values. The voice, the individual experience of the transpersonal, which is particularly strong in childhood, is renounced in favor of conscience. When paradise is abandoned, the voice of God that spoke in the Garden is abandoned too, and the values of the collective, of the fathers, of law and conscience, of the current morality, etc., must be accepted as the supreme values in order to make social adaptation possible. (*The Origins and History of Consciousness*, p. 403.)

Here conscience is a barrier to wholeness. In Joyce conscience is that very wholeness which constitutes judgment. On what? Everything. On what is it based? It is based upon the fruit of the sensorium, a region which constitutes our unconscious, and in which fruit grows from the seed of the intellect. Joyce says nothing creative happens whether amateur or professional unless the power of the intellect impregnates the rich sources of the imagination whose images as we know arrive by many paths: one infinite resource is the mysterious unconscious within the human personality. Depth psychology is not as extravagant in its concept of conscience as it is limited: Joyce sees the poetry of conscience; depth psychology records the dialectic of conscience through the traditional image of the term. This for Joyce is limited and a species of *pars pro toto*, assuming the part for the whole. Joyce is an artist of poetic knowledge who knows that

> In the virgin womb of the imagination the word was made flesh.*
> (*Por.* 255)

*Cf. Jacques Maritain, *Creative Intuition in Art and Poetry*, p. 67 f. M. Maritain cites Eric Gill in *The Priestcraft of Craftsmanship* as the originator of this usage of the Biblical image. Gill wrote his essay, *Art*, in 1940. Joyce finished *A Portrait* in 1914.

Chapter VI

WITNESS: THE STIFF WALK

The process of Bloom's nature which we experience during the eleven episodes that precede *Circe* establish him as a man with hungering flesh who mutely craves to adore. The object of his adoration is symbolized by an unfaithful wife and her many counterparts, but in Joyce's *Ulysses* as in Homer's *Odyssey*, human marriage as well as the feminine principle is in the service of a larger revelation. This accounts for the phenomenal perverseness of Bloom's acts from *Calypso* to *Oxen of the Sun.* It is not alone an earthly wife that provokes this man to the secret corrosive lusts of his mind and body, to the self-induced orgasms procured in pollutive masturbation, to the gluttonies, blasphemies, lecheries, to the gallery of depravities we see in him hour by hour. In Homer, the unconscious and the irrational part of man is explained by means of the supernatural. Odysseus' reversals are all caused by powers (gods, goddesses, magic animals, giants) above the natural which the Greek poet objectifies in the myth. Calypso is like man's tendency to forget his high born destiny; in the poem she is fully identified as a separate being who exerts her full magic charm on Odysseus to make him forget Ithaca, his home. In Joyce this is no less true. He imitates the psychic action of the *Odyssey* in a uniquely twentieth-century modern mode.

Circe is intellectual cinema written in scenario form projected on a mental screen to reveal the object of Bloom's adoration. Joyce's own scheme for the episode is helpful in organizing our perception of it. He tells us first of all that the scene is a brothel; that the time is midnight; that the organ of the body imitated is locomotor apparatus; the art, magic; the symbol, a whore; the technic, hallucination; and that Bella Cohen is Circe. (See Schema)

Intellectual cinema depicts the equations between the emotional content of thought and the essence of abstract concepts. It is the filmic approach to the interior monologue whose form is created by the metamorphic power of the mind communicating with being in the unconscious. Intellectual cinema gives shape to this form. Sergei Eisenstein, the innovator of film montage, considered Joyce the single exponent of filmic depiction in literary art.

> It has been left to James Joyce to develop in literature the depictive line of the Japanese hieroglyph.[1]

The Japanese hieroglyph as Eisenstein demonstrates gave the cinema its basic principle of operation, the ideogram.

> Thus we have seen how the principle of the hieroglyph — "denotation by depiction" — split in two: along the line of its purpose (the principle of "denotation"), into the principles of creating literary imagery; along the line of its method of realizing this purpose (the principle of "depiction"), into the striking methods of expressiveness used by Sharaku.[2]

A picture of water plus a picture of an eye means in Japanese "to weep;" the picture of an ear near the drawing of a door means "to listen." From separate depictables comes the ideogram. The combination of two depictables equals the representation of something that is graphically undepictable. In cinema, shots which are depictive and single in meaning, neutral in content are arranged into a series of intellectual contexts. An example from Joyce: In *Circe* shots of Mary Driscoll, scullery-maid, are single and depictive in meaning, neutral in content until they are placed next to Beaufoy's plagiarism charges to Bloom and coupled with Stephen Dedalus' early charge[3] against the Irish church calling her "the scullery maid of Christendom." Now, why should Bloom at this point have access to Stephen Dedalus' thought life? This is Joyce's direct implication that by means of magic in *Circe* the poet-intellectual will be linked to the poet-*l'homme moyen sensual* and that poetry will unite them as one man.

The intellectual cinema of *Circe* (pp. 422-466) begins with Bloom's trial by Dublin jury in which he is found guilty and sentenced to hang by the neck until dead. Not anyone at the trial is present in the flesh except Bloom, and everyone who testifies against him is a hallucinated presence who speaks, thinks and acts like the real person who resides in Bloom's unconscious. The trial then is an ideogram for Bloom's condition of soul at the end of fifteen hours of his habitual thought life. The beings of his being bear witness that he has or has not done something. The whole segment is informed by a sign: the stiff walk. Unless we know Bloom is the Chaplin clown, this ideogram is lost, so is the sand strewer, so is Stepaside, "write the stars and stripes on it!", and while the trial scene evokes a moral chaos, still the illuminating dimension by which we see it as conscience is missing. For like the whole of *Ulysses*, *Circe* is comedy.

Bloom's comedic agon depends on the Chaplin signs for its evolution toward a total or race conscience. The first segment or "Witness" gives testimony about Bloom's stiff walk, man's stiff walk. When we see Bloom and man as the Chaplin figure, license to pursue the whole squalid category of causes and effects is not an evil but a blessing.

Before he steps into his self-styled dock, Bloom is seen to masturbate on the beach by his own choice in the nearby presence of a young lame girl. He has an idea chastity is avoiding adultery; he has no idea that a self-induced orgasm is anything but his own business. This is why he can go blithely to a hospital where a child is to be born and extol the miracle of birth without realizing his own paralyzed condition. His awareness, swine-fatted as it is with a constant lust, does not admit judgment. He is a blythe spirit which condition is not to be confused with lightness of heart. He is as his counsel later puts it "not all there". But such insanity is a constant state of the human race. Self crimes rarely prevent the gentleman or lady from donning immaculate linen and joining the elite at dinner, from scrubbing up, going to the concert and discussing higher realms of music, from cleaning the fingernails and discussing the art of philosophy or the science of God. Human inconsistency is so painful a truth, the only possible sane reaction is laughter. But in the laugh, if it is conscious, there is the abyss of tears at what seems a wilfully irreversible condition.

Bloom is on trial because he procured the public boon of darkest Stepaside. "I who lost my way and contributed to the columns of the Irish Cyclist the letter headed, *In darkest Stepaside.*" A moment before the ideogram in the frames was Bloom swerved at by two cyclists and then stepping aside from a sackshouldered ragman. The scavenger ragman tries to claim Bloom, but he'll have no such indignity. But this is not what brings him into court. A dragon sandstrewer all but runs him down, and the motorman yells an obscenity at him about his stiff walk.

THE MOTORMAN

Hey, shitbreeches, are you doing the hattrick?

BLOOM

. . . The stiff walk. True word spoken in jest. That awful cramp in Lad lane. Something poisonous I ate. Emblem of luck. Why? Probably lost cattle. Mark of the beast. (428-29)

This does bring him before the law.

In the snaky riverfog of Nighttown, Bloom meets his father in the cliché of a boyhood rebuke, his mother in the cliché of her talisman bequeathed to him: a shrivelled potato, panacea for all ills. "Keep your clothes clean and your belly full, Leopoldenben, and we'll be proud of you;" this is what he did so the mark of the beast did not show. Nor did it show when Marion, his wife, found him an old stick in the mud and told him to see the world. He bought her some soap and in the filmic development of the case of Bloom versus Bloom, the soap materializes:

> We're a capital couple are Bloom and I
> He brightens the earth, I polish the sky. (433)

Hygiene has lathered over the sign of the beast. Bloom in the meantime has hidden his midnight snack, a lukewarm pig's crubeen and a cold sheep's trotter, in his overcoat. As he journeys the hot and cold slough of memory toward a self-hammered dock, the feel of warm and cold feetmeat reassure him.

Like a rhythmic tide controlling this sea of the unconscious which Bloom fears, periodic bursts of Chaplin song ebb and flow. The first of these is Mrs. Breen, the former Josie Powell, "her roguish eyes wideopen, smiling in all her herbivorous buckteeth" (435). In the early years Josie has been mildly cooperative in branding Bloom with the mark of the beast, and he is at careful pains to point up her imbecility. Chaplin films often have a hulking woman whom Charlie confounds. *Tillie's Punctured Romance* with Marie Dressler (1914) is undoubtedly the model here. Joyce creates a new office for the soul of the Tillie image in *Ulysses*. The hilarious comedy of the lines and the business in this single scene balance the spectres testifying against Bloom. He is at the height of his comedy here; would any clown alive avoid provoking Mrs. Breen into being "tremendously teapot" (437)? Here is a witness testifying to the strength in Bloom's weakness. Without the mark of the beast, he could hardly bring off this superb bit of comic justice.

Bloom is followed by a whining dog "towards hellgates" which is Bella Cohen's whore house; it will be this dog ironically enough who accuses him of committing "a nuisance". In his history Bloom has copulated with animals, and now though he does not have time to bring it off, he is accosted by the watch for suspected bestiality.

FIRST WATCH

Caught in the act. Commit no nuisance.

BLOOM

(Stammers) I am doing good to others.

Throughout his trial, "I am doing good to others" is Bloom's principal defense against himself. He sees no difference between the sexual gag towards Mrs. Breen and his literal acts of bestiality. This is how he is comic in the midst of lurid recall of past acts and in the presence of genuine testimonies against his manhood.

The friend of man. Trained by kindness. (446)

he says of the spaniel, because the dog has been kind in a monstrous way, although again Bloom is unaware of anything pre-normal. But with the increasing complexity of the assailing images, Bloom's discomfort is acute. Henry Flower is discovered when he takes off his high grade hat. He is pressed for his identity; he slews around in a few lies but once too often. He is asked his profession, and he answers,

> Well, I follow a literary occupation. Author-journalist. In fact we are just bringing out a collection of prize stories of which I am the inventor, something that is an entirely new departure. I am connected with the British and Irish press. If you ring up . . . (449)

At this point in *Circe* Joyce himself enters into Bloom of the flat spaugs and the walk to defend what he has made. The ruse of Philip Beaufoy pulp-writer testifying that Bloom has stolen his best work and defiled it:

> . . . a specimen of my maturer work disfigured by the hallmark of the beast.

creates the comedy of letters as Joyce knew it through his endless chaotic dealings with publishers. The mind of the world has fed on pulp as literature, newspapers as pulp. This has kept the lively brand of the beast on mankind. He is invited daily to wallow in cheap sensation, degrading human images, hollow oratory, cheap and meaningless idealism, romantic impressions of reality, the defiling human image. This sudden displacement directs the poetry to a human image created by another mass media.

Through the magic of intellectual cinema Mary Driscoll, scullerymaid, is roused from unconsciousness. Her case against Bloom-Joyce is that

> He surprised me in the rere of the premises, your honour, when the missus was out shopping one morning with a request for a safety pin. He held me and I was discoloured in four places as a result. And he interfered twict with my clothing. (453)

Mary Driscoll is a reminder here that once long ago Bloom-Joyce called the Irish Church "the scullery-maid of Christendom".[4] It was a bitter reproach when it was born of sorrow, disgust and despair, but here in its new found setting, the bitterness and despair have vanished and only a portion of comic disgust remains. Bloom counters with Mary, "You counter-assaulted"; but Mary grandly and scornfully levels him with,

> I had more respect for the scouringbrush, so I had. I remonstrated with him, your lord, and he remarked: Keep it quiet!
>
> (General Laughter.) (453)

Mary Driscoll more locally calls up Stephen Dedalus' classic comment on Irish art: "the cracked looking-glass of a servant" (8). And here again that Bloom should have access to the thought life of Stephen foreshadows the mythopoetic merging of the two in *Circe.* Irish art as the distorted image of the Irish race through her artists has a specific validity here. Joyce quite personally bears witness to the peasant mind of the world (not only Ireland) which imagines itself too holy to view the image of the beast, too pure to admit its mark, too unconscious to see through to the other side of the coin, the good of the sensible which has one access only into the being of man: his flesh. We remember Stephen Dedalus' view of Davin:

> . . . for Davin had sat at the feet of Michael Cusack, the Gael — repelling swiftly and suddenly by a grossness of intelligence or by a bluntness of feeling or by a dull stare of terror in the eyes, the terror of soul of a starving Irish village in which the curfew was still a nightly fear.
>
> . . . the young peasant worshipped the sorrowful legend of Ireland. . . . His nurse had taught him Irish and shaped his rude imagination by the broken lights of Irish myth. He stood towards the myth upon which no individual mind had ever drawn out a line of beauty[5] and to its unwieldy tales that divided themselves as they moved down the cycles in the same attitude as towards the Roman catholic religion, the attitude of a dull witted loyal serf. (*Por.* 210)

While all the ways of error and stupidity are lyrically intense in *A Portrait,* the same ways in *Ulysses* become freely hilarious. "The accused will now make a bogus statement," the clerk of the crown announces solemnly, and Bloom proceeds to do so with a fullblown waterlily in his hand. What assault by the scullery-maid of Irish art is complete without the private life of Oscar Wilde? Counsel for the defense, J. J. O'Molloy, is cunning, however, and cleverly he brings forth the one important truth in Bloom's defense:

> I put it to you that there was no attempt at carnally knowing. (455)

This defense imbedded so carefully in the high comedy of the trial has several functions. To remind the world that carnal knowledge in its proper dimension is not realized. Because it is not realized, Bloom is unclean, bestial, effeminate and impotent. What carnal knowledge does man have other than a smutty impression of the use of this term in court? Who gives him carnal knowledge in the ordinary work-a-day rearing of children, in the ordinary school, in the ordinary Sunday sermon? Philosophy has this carnal knowledge to give:

> . . . the soul must be a substance in the sense of form of a natural body having life potentially within it.[6]

> . . . the intellectual soul had to be endowed not only with the power of understanding, but also with the power of feeling. Now the action of the senses is not performed without a corporeal instrument. Therefore it behooved the intellectual soul to be united to a body fitted to be a convenient organ of sense.[7]

History gives us the carnal knowledge of humanism. The Bible is the image of the thought life of ancient peoples which life was housed in bodies and which bodies were not condemned as evil. The Song of Solomon would not be among its books if the Bible witnessed that man's body was evil. In *A Portrait* Stephen Dedalus' shame and confusion at the growth and urgencies of his own body will forever symbolize the peasant mind of the world transmitting its puritanic stamp of shame upon the God given "corporeal instrument" of the body. No feeling is possible without this beautiful instrument and instrument of the beautiful. How much awareness does the human race have concerning the power, beauty, fitness, propriety and glorious fact of its body? Rather the more tragic aspect of the question: How many human beings have defiled themselves because carnal knowledge does not inform carnality?

The high spoofery of the existent, confused morality of the human body continues through Bloom's defense by counsel. We are indeed on a Chaplin kick in these passages:

> My client is an infant, a poor foreign immigrant who started scratch as a stowaway and is now trying to turn an honest penny. [Chaplin's meteoric rise to fame in one year]. (454)

> . . . such familiarities . . . being quite permitted in my client's native place, [England and the mark of the beast]. (454)

> If the accused could speak he could a tale unfold one of the strangest that have ever been narrated between the covers of a book. [Chaplin's pantomime].
>
> Not all there, in fact. (455) [A zany understatement][8]

Bloom drools and sputters baby talk in a few frames to remind us often that the man-child is a comic deformity. The Chaplin myth in pointing up universal tendencies as they relate to a lack of carnal knowledge surpasses Homer. A major tendency constitutes the climax of the first segment of the intellectual film, the stiff walk as witness.

Three Dublin dames, high society, lace curtain, titled, appear to accuse Bloom of sullying their minds with swinish indecencies. His response is a favorite sublimation. He adores being whipped by women for his naughtiness. It gives him sexual pleasure, phallic excitement and extends his image of himself as eternal creature of the womb. The comedy turns on the high seriousness of the three witnesses in the matter of whipping the accused. Bloom wanted just a refined birching to stimulate the circulation, but the women screech that they will flog him without mercy:

> Write the stars and stripes on it! (459)

This is, of course, deliberate placing of Chaplin as is the denouement which is swift and typical. Bloom is saved by a knot of ragged newsboys who interrupt the Sacher-Masoch ceremony with a cry of headlines, "new addresses of all the cuckolds in Ireland." We are reminded sharply by these urchin witnesses that *l'homme moyen sensuel* is he for whom all witnesses are accomplices and he for whom there is no carnal knowing only carnal being. Bloom's unconscious has communicated by means of the metamorphic powers of his consciousness to form the first phase of the uncreated conscience Joyce brings into being in *Ulysses.*

Bloom does not hang by the neck, a sentence essentially pronounced on himself by himself, because a voice from the dead, Elpenor Paddy Dignam, emerging from a beagle's snout cries out:

> Pray for the repose of his soul. [Dignam's] (465)

Odysseus' ordeal to get home is marked by recurring temptations to forfeit his life rather than struggle against inhuman odds. The odds in the myth are analogues to the unchartered, monster-infested sea of the unconscious. In all antiquity no array of man's irrational nature so captures the imagination or so convinces the intelligence as Homer's poem precisely because man suffers the same agony today. But man's irrational nature has for centuries had an illuminative beacon trained on it: this beacon is human judgment in the moral order which we can call conscience, and the steady upthrust whether we will or no, of man's consciousness in the evolutionary character of the world. Human acts or the knowledge which conscience acts upon convolute to a region of unawareness; we forget the time, the place, the hour. We could not understand the significance of the way in which we exercised the act of our existence *in this hour*. New awareness of new things covers like the snow the footprints of an hour ago. Bloom at thirty-eight is hard put to locate those tracks by which he has become his own most vocal witness. With consciousness now in ascent, he must assimilate the buried being of his existence. When the witnesses attempt to hang him, he suddenly reminds himself to be a little quieter about his combat with his poseidon-infested past deeds and pray a prayer. To perish in the sea of the unconscious, to despair at quantity, quality, shape or depth of transgression against human nature is a fate worse than death. As Bloom stands in front of Bella Cohen's, the place he was bound to seek, he hears Stephen's music:

> A man's touch. Sad music. Church music. Perhaps here. (466)

It is dialectic music, intellectual; eventually it draws him into the music-room where it is generated and into the poetry which is conscience.

The intellectual cinema scenario, Part I *Circe* is the oldest of the methods in art conceived in a new technique which the world knew and loved in Chaplin and the Greek world sensed and admired in Homer. But Joyce has in mind a new twentieth century, metaphysical myth through the mythopoetic parents of Greek poetry and twentieth century cinema. We must see the whole picture, however, before the myth is intelligible or the forbears introduce their offspring, the carnal knowledge myth through the Kleigs of *lex aeterna.*

Chapter VII

JUDGE: THE OLD MAN

In the remaining reels of *Circe* Bloom is at the mercy of feminine corruption. He all but suffocates from its vileness and depravity, yet we are made aware again and again that in reality he does battle with himself. How do we read this condition? He battles with a corrupt intuitional system in his nature. Intellectual cinema, more than any other art used to communicate *Ulysses,* serves Joyce accurately because he insists upon separating human beings into separate images of themselves before he unites them into final whole personalities. Film is the one art form that can convey the sense of simultaneity needed for this vision. While Stephen Dedalus and Leopold Bloom each maintain an individual existence at novel's end, they serve the total vision of the work as one person. The mind is embodied; the flesh is embodied; fully created they exist in divided worlds (like our own intellect and flesh) until such time as they are brought together in an image of coition (gate lock, 688). Finally, it is the poetry of the nature of man Joyce creates. Philosophy calls soul the act of the body or that which gives form to the body. Joyce has Stephen Dedalus use this definition in "My soul walks with me form of forms" (45). The soul cannot scorn the body's indispensable service of feeling, cannot reject its sensual power, cannot ignore its complementary control of sensible reality. If the soul does reject its flesh, that flesh — feminine in nature because fertile — becomes corrupt.

Bloom of *Ulysses* is the man with hungered, spiritually starved flesh. Hunger is the single form of human torment that cannot, will not be endured. A man will kill, rob, plunder, accept a dictator, embrace an ideology, pervert every ideal he ever held for food. Bloom perverts woman, womanicity, the feminine, the feminine principle, prudence, fortitude, temperance, chastity precisely because the spiritual act of the flesh is paralyzed. He is of course not a happy man. But he is a comic one and relentlessly has Joyce shouted this to us over and over in *Ulysses*.

Reel two of *Circe* shows Bloom to be the "funniest man on earth" (481). What else has the world called Chaplin? Bloom as human clown is made to have one hey-day here (466-491) for he tells the world, and whenever a clown tells the world, we are bound in our amusement to see ourselves in his same ridiculous light. As fantasy-farce the new Bloomusalem sequence is wilder than the most ideal Keystone, so it is good to know Mack Sennett is divided and put into the act. On page 466 Bloom asks Zoe Higgins, "Is this Mrs. Mack's?" And on page 471 in the midst of a monstrous Hibernian parade, "Four buglers on foot blow a *sennet*." No one could mistake what Joyce had in mind for the reel as farce or fantasy, but as always the reel as part of the esthetic moment locates another segment of Joyce's artistic vision.

That artistic vision, like Homer's, is the image of the wholeness of man. Charles Taylor calls Odysseus the wholest man in literature.

> For Homeric man, both the spirit and the flesh are indispensable, and this is why Odysseus refuses the immortalities both of Calypso and of Hades. Put another way, man must be conscious to be human, but he must come to terms with the unconscious to be whole.[1]

It is in the unconscious layers of the human race we find the promise of fulfillment for humanity. Joyce's ardent concern with the complexity of human consciousness which he saw to be a condition in process and which he himself demonstrated in his art relates him closely to Pierre Teilhard de Chardin, the French paleontologist, whose *Phenomenon of Man* is considered to be the great scientific synthesis of the twentieth century. In *Claybook for James Joyce,* Louis Gillet speaks of Joyce's friendship with a French Jesuit with whom he found intellectual identity on matters of language and philosophy. Chardin was born in 1881, Joyce in 1882; Joyce went to Paris in 1920; Chardin was at the Paleontological Laboratory of the Paris Museum during 1919-1922 and had by then published articles in *Etudes* which foreshadowed his mature scientific thought on man as phenomenon. By the time *Ulysses* was published in 1922, Pierre Teilhard de Chardin had published an article in *Etudes* (March, 1921) whose shock of wisdom was widely publicized. The article contained this paragraph:

> The letter of the Bible shows us the Creator fashioning the body of man out of the earth. Conscientious observation of the world leads us to see today that by this "earth" we must understand a substance that has been slowly elaborated by the totality of things, in such a way that man, we should say, has been drawn out not exactly from a little amorphous matter, but by a long effort of the whole "earth".

In *The Phenomenon of Man* Chardin reconciles the fact of evolution with the Christian position. He demonstrates as a scientist from his studies of Pre-History that in the beginning the Earth contained all it would realize in space and time. At the birth of reflection man is observed as conscious and his history in the thousands of years on earth proves an increase in that consciousness. The increase constitutes a complexity and the complexity is an irreversible condition in evolution. The whole of creation is convergent upon a point which he calls the Omega Point, and this combined with Alpha, the beginning, is the human process from the Creator to the Creator.[2]

Man's unconscious, while ever in reserve, lessens as the world evolves, and in this lessening he becomes more aware. Awareness is the product of consciousness communicating with the unconscious. In the unconscious is buried the knowledge upon which consciousness works, the knowledge upon which judgment performs. In this sense, the result is *cum alio scientia* or conscience. Conscience is a much wider sphere in Joyce's vision than the simple, catechical examen man might subject himself to at the end of the day. Conscience is the delivery of man through science to a full human integration. The human unconscious narrows with knowledge of history, archeology, philosophy, psychology, aesthetics and theology. Joyce envisions conscience not only as a means of moral truth, but also a channel toward total truth which is of course the evolutionary approach to this human power of reflection.

As denizen of feminine corruption Leopold Bloom makes a stump speech. The way we must see this stump speech of his unconscious is by relating it to the stump speech of his consciousness. In the *Cyclops* episode which takes place earlier in Kiernan's Public House, he held a stump cigar and uttered these immortal words to the Irish Fenian and pubmates:

> — And I belong to a race too, says Bloom, that is hated and persecuted. Also now. This very moment. This very instant.
>
> Gob, he near burnt his fingers with the butt of his old cigar.
>
> — Robbed, says he. Plundered. Insulted. Persecuted. Taking what belongs to us by right. At this very moment, says he, putting up his fist, sold by auction off in Morocco like slaves or cattles.
>
> — Are you talking about the new Jerusalem? says the citizen.
>
> — I'm talking about injustice, says Bloom.
>
> — Right, says John Wyse. Stand up to it then with force like men.
>
> . . . And then he collapses all of a sudden, twisting around all the opposite, as limp as a wet rag.
>
> — But it's no use, says he. Force, hatred, history, all that. That's not life for men and women, insult and hatred. And everybody knows that it's the very opposite of that that is really life.
>
> — What? says Alf.
>
> — Love, says Bloom. I mean the opposite of hatred. (326-27)

Here Bloom says all the right things — as he says, to keep to the right, right, right, right. Now relate this conscious, passionate hungering flesh speech to what Leopold says to Zoe in front of Bella Cohen's. Bloom is human in the *Cyclops* outburst; to become whole, he must come to terms with the fantasy and farce he lives with in his heart of hearts. Here is his dream of love for humanity; this is the good that incites him.

"Mankind is incorrigible," Bloom says as the man on the street scratching at the thin surface of history, "Sir Walter Raleigh is to blame for our death in life: he brought us the twin poisons of tobacco and the potato. The result? Suicide and lies — all are habits of public life." For this less than conscientious speech Bloom is made alderman, and he suggests his first stunning reform.

> . . . run a tramline, I say, from the cattle market to the river. That's the music of the future. (469)

For this perception in better living, Alderman Bloom is made Lord Mayor of Dublin (and the world), and a parade such as the world has never seen passes by with His Honour the object of wild excitement. So classic a face does he possess that he is immediately elevated to the monarchy and called Leopold the First. Every Churchman rejoices as hair oil is poured on Bloom's head by Michael, Cardinal Logue Archbishop of Armagh, and the peers of the realm bend the knee and say,

> I do become your liege man of life and limb to earthly worship. (473)

As ruler supreme of the realm, the King declares his plans:

> My subjects! We hereby nominate our faithful charger Copula Felix hereditary Grand Vizier and announce that we have this day repudiated our former spouse and have bestowed our royal hand upon the princess Selene, the splendour of night.
>
> (The former morganatic spouse of Bloom is hastily removed in the Black Maria)[3]
>
> My beloved subjects, a new era is about to dawn. I, Bloom, tell you verily it is even now at hand. Yea, on the word of a Bloom, ye shall ere long enter into the golden city which is to be, the new Bloomusalem in the Nova Hibernia of the future.
>
> [The new Bloomusalem is a colossal edifice built in the shape of a huge pork kidney, containing forty thousand rooms. Space must be cleared, so old institutions, residences and even part of the walls of Dublin must go.] (475)

The Court of Conscience, conducted by His Most Catholic Majesty sees open air justice administered. The King declares this not a festivity but a sacrament.

> Free money, free love and a free lay church in a free lay state.

(Bloom explains to those near him his schemes for social regeneration . . . the nine new muses of Commerce, Operatic Music, Amor, Publicity, Manufacture, Liberty of Speech, Plural Voting, Gastronomy, Private Hygiene, Seaside Concert Entertainments, Painless Obstetrics and Astronomy for the People.) (480)

But King Bloom has been too bold. The Church cries out "seeking to overthrow our holy faith." This turns the Irish Catholic Lace Curtain against him and the peasant, but the pub still reveres him and a prophetess, the Veiled Sibyl:

I'm a Bloomite and I glory in it. I believe in him in spite of all. I'd give my life for him, the funniest man on earth. (481)

The Chaplin figure winks and says "I bet she's a bonny lassie." But the trouble has just begun. Theodore Purefoy accuses Bloom of employing "a mechanical device to frustrate the sacred ends of nature" at which the Veiled Sibyl gladly stabs herself and dies with the triumphant words, "My hero god!" The Church has spoken, now religious fanatics led by Alexander J. Dowie cry out that Bloom must burn (which is a wonderful travesty on his already flaming condition). A medical discussion in defense of Bloom announces him to be "a finished example of the new womanly man" and appeals for clemency on the sacred grounds that "He is about to have a baby" (484). Eight male yellow and white children are immediately born and appointed to positions of high public trust in several different countries such as managing directors of banks, traffic managers of railways, chairmen of limited liability companies and vice chairmen of syndicates. A solacing murmur streams up to his ear,

Bloom, are you the *Messiah* ben Joseph or ben David?

BLOOM

(Darkly.) You have said it. (485)

"Then perform a miracle," squeezes Brother Buzz. Bloom's miracle is the apotheosis of Chaplin high comedy mimicry in pantomime that ends with "turns each foot simultaneously in different directions, bids the tide turn back, eclipses the sun by extending his little finger." (485)

A genealogy ending with "Szombathely begat Virag and Virag begat

Bloom *et vocabitur nomen eius Emmanuel* (486) comes to him as through a mist, but the way of glory is accompanied by the way of error, and again Bloom is attacked by reminders of his heinous obscenity and seats himself (wearing asses ears) in the pillory. He is scourged with pantomime stones and finally accused in the name of the ages,

> And they shall stone him and defile him, yea, all from Agendath Netaim and from Mizraim, the land of Ham. (487)

He is part of all he has met, and as their product, he, as Lieutenant Myers of the Dublin Fire Brigade, sets fire to himself (488); he does himself one more service: he puts on a seamless robe marked I.H.S. and stands upright amid the phoenix flames. The Daughters of Erin he brings in for a litany of his many merits and they chant,

> Kidney of Bloom, pray for us.
> Flower of the Bath, pray for us. . . .
> Sweets of Sin, pray for us. . . .
> Friend of all Frillies, pray for us. (488)

as a Bloom gathered choir of six hundred voices sings the Alleluia chorus. The last shot: "Bloom becomes mute, shrunken, carbonised."

Zoe's ingenious line, "Talk away til you're black in the face." ends the Stump Speech sequence, and the funniest man on earth has judged what should be done to defeat injustice. He has been incited to his version of the good.

If *Circe* is not seen as intellectual cinema whose series of ideograms build toward psychological illumination, it is easy to mistake Bloom for the Christ figure. Disproportion through close-up, fragmentation, disassociation, and discontinuity through medium, long and short shots is the manner of montage. Joyce conveys by this Reel of *Circe* and its analogy to the *Cyclops* episode that Bloom's consciousness is a cliché as old in the human race as the birth of thought. That cliché is "Everyone is out of step but me." But the cliché splits like an atom when the conscious and the unconscious meet, for then conscience is born.

Bloom, an emigrant's red handkerchief bundle in his hand, leading a black bogoak pig by a sugaun, with a smile in his eye, now says to Zoe from the depths of the new misery of conscience,

> Patriotism, sorrow for the dead, music, future of the race. To be or not to be. Life's dream is o'er. End it peacefully. They can live on. (He gazes far away mournfully.) I am ruined. . . . No more. I have lived. Fare. Farewell. (489)

As we said in Chapter VI, Odysseus rather than come to terms with his unconscious more than once is tempted to end it all. But corrupted femininity has cheek, wit, talon strength, and in less time than it takes a drop of swinefat to drop from Zoe's armpit, Bloom apologizes and says,

> I am very disagreeable. You are a necessary evil. (489)

Witnesses to his deeds have converged, he has made an impassioned plea for a new order built on an old comedy, the burning flesh, and the funniest man on earth has burnt himself in effigy as a Saviour. He has a third peril awaiting him before conscience, in the dynamic form of accusing, tormenting and rebuking, assails the structure of his being. That peril is a test of his judgment about what to avoid if he would bind himself to the good.

Chapter VIII

MUSICROOM: PLACE OF POETRY

We have now experienced in the Intellectual Cinema of *Circe* what Joyce means by magic, and it is poetry; what the service of hallucination, and it is to serve poetry; what context "Whore" is to be taken, and it is in the context of the inner sources of poetry; why the organ of the body created is "locomotor apparatus", and this predicts the circumference of the poetic knowledge, for in *Circe* we have seen how Bloom does walk and what its origin; we can expect to see intellectual movement arise from the physical stiff walk in ever larger structures not only for Bloom but for Stephen as well. But we have so far been only in the atmosphere of poetry; we have not entered its place nor have we met its famous magician, Circe. We have not entered the musicroom. Joyce supplies us with every conceivable reason for creating a music situation in the brothel. First, a "pianola" is standard pleasure equipment for preliminaries in any gathering place, brothel or not. Next, Stephen Dedalus sings and plays the piano. Supplying him with appropriate props in Nighttown could keep us on this level of awareness about the meaning of musicroom and pianola through the rest of *Circe* which would be confusing to say the least. But Joyce at no time in *Ulysses* is at fault if this happens. He supplies every nuance we need for the simultaneity of the particular and its universal significance provided we exert the organ of consciousness to do so. Zoe asks Bloom just before she takes him in to the brothel, "Are you coming into the musicroom to see our new pianola?" (490). We won't know why a "new" pianola unless it occurs to us right then that Joyce has all through *Circe* been using a new instrument to play his music, his poetry; we must admit the full novelty and invention in Reels one and two of the intellectual cinema, but this is epiphanic in its directness — the *new pianola.*

The musicroom itself, however, written as one word, the scene of foreshadowed movements, expiations, struggles and outcomes ought to impress us at once as to its character. The very setting composed as it is of all the essentially dramatic rhythms of both Bloom and Stephen with its escaping, colliding, constantly flying moth, its floor mosaic of jade, azure and cinnabar rhomboids, its endless footmarks, its yewfronds; these all help us to understand the music of the musicroom. It is, as we continue to see, Plato's *mousike* shifting and changing, revealing and transforming. In the *Symposium* Plato wrote:

> "You know that the word *poièsis* means many things: for every activity causing a passage from non-being to being is *poièsis,* so that the works produced by any kind of art are *poièseis,* and the workmen who achieve them are all *poiètai* or makers. You know, nevertheless, that they are not called *poiètai,* poets, rather they have other names; and only that portion of the whole *poièsis* (in the general sense of art) which is separated from the rest and is concerned with music (mousikè) and melodic measures, is called poetry, and those who share in its possession are called poets."[1]
>
> *Music,* thus, in Plato's vocabulary, does not mean only music, but every artistic genus which depends on the inspiration of the Muse. And he perceived that all the fine arts are the realm of *Mousikè,* and are appendent to poetry, which quickens painting or architecture as well as poetry in the strict sense of the word.[2]

With this preparation to receive poetry in the place of poetry we rejoin

Bloom to see in what manner, if at all, he is bound to the good and what, from the evidence we have seen, he will now call "the good".

On the conscious level Bloom loves love which he has heard is the opposite of hatred. Before his experience of Reel 2 of *Circe*, he imagined it to be an ideal, remote condition somehow existing in Asia Minor, the cradle of civilization, which condition you journeyed to in mental space by the energy of sighs. But after he burned himself at the stake and imagined himself redeeming the world by his sacrifice, he is no longer sure love is the life for man and woman or even that love is all he thought it was, for now he bitterly reflects,

> Man and woman, love, what is it? A cork and bottle. (489)

Zoe, however, who depicts Bloom's feminine capacity as diseased, says quite naturally,

> Give a bleeding whore a chance. (489)

This natural request in Dublin's Nighttown by a Bella Cohen whore so perfectly serves its twin purpose as does the whole life of the series of frames from pages 491 - 515; we are overwhelmed by Joyce's genius for, as he puts it, "the re-embodied image".[3] Bloom's corrupt feminine (the sensible in the flesh) is a bleeding whore at this point. All his old wounds gape, there is no sign that the bleeding will stop; his pain gathers; he is a man stabbed many times by the dagger of his own flesh. On the screen of our minds, the symbolic "bleeding whore", Zoe Higgins, is that feminine sensitivity inherited from Ellen Higgins, Bloom's mother, and the Higgins line which predates the Firbolgs in Irish history, passes back through the Spaniards and descends beneath their roots. The space-time power of the image comes to us in its brooding extensive quality, in the brilliant co-extensive existence of the Chaplin figure in Bloom who makes possible the psychic similarity between Joyce's Ulysses and Homer's Odysseus.

As stated in the conclusion of Chapter VII, however, our man of the raw wounds must now profess what he will avoid in order to bind himself to the good. This appears through the prefabricated presence of his male progenitor, Lipoti Virag, his grandfather. Before he is dredged up, however, Bloom is granted a moment of relief which he uses comically to gag up his fatal entrance to the inner portals of his unconscious, the musicroom, Number 81, Mabbott Street, Mrs. Bella Cohen's Brothel.

He jovially hesitates to go in because "Somebody would be jealous if she knew." Flattered, Zoe comforts him, "What the eye can't see the heart can't grieve for." But now a boyish ideal embarrasses him, and he remembers purity, "The hand that rocks the cradle." Zoe fondly calls him "Babby!" He drools and is silent. With little parted talons she captures his hot hand. He hesitates. She draws him by the middenmist of her person up the steps, past two sister whores. He bows. He trips awkwardly. Zoe says, "Don't fall upstairs." He stands aside, "After you is good manners." She crosses the threshhold. He hesitates. She draws him over. He hops. He takes off his hat. A door is thrown open; Bloom averts his face and bends quickly to examine something on the hall table. All of this is accurate Chaplin and Joyce meets us honestly on it. A moment later Bloom follows Zoe into the musicroom and turning the gas full cock in the chandelier, she says with showmanship,

> More limelight, Charley.[4] (492)

Lynch's deep rejoinder, "Enter a ghost and hobgoblins," points "Charley" right back into Bloom, however, for he's bleeding internally, we remember, and he is peopled with swarms of hobgoblins still to be released from the Gomorrah of his unconscious. Miss Higgins takes the credit, "Clap on the back for Zoe," she says, and the diseased feminine is in the presence of its sullen masculine, Stephen Dedalus. Bloom and Stephen are in the same room at the same time, but space time has made them strangers. They are in the beginning, then, two men ignoring each other importantly. Stephen is the first to articulate his own importance. This is a shooting script, Reel 3, Intellectual Cinema (493-494):

(TITLE)	The rite is the poet's rest. (Technical abbreviations used here stand for: close-up, CU; medium shot, MS; and long shot, LS)
1. (LS)	Of Musicroom to focus Stephen Dedalus and through him Florry on tatty couch; Lynch at peacock in grate through Kitty on table through mantle mirror; Bloom and through him Zoe Higgins.

2. (MS) Of peacock along azure rhomboid to Stephen, back along jade rhomboid to Bloom, back along cinnabar rhomboid to Lynch.

3. (CU) Of moth flying, colliding, escaping.

4. (MS) Stephen Dedalus stands at the pianola, fingering a phrase. He goes to Florry.

5. (CU) Top of pianola: hat and ashplant of Stephen Dedalus.

6. (LS) Bloom smiles sheepishly at hat and ashplant.

7. (MS) Lynch on floor at fireplace works Kitty's petticoat with poker wand as Zoe lights Bloom's eyes with chandelier and causes Florry Talbot to squirm in sofa corner.

8. (CU) Stephen leaves her to play series of empty fifths with two fingers standing at pianola.

9. (CU) The two fingers play sullenly at bottom of frame.

10. (MS) Stephen says to Lynch, "The rite is the poet's rest." and the psychic energy refracts from Bloom's face made long in the mirror above the fireplace.

11. (MS) Stephen speaks with detachment about his two-finger exercise as hymn whose origin is immaterial. What counts is its susceptibility of far apart modes . . . .

12. (CU) Stephen says as he plays, ". . . hyperphrygian . . . ."

13. (LS) Bloom has moved two steps to table, his back hunches as if turning slowly on a spit. . . . Stephen says as he plays, ". . . mixolydian . . . ."

14. (CU) Lynch gestures with cap, "Bah!"

15. (MS) Stephen stops playing suddenly to stare at the cap. ". . . whetstone? . . ."

16. (CU) Lynch twirls the cap; it ends back to front again. Bloom stares fixedly at the light which plays on Kitty's henaed hair.

17. (MS) Stephen fingers as he says, "Here's another for you."

18. (CU) Bloom's wide face in the mirror as Stephen gestures on keys, ". . . the fundamental and dominant are separated by the greatest possible interval . . . ."

19. (LS) Through Bloom's face a barren land, bare waste, Volcanic lake, the dead sea: no fish, weedless, sunk deep in the earth. A dead sea in a dead land, grey and old. It bore the oldest, the first race.

20. (MS) Bloom's interior voice says: "The oldest people. Wandered far away over all the earth, captivity to captivity, multiplying, dying, being born everywhere. Dead. An old woman's: the grey sunken cunt of the world. Desolation."

21. (CU) Grey horror . . . . Bloom's head in mirror. Stephen (with effort): ". . . is the greatest possible ellipse. Consistent with. The ultimate return. The octave."

22. (LS) Of jade, azure, cinnabar rhomboids on floor up through Zoe, Florry, Kitty through window to blare of gramophone outside, "Holy City". Stephen goes to window.

23. (MS) Stephen at the window, arc lamp squaring his forehead, "What went forth to the ends of the world to traverse not itself. God, the sun, Shakespeare, a commercial traveller having itself traversed in reality itself, becomes that self. Wait a moment . . . ."

24. (CU) Arc lamp shattering forehead and gramophone blare rising, ". . . wait a second. Damn that fellow's noise in the street."[5]

25. (LS) Through the window the trails of midden fog push Stephen inward, caress softly faces of all and come to rest on Bloom near Zoe, ". . . Self which itself was ineluctably preconditioned to become."

26. (MS) Stephen strikes an octave, ". . . Ecco! . . ."

27. (MS) Lynch with a mocking whinny of laughter grins at Bloom and Zoe Higgins. ". . . What a learned speech, eh?"

28. (CU) Zoe pushes past Bloom to spit out at Lynch. ". . . God help your head, he knows more than you have forgotten . . . ."

What happens, of course, on the screen of the mind is that we ourselves create dimensions of awareness from the analogies to Bloom's and Stephen's act of existence and its potentiality as it unfolds up to this time. The seer of *Ulysses* is the essential *montageur.*

Bloom's importance can in no way be expressed by him in a brief epiphanic revelation like Stephen's music analogy. As we know, he does not think, he feels his way, so to communicate Bloom's feelings, Joyce creates equative beings who speak for him. The end-of-the-world sequence (494-500) is a good example of this technique as it applies to Bloom's unconscious. Real as is their presence, Kitty, Florry and Zoe, the three whores at Bella Cohen's, create a symbolic presence of the feminine corrupt in the natures of Lynch, Stephen and Bloom. Each of the women has a mark linking her to her man and the kind of mark indicates the kind of obstacle to wholeness each man must surmount. Florry has a stye in the eye: Stephen's vision (interior) is paralyzed, and for reasons which evolve in Chapter IX the azure rhomboid is his symbol of wandering. Kitty has henaed hair, Lynch is the serpent figure attached to Stephen; his traditional color is red — the cinnabar rhomboid is his; Zoe's flesh glows green and she has green teeth; the jade rhomboid and Zoe are Bloom's corrupt flesh condition. The three whores' dramatized interior monologues become beings and situations not to be seen on land or sea, and by their very grotesquerie involve us on their deeper level of symbol. Their combined picture of the end of the world, for instance, is a two headed octopus in gillie's kilts, busby and tarton filibegs, whirling through the murk, head over heels in the form of the Three Legs of Man. Elijah appears as a revivalist who moves them to testimonial that they have sinned. They speak for Bloom. Stephen's interior monologue dramatized spans the arc from faith to superstition as it relates to the end of the world. From St. John's gospel of the Word to the human fallibles, Lyster, the Quaker, and John Eglinton, the Protestant, down to Manaanan Maclir up to the sea of Irish myth, Stephen traces his course to return by way of a wailing gasjet, thin light of his choice (498). This speaks for Bloom, too, in demonstrating what he lacks. Now we are ready to understand how Bloom is bound to good or what he will avoid in the name of the good. For this we distill the experience of pages 500-515, *Circe,* Reel 3, Intellectual Cinema.

As Bloom stands, smiling deliriously, twirling his thumbs, appraising the value of the three feminine corruptees, his grandfather, Lipoti Virag of Szombatheley, leaps out of him converting an interior monologue to an exterior dialogue whose pity and terror drive inward as its comic exuberance drives outward, and we are shocked into a new wisdom about the shrewd animality of the Flesh. Lipoti Virag enters the musicroom[6] as a basilicogrammate which I take to be a rather imperious grass eating being,[7] identifies himself at once to his grandson and begins his forefatherly instruction on how to choose the best corruption. When Bloom hesitates through a show of sorry regret for his condition (only a moment, see p. 504, l. 5) and is in the periphery of an identity specifically his own, his grandfather works fast and hard to keep him in bondage:

> Nightbird, nightsun, nighttown. Chase me, Charley! Buzz! (504)

Whenever the truth of the image offends, Joyce saves the comedy by reminding us that Charley will do the graceful thing though the midden fogs wrap him round and the stench suffocates. In this case grandpapachi's principles agitate Bloom to pronounce,

> Instinct rules the world. In life. In death. (505)

The moth now becomes Virag's sole concern. He has worried it into the light so consistently that only a matter of time separates it from death. But before he kills it, Henry Flower materializes from the moth to strum a few last bars on his guitar. He "has the romantic saviour's face with flowing locks, thin beard and moustache" (506). To see at this point the sad modern anomaly derived from the animal nature of Lipoti Virag in the romantic mask of the Saviour is Joyce's deft blow to the sleeping racial conscience that has transmitted its maimed manhood to an age that can comfortingly say, "I am doing good to others; I am saving them from loneliness, anxiety, hysteria." The age has fully romanticized the Saviour of the world, so its figure of him lacks the gravity of a solid body, lacks the divinity of the Supreme Being. The minds that have conceived the "romantic Saviour" must end by disowning the conception. In the trimmest moment of Reel 3 the Chaplin figure in Henry Flower makes us see this by his perfect touch:

> There is a flower that bloometh. (506)

Bloom begins to struggle against the evil in his ancestry.

What will Stephen avoid to regain his wholeness? Ever aware that he is helpless before the flesh, he takes sober stock in his partial drunkenness, "Steve, thou art in a parlous way" (506). Joyce's wonderful division and subdivision of states of consciousness which carry on the most lively dialogues with separate names and separate faces are ever a mainstream to discover all of *Circe.* Nowhere is the technic more valuable than in the Philip Drunk-Philip Sober scene following Stephen's assessment of his perilous state. They are presented as Siamese Twins, Oxford dons with lawnmowers wearing Matthew Arnold faces. We must know, of course, they are aspects of Stephen's consciousness as he experiences the musicroom and its inmates. The information it contains is voluminous and the poetry it contains is lyrically intense: Your houseguest will leave if you cut off the food. Observe the guest, the old man.

The first economy to detect is the lawnmower. Virag leaped forth from Bloom as basilicogrammate, a grass eater. The lawnmower action in the sequence is food for the old heckler. This is a little symbolic lesson in prehistory; Virag goes back to that moment in human evolution when thought was born. The Siamese Twins are, of course, the inseparable states of consciousness and unconsciousness. Stephen is partially drunk which heightens his lowered awareness and lowers his heightened awareness. Somewhere in the exchange he sees himself in Bloom,

> Reduplication of personality. Who was it told me his name? (His lawnmower begins to purr) (507)

And again "Mac Somebody" and "Unmack" turn up to slip the whole reel back to Mack Sennet who told us Chaplin's name.

> He told me about Swinburne.

Joyce could hardly resist the elegance of "The spirit is willing but the flesh is weak" as an old human adage to which we have ever paid lip service. But the frame next to it of Florry lolling near him and saying,

> Are you out of Maynooth?

localises the lip service and gives Philip Drunk and Philip Sober the cut of their lives.

> (Their lawnmowers purring with a rigadoon of grasshalms)
> Clever ever. Out of it out of it. . . . Keep in condition. Do like us.

The Oxford don is Stephen's nickname and in ways his image of himself, but it is the mask of Matthew Arnold, the real Oxford don, that economizes for Arnold's position in *Culture and Anarchy* in which he creates the terms Hebraism and Hellenism to describe the poles of society and their relation to culture. Hebraism is the way of conscience and religion; Hellenism is the way of intelligence and culture, and while Arnold's qualified meaning of each term presents a fairly sound thesis, the joke of using him here to mow the grass serves the twin purpose of criticism and a new concept of each of the above terms. Hebraism indeed is the way of conscience and religion which has transmitted a Bloom through the centuries, but the transmission has been anything but mechanical. Hellenism has made a Stephen sometime free, but his "free play of consciousness" has given him anything but "sweetness and light". Joyce must perform the extraordinary trick of uniting the Hellenist with the Hebraist, and when he does, it will not be on Arnold's terms. That is why just the mask of Matthew Arnold is employed. Beneath the mask is a sober-drunk fellow to be sure, but he has a vision. Mulligan, we'll remember, approached Stephen early that morning on the subject,

> God, Kinch, if you and I could only work together we might do something for the island. Hellenise it. (9)

Mulligan is the champion of Hellenization, but it is Stephen's energy that mows the grass. He feeds Virag well; whereas Mulligan is more likely to eat with the character. When we remember Arnold's concern with energy, Joyce's fillip becomes even wittier.

But the implications gather. Virag begins to rave in his pursuit of the moth and to blaspheme in the manner of Satan. The lust of a priest is mentioned and in a transforming spasm we see Virag lifting a mooncalf nozzle and howling out against God.

> (He leans out on tortured forepaws, elbows bent rigid, his eye agonizing in his flat skullneck and yelps over the mute world.) A son of a whore. Apocalypse. (509)

Bloom's forebear has worked through generations of old men to the real "old man", Beelzebub, who has led Bloom step by step to all but total corruption through his Flesh. Kitty tells of a girl friend's illegitimate child who was smothered in its mattress.

Matthew Arnold's Parisian mask comments:

PHILIP DRUNK

(Gravely.) Qui vous a mis dans cette fichue position, Philippe?

PHILIP SOBER

(Gaily) C'ètait le sacrè pigeon, Philippe.

Bloom, Lynch and Stephen are now species of Virag's heirs. Virag-Beelzebub is agueshaken; we hear baboon cries from him as he sees Henry Flower holding and caressing only a feminine head, a far too wholesome activity:

> (Sloughing his skins, his multitudinous plumage moulting.) Rats! (He yawns, showing a coalblack throat)[8] After having said which I took my departure. Farewell. Fare thee well. Dreck! (511)

Henry goes to the door; Virag gains the door; he butts a pusyellow[9] flybill on the wall. He unscrews his head. Henry says, "All is lost now." The head says, "Quack!" And they "exeunt severally." Bloom's ancestral "old man" makes a show of his hypocrisy. The head under the arm and the shout of "Quack" shows us what Bloom and therefore Stephen will do toward the good. They withhold food (grass) and consent from Satan.

As if nothing had interrupted the flow of conversation about the fallen priest, Stephen pursues the subject with a show of church history. Florry pierces him, "I'm sure you are a spoiled priest. Or a monk." (512); Lynch jokes, "He is. A cardinal's son." Stephen puns, "Cardinal sin. Monks of the screw." A sudden fantasy of Simon Stephen Cardinal Dedalus, Primate of all Ireland in procession as Cardinal Sin attended by seven dwarf simian acolytes, also in red, cardinal sins. Round his neck hangs a rosary of corks ending on his breast in a corkscrew cross. His voice is heard mellow from afar, merciful, male, melodious as he sings:

> Shall carry my heart to thee,
> Shall carry my heart to thee,
> And the breadth of the balmy night
> Shall carry my heart to thee.

As the trick doorhandle turns, Zoe says, "The devil is in that door." Bloom who has not spoken for six pages makes an occasion of it. In his Svengali overcoat and with folded arms and Napoleonic forelock he frowns in ventriloquial exorcism with piercing eagle glance at the door. With an impelling sign of past master — Bloom is crafty —:

> Go, go, go, I conjure you, whoever you are. (514)

And a male cough and tread are heard passing through the mist outside. Bloom is a changed man. The procession of witnesses who testified that Leopold Bloom defiled the seed of his manhood tempts him to "be hanged by the neck until dead"; the terrifying spectacle of his judgment on the good of society burns him on the stake of his own Flesh with the despairing knowledge that his whole existence is a hollow Saviour's pose; but what essentially binds Bloom to good at the still center of his corrupt nature is a long look at the Devil's role in human heritage. Even Bloom, the moral cripple, locates a power beneath the unconscious to assail this being by somehow apprehending through the passions that dismissing him is possible. This time Bloom does not think of destroying himself but instead for the first time, asserts himself. This assertion will make it possible for him to accuse himself; he will be tormented by the accusations, and he will rebuke himself. He must conquer Bella Cohen before he becomes whole. Bloom places a hand in his waistcoat and poses calmly. The flower of the feminine corrupt is gone; now to its roots.

Chapter IX

TORMENT: CONDITION OF POETRY

The good of the Flesh is corrupt in Bloom because the malice and snares of Satan have ruined his line. He is the Flower of corrupt generations whose hungering Flesh was assailed, for whom the object of adoration was obscured, for whom the dark substitute was popularized. It is upon his brain that a heavy plumpness settles, and for him is laid the beguiling snare,

> Perfume of embraces all him assailed. (166)

He embraces himself, and in a lonely secret lust, he begets the stiff walk.

The feminine corrupt in Bloom spun out in the magic of Joyce's language and the genius of his invention has a logic which comes to us in his esthetic. He does not enumerate esthetic principles; he shows them in process in *A Portrait of the Artist as a Young Man,* and they animate the order of *Ulysses.* This gives the principles the advantage of full conception and us the advantage of understanding them through experience.

Artistic conception for Joyce is the intellect's impregnation of the imagination whereby new being is formed. The idea is not new. St. Augustine divides the blessings of this life into two categories: *propagation* and *conformation.*

> By the first of these blessings man is enabled to reproduce his kind and thus ensure the continuation of the human race. But without the second of these goods the offspring of human generation would hardly rise above the level of the beast. It is God alone who "conforms" the human spirit with its body, "copulating and connecting, in wondrous ways, the incorporeal and the corporeal natures, the one in a superior position and the other inferior, so that the result is an animate being."[1]

Transmuted by poetry, the philosophic truth becomes:

> In the virgin womb of the imagination the word was made flesh.[2]

Preceding the mystery of esthetic, however, are the basic acts of consciousness: to discriminate, to distinguish, to mark off, to isolate oneself from the surrounding context.[3] This the young hero artist, Stephen Dedalus, does with motive intensity throughout *A Portrait*:

> . . . art was the human disposition of intelligible or sensible matter for an esthetic end . . . .[4]

> — Aquinas — said Stephen — says that is beautiful the apprehension of which pleases. —
>
> Lynch nodded.
>
> — I remember that — he said — *Pulcra sunt quae visa placent.* —
>
> — He uses the word *visa* — said Stephen — to cover esthetic apprehensions of all kinds, whether through sight or hearing or through any other avenue of apprehension.[5]

> . . . the true and the beautiful are akin. Truth is beheld by the intellect which is appeased by the most satisfying relations of the intelligible: beauty is beheld by the imagination which is appeased by the most satisfying relations of the sensible. The first step in the direction of truth is to understand the frame and scope of the intellect itself, to

> comprehend the act itself of intellection. Aristotle's entire system of philosophy rests upon his book of psychology and that, I think, rests on his statement that the same attribute cannot at the same time and in the same connexion belong to and not belong to the same subject. The first step in the direction of beauty is to understand the frame and scope of the imagination, to comprehend the act itself of esthetic apprehension.[6]

> . . . though the same object may not seem beautiful to all people, all people who admire a beautiful object find in it certain relations which satisfy and coincide with the stages themselves of all esthetic apprehension. These relations of the sensible, visible to you through one form and to me through another, must be therefore the necessary qualities of beauty.[7]

> . . . the most satisfying relations of the sensible must therefore correspond to the necessary phases of artistic apprehension. . . . Aquinas says: *Ad pulcritudinem tria requiruntur integritas, consonantia, claritas.* I translate it so: *Three things are needed for beauty, wholeness, harmony and radiance.*[8]

> . . . here the imagination has contemplated intensely the truth of the being of the visible world and that beauty, the splendour of truth, has been born.[9]

Joyce performed the economy of creating a young artist determined to understand art, his own gift and how best to use it, all the while employing those very principles to create Stephen Dedalus and his doctrine of esthetic. Apprehension is the good of the intellect; contemplation is the good of the imagination. When the two unite, their act is analogous to the human act of begetting a child. The woman conceives; the human image-making power conceives. Both beget a being. The being of psychic conception no less than the being of the feminine womb must develop in a healthy vessel. Bloom's imagination is not a healthy vessel. The being he begets is a product of the corrupt feminine in his nature. For everything that issues from Bloom's imagination is tainted with a perversion toward women as we know: there never has been so total an expression of sensual man's deviation, prodigality or *shuffling*. The esthetic image to convey this poetry of conscience does encompass all masculine-feminine relations from marriage in the real world to symbolic individual spiritual marriage within the single human personality. The deliberate perfidy of Bloom's wasting generative seed is small indeed to the deliberate perfidy of mankind wasting the generative seed of his intellect instead of depositing it into the vessel of his flesh, the imagination, that the being of liberation may be born. Sterile intellectuality which condemns the flesh; romantic intellectuality which sublimates the flesh; infantile intellectuality which abuses the flesh; reptilian intellectuality which seduces the flesh — all these dishonor the nature of man. A maturing, arriving intellectuality which honors the flesh and holds it sacred; an intellectuality in evolution which cherishes the flesh as he would a marriage partner, or the one loved most dearly, belongs to a man or woman who might in this day of an increased complexity of consciousness be described as "an incarnate spirit".[10]

"Pornography fails because whores are bad conductors of emotion," Joyce writes in his Notebook, 1904-1914.[11] *Circe* far from being a vehicle to arouse sexual desire is an art form to establish healthy, productive, creative sexual relations physically, if you like, intellectually and, of course, morally with another: principally and symbolically in the human personality. This is the endued poetry of conscience which animates *Ulysses.*

Bella Cohen the giant whoremistress of Reel 4, *Circe,* intellectual cinema, is the final hematoma in Bloom's mutilated unconscious which must be drained and disinfected before he can come to terms with that mysterious organ of perception and become a whole man. She accuses him. The accusation of Leopold Bloom (by himself in the center of analysis) is a comedic agon so pathetic and so ludicrous we are grateful indeed the Chaplin figure plays it. Everything Charlie implies in his total canon is here concretized and brought to artistic time by Joyce; everything Homer idealized and made graceful in Odysseus' adventure with the magician, Circe, is here realized and made active by Joyce. This is because Joyce has in his scrupulous artistic consistency made Homer the masculine intellect and Chaplin the feminine imagination to beget a living thing: "a new soaring impalpable imperishable being"[12] — the poetry of conscience, the poet's word made flesh in *Ulysses.*

Bella Cohen is a corrupt feminine monsteroid who converges upon Bloom's imagination, pursuing him through the deep ruts of his past so that she can get him in goring position. Her chase is a series of minor victories, because she uses the long handle of Bloom's central weaknesses to bring him to his knees. Once on his knees in an act of lecherous adoration — lacing her boot for its many pleasures of sight and smell — he assumes the role of Bella's slave. Joyce describes his action,

(. . . Bloom, stifflegged, ageing, bends over her hoof and with gentle fingers draws out and in her laces.) (517)

As soon as he becomes her slave,

His eyes grow dull, darker and pouched, his nose thickens. (518)

and at this moment Bloom yields the masculine principle to the great whoremistress who is henceforth known as Bello, the supra-human despot.

BLOOM

(Mumbles) Awaiting your further orders, we remain, gentlemen . . . .

BELLO

(With a hard basilisk stare, in a baritone voice) Hound of dishonour! (518)

The first moments of Bloom's enslavement epitomize all his erotic thrills in total subjection, and he says, "I promise never to disobey" (519). But Bello has no lap dog state in mind for Bloom. He is pure sadist. His delight in slavey Bloom from this time forward is to see him writhe, suffocate, shamed, and this Bello will accomplish by accusing Bloom of unnatural vice in all its species and tormenting him with a fiendish excess of each kind. "I'll make you remember me for the balance of your natural life" (520), Bello cries savagely as he subjects Bloom to a gross travesty of the unnatural copulation he practiced with his wife and other loves.

BELLO

Henceforth you are unmanned and mine in earnest, a thing under the yoke. (523)

Bloom is now Ruby Cohen, "a charming soubrette with dauby cheeks, mustard hair and large male hands and nose, leering mouth" (524). We are sharply reminded in this sequence of the one film in which Chaplin played a woman,[13] also a charming soubrette, whose principal gag was to keep losing her falsies whenever her virtue was attacked. The quality of Bloom's sudden comic response to "silks-crinkly, scrapy" (523), and the pantomimic movement of the duologue establish both Joyce's knowledge and use of this Chaplin film. For Joyce it is the mode of expressing Bloom's effeminacy:

the sundry ways in which he procured pollution without copulation for venereal pleasure. In a medley of voices the sins of his past accuse and torment Bloom into a crouch of abjection. Now Bello gores him: she commands him to confess the most revolting piece of obscenity in all his career of crime. Goaded, Bloom finally admits it was unnatural copulation with him, Bello Cohen. Nothing could have prepared Bello for this brand of courage from her bondslave, but he retaliates by promising a life of filthy degrading for Ruby Cohen among the whores. But Ruby's "inflection toward the gag" is a perverted triumph that goads Bello to conjure up Bloom's impotency is his marriage and that he is cuckolded by Blazes Boylan. Bloom's pain is transformed to sorrow.

BELLO

> You have made your secondbest bed and others must lie in it. Your epitaph is written. You are down and out and don't you forget it, old bean. (531)

When Bello sketches the brutish burial he will receive under the Cohen flag, Bloom cries out, "My will power! Memory! I have sinned! I have suff. . . ." and he weeps tearlessly (531). It is at this point in the space time of his conscious-unconscious duel that he breaks with his ancestors' heritage of the flesh and they bury him. The scene is a magnificent example of Joyce's artistic economy. In a short scene of four spoken lines and three shooting descriptions, he encompasses the generations who have transmitted to Bloom the prostitute imagination. (532)

Dying to his ancestors through a consciousness that he has done evil and avoided good is one leg of the journey; the other is living up to the superstition about the good. Philosophy would term it the apparent good, and distinguish it from the real good. For the nymph has nourished Bloom into a way of false beauty. She comes to him now on his ancestral pyre to lure him back to the false heights she made him ascend in the halcyon days before Bello and before "I have sinned." Along the way, we reminisce with Bloom on his casual transgression of copulating with a beast (536-37). Now he is not so casual. He is conscious. The nymph reminds him lovingly of his sodomy. Now the beauty of the act escapes him. *Peccavi*! And finally the nymph who has been his life guide to the beautiful, seeing no other way, beguiles him with a change of costume and a change of tune. She comes to him as Sister Agatha of Mount Carmel and says, "No more desire. (She reclines her head sighing) Only the ethereal. Where dreamy creamy gull waves o'er the waters dull" (539). This shakes the very foundation of his being as its counterpart, the Mananaan Maclir superstition, "I am the light of the homestead, I am the dreamery, creamery butter" (499), reviled Stephen Dedalus, and

> (. . . His back trousers' button snaps.) (539)

We have arrived at the sagging Chaplin trousers.

Bloom rejects violently the nymph's "ethereal" persuasion, attacks her; she flees, ("her plaster cast cracking, a cloud of stench escaping from the cracks.") (540)

> BLOOM
>
> I have sixteen years of black slave labor behind me. (540)

Bello has lost his command, but Bella tries her wiles once more. Bloom with an ego consciousness born of self-accusation and remorse, places her in time and in space. He is cool, civil but scornful and direct. He calls her "Pox and gleet vendor!" (541). She turns to the others in the musicroom and demands to know, "Which of you was playing the dead march from *Saul?*" Bloom has expelled the feminine corrupt and in so doing has in St. Paul's sense "put off the old man," the devil. Joyce's use of St. Paul's exhortation in *Ulysses* is done here as elsewhere with expert subtlety, and once the habit of Joyce's subtlety becomes our own we are no longer satisfied in that living sense with anything less arduous. What makes the subtlety so engaging is its verisimilitude to consciousness itself. All great artists hold a mirror up to nature, but who before Joyce transformed the mirror to a looking glass thinly veiled?

Zoe had been playing that selection from *Saul,* we learn, and quite properly since she is Bloom's maternal line and the direct evidence of his former state of feminine corruption. He quietly demands from her his potato panacea. Since he no longer depends on a talisman from evil, he can employ it as a reminder. Zoe relinquishes it contemptuously.

The sequence now shifts to Stephen Dedalus' struggle with his unconscious. Bloom lacked consciousness; Stephen lacks imagination. Joyce gives us the psychic state of affairs through Stephen's yielding money for three whores; Bloom trumping him by quietly paying the bill. Stephen in sensual unrest demands a cigarette; Bloom wants him to eat; Stephen restless for self-knowledge lets Zoe read his palm.

STEPHEN

> (Murmurs) Continue. Lie. Hold me. Caress. I never could read His handwriting except His criminal thumbprint on the haddock. (548)
> [He refers of course to God]

When Zoe asks Stephen what day he was born, he answers prophetically, "Thursday. Today."[14] Zoe tells him Thursday's child has far to go. Florry — who is Stephen's feminine corrupt — speaks unconsciously, the most contextually conscious line in the novel, "Imagination". Stephen complains he cannot read God's signs. From the mouth of the feminine corrupt and no other he must hear that he has far to go before he will be able to read them — he will have to use Imagination. Now for the moment Zoe hesitates in the reading. She sees something that might shock Stephen. Bloom comes quietly to his aid. "Here. Read mine" (548). Bloom only toys with the palmistry, however, for he has self-knowledge enough for the present. He dodges Zoe's questions and talks about the weal on his hand for Stephen's benefit. "Fell and cut it twenty-two years ago. I was sixteen." Both Joyce and Stephen declare exuberantly,

> See? Moves to one great goal. I am twenty-two too. Sixteen years ago I twenty-two tumbled, twenty-two years ago he sixteen fell off his hobbyhorse. (549)

At this Bloom quite quietly withdraws his hand and writes idly on the table in backhand, pencilling slow curves. But the curvaceous reverie vomits forth a sudden spasm of torment in Bloom's newly awakened consciousness: he has a vision of his status as cuckold husband (550-553) the fantasy of which is not paralleled in the entire Bloom ordeal in *Circe.* But to have seen himself as cuckold and effeminate is a torment of conscience he was bound to suffer in the light of his awakening. This is the necessity that animates the scene.

Stephen and Bloom stand together for the first time in *Ulysses,* side by side and look in the mirror. Shakespeare's face appears and speaks to them. He says to Stephen, "'tis the loud laugh bespeaks the vacant mind." Stephen is notorious for his unrestrained youthful laugh in *A Portrait, Stephen Hero,* and *Ulysses.* His amusement is heartiest at sudden revelations of stupidity. To Bloom Shakespeare says, "Thou thoughtest as how thou wast invisible. Gaze. Iagogo! How my Oldfellow chokit his Thursdaymomum. Iagogo!" You thought, Mr. Bloom, no one saw you. Villain. You're just like Othello, another creature of the flesh who choked his wife, Desdemona: to the Thursdaymomum next to you there, Stephen Dedalus, you are a choker, a killer. He sees no way of life with you, the flesh. He's an Iago too. Shakespeare has only one other comment. It is delivered in paralytic rage, "Weda seca whokilla farst" (554). The Italian dialect is a gag but at the same time, were Shakespeare writing the story of Bloom and Stephen he would seek the villains in the order of their villainy: did Stephen kill his imagination before Bloom killed his intellect? Who died first Stephen or Bloom?

Stephen who has far to go before he will reclaim the original good of the image-making power of his mind must like Bloom come to fuller terms with his unconscious. To experience what is happening to Stephen it is best to know his personal history in the *Portrait.* His Bloom there is the violent ravish of his soul by lust and his desperate attempt to free himself of its power. Joyce is at careful pains in *A Portrait* to make clear that Beelzebub enters Stephen's being.

> He felt some dark presence moving irresistibly upon him from the darkness, a presence subtle and murmurous as a flood filling him wholly with itself. Its murmur beseiged his ears like the murmur of some multitude in sleep; its subtle streams penetrated his being. His hands clenched convulsively and his teeth set together as he suffered the agony of its penetration. He stretched out his arms in the street to hold fast the frail swooning form that eluded him and incited him: and the cry that he had strangled for so long in his throat issued from his lips. It broke from him like a wail of despair from a hell of sufferers and died in a wail of furious entreaty, a cry for an iniquitous abandonment, a cry which was but the echo of an obscene scrawl which he had read on the oozing wall of a urinal.[15]

To further document the Beelzebub penetration, Stephen's visit to Nighttown, which follows the above passage, is part of a larger sequence which is a vision during an erotic dream or an auto-erotic ecstasy. We arrive at this information in two ways: (1) the dream quality of the Nighttown passage, page 113 of the *Portrait,* where in the raw November weather, for instance, the whores go from house to house "in long vivid gowns", he meets a young woman "in a long pink gown", and we know he was painting his room pink and had left it unfinished, and that he is in a speechless torpor during the dream fornication. (2) In his confession (166), the priest exhorts him about "that" sin and describes it as "dishonourable and unmanly", a "wretched habit." The exhortation continues about "that sin" and "when that sin comes into your mind." Obviously the sin forgiven is uncleanness or effeminacy, not fornication. Had it been, the priest would have used the term, "woman or women" in his exhortation.

In *Ulysses* Stephen dreams a recurring dream, "After he woke me up last night same dream or was it?" (47)

STEPHEN

Mark me. I dreamt of a watermelon.

FLORRY

Dreams go by contraries.[16]

STEPHEN

(Extending his arms) It was here. Street of harlots. In Serpentine Avenue Beelzebub showed me her, a busby widow.

BLOOM

(Approaching Stephen) Look . . . .

STEPHEN

No, I flew. My foes beneath me. And ever shall be. World without end. (He cries) *Pater!* Free! (556, 557)

Stephen's flesh prompts him to be quiet; his intellect bids him recall. He conjures up the old reality; he exults in it as he did six years ago; he says he flew and his foes were beneath him — as they always will be. The world will not end for him in Beelzebub. This father freed him. But at once a series of father events well up, frames of the confused father image in this proud young god's unconscious: his own father gaily tells him, "Keep our flag flying! An eagle gules volant in a field argent displayed." (557); the fox who buried his grandmother (Stephen who buried Erda); Deasy who gave him a horse, (a teaching job, such as it was, to maintain himself while he thought things out), all of which focus sharply on Stephen's conflict with the Enemy which at this point is courage. He has the Thought, the Memory, and the gloom of the Wanderer, and he has in a sense the intuition that his twilight has been overextended. He knows in the heart he neglected that his ashplant, the augur's stick which shakes the earth, will soon be in mortal combat. When it goes, so will he. In the interim, Stephen, the Wanderer, hearing a "noise in the street" refers to it as "our friend." His definition for God is a noise in the street. Without imagination he cannot fathom the wisdom of his statement, of course, but we feel with him the cracking of internal layers of the strata that separate Stephen from "his friend" and an ominous foreboding of the upheaval of that strata in the "dance of death." Before he will do the dance, however, Stephen cries for his weapon, his "augur's rod," the ashplant, and when he has it, he beats his foot in tripudium, Buck Mulligan's gesture. During Stephen's exhibition Bloom stands aside (560), and as we see his privation (consciousness) in action there are some miraculous moments of comedy. Imagining the Chaplin figure's reaction to Maginni, the dancing master, for instance, and the solemn mimicry that ensues; his pantomimic play with the Hours of the Day; his own shy movement in the dance — all this is brilliant integral clowning. Anyone who has seen Chaplin's dance in the *Gold Rush*[17] will easily transfer the mood he brings to ballroom ceremonies.

The morning, noon and twilight hours retreat before the night hours who steal to last place. "They are masked with daggered hair and bracelets of dull bells. Weary, they curchy-curchy under veils."[18] As the excitement mounts, the whirligigging gigs, all reel exhausted, Stephen stops dead (564). As we know, his mother rises through the floor in leper gray to plead with him — like the Erda of old who counselled her son, Wotan, to give up that which cursed his youth, the fatal loveless Ring — to abandon his hardness of heart, to renounce his loveless state, to repent his folly, to reclaim his youth. She surges toward him and "a green crab with malignant red eyes sticks deep its grinning claws in Stephen's heart" (567). Here is the Loki he has lifted from his evil brood long ago and made his friend and counsellor: the demon of fire, mischiefmaker, traitor, the spirit of cunning: the condition of exile; the motion of silence.

> ***Ah non, par exemple!*** **The intellectual imagination! With me all or not at all. *Non serviam.***

I will not serve as a human. I am an earth shaker. Kinch, the superman.

THE MOTHER

(Wrings her hands slowly, moaning desperately.)
O Sacred Heart of Jesus, have mercy on him! Save him from hell, O divine Sacred Heart!

STEPHEN

No! No! No! Break my spirit all of you if you can! I'll bring you all to heel!

THE MOTHER

(In the agony of her deathrattle) Have mercy on Stephen, Lord, for my sake! Inexpressible was my anguish when expiring with love, grief and agony on Mount Calvary.

STEPHEN

Nothung!
(He lifts his ashplant high with both hands and smashes the chandelier. Time's livid final flame leaps and, in the following darkness, ruin of all space, shattered glass and toppling masonry.) (567)

Wotan, the earth-shaker, is in conflict with the light — the light of fortitude, of love. They struggle: *Nothung* against sacred spear of ash.

(Stephen, abandoning his ashplant, his head and arms thrown back stark, beats the ground and flees from the room past the whores at the door.) (568)

The god vanishes in darkness.

The hero (Leopold Bloom), light-hearted, blowing his horn, beats Bella Cohen to the draw about the broken lamp chimney by a little device of blackmail:

And if it were your own son in Oxford! (Warningly.) I know! (570)

Like the ancient Circe on the Aegean, this evil woman is stripped of her powers,

Who are you incog?

This new little man with fleet step of pard, dark suit, sagging trousers, derby hat and, finally the cane (the ashplant marks his stride), makes his get-away from the brothel only to find a drag behind him of all the known Dublin world hunting him with a pack of blood hounds.

THE HUE AND CRY

> He's Bloom! Stop Bloom! Stopabloom! Stopperrobber! Hi! Hi! Stop him on the corner! (571)

Bloom is a robber, of course, because he has claimed the Irish intellect which the gang says has nothing to do with the vile body, and he has claimed his role in the world as the noble role of the Flesh. The world joins in the chase. Joyce stops Bloom just before he goes around the corner, for to have him actually execute the famous Chaplin-rounding-a-corner gag (one leg outstretched as he bounces on the other) would rob the moment of its suggestion. We round the corner. But the Chaplin touches are in the texture: "Whatdoyoucallhim, Strangeface, Fellowthatslike, Sawhimbefore, Chapwith" (571), and in the super-Sennett free-for-all, "on the fringe of the noisy quarrelling knot, a lot not knowing a jot what hi! hi! row and wrangle around the whowhat brawlaltogether."

But the young man who had allowed Satan to control his keen mind, and who had for a period of time been masquerading as a gloomy, loveless Earth-Shaker now finds himself in some darkness still. The thread of light for the alert viewer will be the continuity in Homer. Circe directs Odysseus and his men to Hades and Teiresias; so does Joyce. They, too, arbitrate in the kingdom of the dead that they might learn how to get home. Joyce has used the visit to the underworld as an economy for the poetry of restitution as it relates to conscience. It is necessary for Stephen especially to become the fearless Siegfried: he must give all or not at all. He has, as we remember, far to go in coming to terms with the volatile debilitations of his unconscious.

> But in here it is I must kill the priest and the king. (574)

Satan and Wotan still have his mind. How does he free himself and like Siegfried learn who his father is? Joyce has a great deal of fun with the king image as a step toward wholeness. Stephen's famous sublimity begins to dissolve in a jujube sucking king of lewd revelry in the guise of Edward the Seventh. As always, of course, images draw one another and before

Joyce is finished with any one scene, a remarkable host of evocative analogues have clustered together in depth. The verisimilitude in Joyce's art to the complexity of modern consciousness is one aspect of his genius that separates him from everyone else in the twentieth century, and it most surely links him to the tradition of the great artists. He is of his time.

Stephen's argument with the dead in this scene is not so much a combat with the stupidity of Privates Carr and Compton as it is with his own dead images, the attitudes, inclinations and tendencies which he indeed tries to beat back from his blood, as in Homer, until such time that a Teiresias should appear to counsel him on the homeward journey. Circe, the original goddess, tells Odysseus to dig a trench when he arrives in Hades a cubit in length and breadth. Bloom elbows through the crowd; Homer's Circe directs her Odysseus to pour a drink offering about the trench to all the dead: (1) with mead, (2) sweet wine, (3) water sprinkled with white meal. Stephen complies by speaking "honied" words to the roistering English soldiers, overturing to them in a variety of ways while at the same time doing ceremonious responses to the king figure of his unconscious, Wotan, Earthshaker. Circe warns Odysseus to sit with drawn sword "suffering not the strengthless heads of the dead to draw nigh the blood ere thou has word of Teiresias."[19]

The remnant king Wotan in Stephen rebukes him with

> My methods are new and are causing surprise.
> To make the blind see I throw dust in their eyes. (576)

Stephen is repulsed at this light on his great thoughts while at the same time, he is shocked by its truth. As he says to Bloom, his intelligence is provoked (577). That provocation suffers the rebuke of a look at old Ireland through the new light. He converses with Biddy the Clap, Cunty Kate, Old Gummy Granny whom he twits with his former phrase of contempt, "The old sow that eats her farrow" (579). Circe in Homer further instructs Odysseus, "sacrifice apart, to Teiresias alone, a black ram without spot, the fairest of your flock." Stephen prepares the sacrifice on the altar of renunciation.

> The harlot's cry from street to street
> Shall weave old Ireland's winding sheet. (582)

With gratitude to Cissy Caffrey, the prostitute who is the object of the quarrel, Stephen gives her two lines of the love lyric he praised on the beach that morning,

> White thy fambles, red thy gan
> And thy quarrons dainty is. (582)[20]

The black ewe, fairest of Stephen's flock, is ready for sacrifice to Teiresias, "Who hath been given judgment, even in death, that he alone should have understanding." That black ewe is the dream sequence of the Black Mass rising in steady stench from the fire of Stephen's unconscious. In it he renounces the pomps and the works of Satan who presented him with the scoffer, Buck Mulligan, for boon companion. As Adonai, Stephen is midway between hell and heaven (584); with the damned he blames the dooooooooooog for startling the boar who gored him. With the blessed he praises Goooooooooood for wounding him with his love. That both Bloom and Stephen are gored to their destiny as individual men and composite man is realistic and significant. No man will find the struggle to maintain human identity easy; he must be spurred; if his identity is double — Intellect and Flesh, he must be gored to effect their unity. Stephen's knock-out blow is similar to the agony of penetration he knew when Beelzebub entered his being; the demon's exit leaves him unconscious. The organ of perception begins its nuptial ceremony with the conscious mind of Stephen Dedalus through a hymn of hope from Yeats. He will brood no more on love's bitter mystery; he knows now who it is

> . . . rules the shadows of the wood,
> And the white breast of the sea.

He understands dimly now what he always knew: God alone animates the world. This is the Teiresias. He sees his relation to God in the new light of "Nothung"; he sees the mystical relation of his intellect to his senses. What is inestimable, however, is the greatest good of all to Stephen Dedalus who had only a short time ago insisted upon the intellectual imagination only: he sees now that the good of his flesh is service. Bloom, fair little fellow, is solicitous, attendant, protective, compassionate as the flesh should be. He's a little thin on memory as we see in his quotation of the Yeats lines (593) and a little impulsive in assigning a meaning to them, but this is the state of the Flesh when the intellect is absent even temporarily: it is like a comic gag but without inflection.

Never let it be said, however, that Bloom fails in his inflection toward the gag; Chaplin does not allow it. After shredding Stephen's poetry of the unconscious, he tops his master with shredded poetry of his own. The last frame in the intellectual cinema of *Circe* shows a fairy boy of eleven, a changeling, kidnapped, dressed in glass shoes and a little bronze helmet. He holds a book which he reads lovingly. Bloom calls inaudibly, "Rudy!", but the little dead Bloom son gazes unseeing into Bloom's eyes and goes on reading. His buttons are diamond and ruby. He holds a slim ivory cane and a white lambkin peeps out of his waistcoat pocket. That he reads with love and devotion makes him a very young archetype of the intellect; that he has the cane and the symbol of purity, the lamb, makes him a very young archetype of the sensible. He is the one, new, kidnapped child Stephen and Bloom have become through the poetry of conscience.

Chapter X

METAPHYSICAL MYTH

The theme of Joyce's *Ulysses* is the human ascent to consciousness through the coaction of intellect and feeling which generate the creative act of life. His general artistic mode is to concretize with scrupulous accuracy the nearest verisimilitude to the theme of his vision; therefore, a creative artist and a gifted clown compose the hero, a vast indifferent *Weib*[1] is the heroine, and as a vital trinity, they perform the ascent to consciousness which is the novel's theme. The gifted clownman, Leopold Bloom, through the psychic similarity to Odysseus and the sensate similarity to Chaplin of the movies becomes the incarnate "feeling" of the theme; the creative artist, Stephen Dedalus, becomes the incarnate intellect. The coaction between Stephen Dedalus and Leopold Bloom becomes the ascent to consciousness within the theme, and Molly Bloom surrounds them both as the indifferent fertility surrounding the creative act of life.

Joyce's closest affinity in the literary tradition is the Old Testament poet. As John McKenzie, S.J., has demonstrated in *The Two Edged Sword*[2] and elsewhere, the Hebrew poets of Scripture revealed the thought life of ancient peoples:

> All they could do was to represent through symbolic forms the action of the unknown reality which they perceived mystically, not mythically, through His revelation of Himself.[3]

Joyce's similarity to the poets of Scripture is essentially mystical perception of God through his creature, man. Like them he represents in symbolic forms the action of God in men, and like them he writes a narrative to express God's revelation of Himself through man. In the four thousand years that separate Joyce from his spiritual fellow artists, the evolutionary character of the world has brought its change but not necessarily in the objective quality of the symbol. The ancient symbols arising from myth, for instance, have merely been freed from a "life mythically bound and fettered to an esthetically liberated life"[4] by the modern artist, and this is how, for instance, Lynch in *Ulysses* resembles a reptile and has the function of the serpent in Genesis, which itself was a new use for a fertility symbol.[5] For the serpent, as Erich Neumann records in his *Origins and History of Consciousness,* is sacred in pre-Christian times.

> Living the cycle of its own life, it is the circular snake, the primal dragon of the beginning that bites its own tail, the self begetting Ουρόβορος.
>
> This is the ancient Egyptian symbol of which it is said: "*Draco interfecit se ipsum, moritat se ipsum, impraegnat se ipsum.*" It slays, weds, and impregnates itself. It is man and woman, begetting and conceiving, devouring and giving birth, active and passive, above and below, at once.
>
> As the Heavenly Serpent, the uroboros was known in ancient Babylon; . . . It is the archetype of the ἓν τὸ πᾶν, the All One, appearing as Leviathan and as Aion, as Oceanus . . . . there are pictures of it in the sand paintings of the Navajo Indians and in Giotto; it is found in Egypt, Africa, Mexico and India, among the gypsies as an amulet, and in the alchemical texts.[6]

The Hebrew poet's story of Eve's temptation by the Serpent is understood by today's Biblical scholars in terms of the mythology which the story rejects. And that mythology is the cultic myth of the serpent representing sex as a god. Appearing in its most radiant form, it persuades the woman that she and the man will be like gods if they follow its instructions. To return to Lynch: he is not only the ancient symbol of fertility seen through Hebrew eyes as perverse, but also the fallen angel or devil symbol which clusters about the Genesis serpent as the Old Testament evolves and mythology ascends in consciousness. To understand the action of God in the Old Testament, scholars now know they must discern the message of the myth through a reconstruction of place, time and mentality; they must, in other words, take the Old Testament Poet on his own terms.

Taking Joyce on his own terms is not easier in many ways than was the task of Biblical Scholars who awaited the evidence of archeology. All Joyce critics are dependent on the Joyce story through letters, documents and manuscript evolution. The second biography has been enormously helpful in gathering much, but we cannot be satisfied with the interpretation of the works Mr. Ellmann gives us, for too often it derives from an early faulty critical structure, and while readers of the biography have thanked him for humanizing Joyce and saying in simple words what Joyce is about, those who respect Joyce's greatness see a disservice to the artist's vision. Here is Mr. Ellmann's description of theme in *Ulysses:*

> The theme of *Ulysses* is simple, and Joyce achieves it through the characters of Bloom, Molly and Stephen. Casual kindness overcomes unconscionable power.[7]

Affixing this absurd theme to Joyce's great work is equivalent to omitting the poetry in *Ulysses* and to omit the poetry is to bypass the vision. The faulty structure upon which Mr. Ellmann's theme rests is accepting the earnest views of such men as Stuart Gilbert, who in his early *James Joyce's Ulysses* was more concerned with its lore than its poetry. He contributed linear expositions of the episodes of the novel and pointed out Homeric parallels; nothing more. His understanding of *Circe* as the place of the novel's poetry has not a hint of radiance or stasis. It is with the other eighteen episodes all of a piece. But Mr. Ellmann and colleagues are not alone in failing to take Joyce on his own terms. For forty years there has been continual controversy in another area. Marvin Magalaner puts it:

> Biography remains the disturbing problem in Joyce criticism. Nor do the recent books on the subject help to uncomplicate it, for they are the

> product of people who are themselves highly individual and complex. The questions remain: what is the true relationship between Stephen Dedalus and James Joyce, biographically; between Bloom and his creator; between Joyce and his family.[8]

A valid solution to the problem of biography is through Joyce's theory of esthetic. If the principles of art as they come to us through Stephen Dedalus in *A Portrait of the Artist as a Young Man* are the information we have as to his manner of creating, then he is Stephen Dedalus. A Joyce critic cannot begin any analysis of his works without those theories and their operation. They demonstrate to us again and again that we can take Joyce at his artistic word, and they prove as conclusively as we need to know that Stephen Dedalus' fictional evolution is an imitation of Joyce's own spiritual and general physical action. Mr. Bloom is less of a mystery after combing the *Portrait* carefully *for l'homme moyen sensuel;* he is no mystery after reading the letters to Nora, 1909, in the Cornell collection. Finally, of course, to see that Chaplin carries the earthy burden for Joyce's earthy self is to see Joyce's wisdom in choosing the most attractive existing dramatization of the flesh; he knew he must continue as Stephen Dedalus for personal reasons and to maintain artistic coherence between *A Portrait* and its sequel, *Ulysses.*

Joyce's artistic promise through Stephen Dedalus, "To forge in the smithy of my soul the uncreated conscience of my race",[9] he keeps with monumental faith. The most pronounced evidence of that faith is the nature and scope of his own consciousness within the work, the presence and operation of his pre-conscious vision, the courageous use of the unconscious as he knows it to be, and finally the suggestion of wholeness of both himself and the fictional characters. *Ulysses* is a very personal as well as a public work of art. But what does Joyce understand the distinguishing mark of consciousness to be? He accepts the evidence that judgment is the highest faculty of the mind, for this way lies the knowledge of being, and judgment always is a pronouncement by the mind. That pronouncement is conscience.

Conscience as all men know it, to proceed like Aristotle, is a knowledge of right and wrong with a desire to do right, a tendency to do wrong. Is this what Joyce sees as conscience? It is, but not all he sees. He sees that a black and white law of morality is meaningless without that degree of consciousness that will behold the distinction between the two realms, actually, humanly and realistically. The consciousness of act as act calls for self-knowledge; the consciousness of being human calls for a knowledge of carnality in its essence; consciousness of the real is consciousness of truth which makes possible that human interior act of the beautiful: intellect enduing and informing the senses and imagination for the creative act of life. Every failure in the moral realm is a miscarriage of consciousness distinguished by conscience; every failure in the esthetic realm is a failure of conscience as the mark of judgment; every failure in the social realm is a failure of creative judgment accomplished by the flesh and the spirit. The uncreated conscience is the conscience that has not come into being in the human realm as yet; the uncreated conscience is the moving potential in store for Ireland, for mankind. This is precisely the remedy for the paralysis Joyce experienced in Ireland and later in other countries, but what comes as a revelation is that he freed himself (fictionally) first, that he might serve the generation into which he had been born by offering it the "gift of certitude".[10] This is the paradox of Joyce.

Joyce traces his own ascent to consciousness both as artist and human being in the two carefully connected works, *A Portrait* and *Ulysses.* They must be experienced in sequence for full intelligibility, and while each is a completed art form, still it is the two which contain Joyce's vision. Even *Dubliners* has a new meaning after Joyce's vision is seen. *Exiles,* Joyce's play written between *A Portrait* and *Ulysses,* is a scrupulous examination of the justice he seeks to create in Stephen Dedalus' final fictional appearance. Again *Exiles* exists as artistic whole, yet is bonded in its being to a larger artistic context.

Frank Budgen's recorded conversations with Joyce during the making of *Ulysses* have directed critics to interpret Stephen as a creation less than Bloom,[11] and to see him as Budgen saw him "pictorially" rather than "in the round" like his counterpart Bloom. Joyce did say:

> I have just got a letter asking me why I don't give Bloom a rest. The writer of it wants more Stephen. But Stephen no longer interests me to the same extent. He has a shape that can't be changed.[12]

"To the same extent" has a new meaning when Stephen's hidden action in *Ulysses* emerges, and "a shape that can't be changed" is Joyce's comic allusion to Stephen as symbol. The intellect cannot be considered in terms of shape.[13]

I want now to trace Stephen Dedalus' ascent to consciousness as he exercises the act of his existence indicating in the process where he achieves greater complexity of consciousness whose distinguishing mark Joyce attributes to conscience and finally to that state of uncreated conscience at which Stephen arrives in *Ulysses.* Myth, language and art, as Ernst Cassirer says, begin as a concrete, individual unity which is only gradually resolved as a triad of independent modes of spiritual creativity.[14] With this in mind I have looked not at the *Portrait* in perspective, but rather the perspective itself of *A Portrait of the Artist.*

Stephen Dedalus' potential consciousness is undertrussed at birth by a pervasive and keen sense of touch whose power is to carry him to the very summit of creation, but not before it has cast him into the most abysmal paralysis of soul where, in a fixed position, he is tormented by the delusion of movement toward his destiny and baffled by the mystery of his impotence.

The sense of touch, as Aristotle tells us, "is not a single sense but a group of senses,"[15] and that "it is to differences in the organ of touch and to nothing else that the differences between man and man in respect of natural endowment are due; men whose flesh is hard are ill-endowed by nature, men whose flesh is soft, well-endowed."[16] This is one of the reasons man is most intelligent among all animals. St. Thomas, in his extension of Aristotle's tract on sense perception, organizes his discussion of the sense of touch this way:

> Now all the other senses are based on the sense of touch. But the organ of touch requires to be a medium between contraries, such as hot and cold, wet and dry, and the like, of which the sense of touch has the perception; thus it is in potentiality with regard to contraries, and is able to perceive them. Therefore the more the organ of touch is reduced to an equable complexion, the more sensitive will be the touch. But the intellectual soul has the power of sense in all its completeness, because what belongs to the inferior nature pre-exists more perfectly in the superior, as Dionysius says (*Div. Nom.* V). Therefore the body to which the intellectual soul is united should be a mixed body, above others reduced to the most equable complexion. For this reason among animals, man has the best sense of touch. And among men, those who have the best sense of touch have the best intelligence.[17]

Touch then in Stephen Dedalus is an index to his intelligence; it is in him, as St. Thomas says above, "reduced to an equable complexion," equal in its intensity through the whole complex sense perception. There was only one blemish on his otherwise perfect sense organs and that was the inheritance of weak eye sight. An early, pre-conscious, highly sensate declaration by Stephen that he would marry Eileen Vance when he grew up, seized upon his most vulnerable asset when his mother told the little boy to apologize for saying a monstrous thing, and Dante, his Aunt, sketched what would befall him if he failed to do so. "O, if not, the eagles will come and pull out his eyes." He was conscious mythically of the crime he had committed, and of his guardians' superior knowledge, and he began to form in his mind the mythic reason for his criminality. His Mother and Dante pronounced for him his earliest Catholic doctrine on his relation to women and with the overpowering excitation that all sight and sound created in him, his keen and potential intellect made an interior mythology of the data which was not to leave him until a night in his twenty-second year when he beheld his flesh in its manifest reality not as ignoble and forbidden but as worthy and his medium of creation. But the medium of touch is the flesh and through his flesh Stephen received earlier than the sensation of criminality, the symbolic form of language which alone among the human joys satisfied him. At the center of his satisfaction, even as a child of six, he had located a source of his joy in language, and that was a vague concept of the Word as one of the divine names. But the dichotomy between the splendour of the Word as God and the meanness of creatures as servants of that God suppressed Stephen's advance in science or logic as a symbolic form, and myth-making aided by language took precedence. Stephen's logic as a student in the Jesuit school, Clongowes Woods, was the logic of feeling, but memory and apprehension made him a superior student and a frail physical beauty made him a winning one.

He came away from three years of boarding school with information and technique, a growing as well as emerging sense of myth, for, from the many confusing human events, one stood clearly as a sentinel, and that was an experience of justice. Stephen had been given the pandy bat by the disciplinarian for lack of preparation in a Latin class; but he had broken his glasses and had permission to prepare the lesson when they were repaired. After public humiliation, the little boy had gone to the President to clear his good name, an unheard of bravery from the Class of Elements. The President reasserted Stephen's innocence, and in the justice that ensued, he was, for the first time, Stephen Hero.

But the hero in Stephen vanished almost at once into his interior mythical existence, for his parents with now five children departed suddenly and without warning from Blackrock to Dublin and replaced comfort, servants and seeming social position with a bare, cheerless house, frugality and anonymity. A sustained and habitual revery related to his reading of the *Count of Monte Cristo* begun in Blackrock became in its new setting a sole source of comfort and through it Stephen expanded his personal myth in the image of a vague destiny he felt born to serve. But the complex sensation of Dublin, the dispossession of family and the long freedom of his day (for there was no school until there was money) separated him almost completely from the symbolic forms science offers, and the power of his intellect was unused while the power of his perception presented to his imagination a new and disturbing unrest, a longing to meet in the real world the image he so constantly beheld. She was a Mercedes of ineffable beauty and compassion, a peerless heroine who would look upon him with warmth and mercy and love, and in their instant of meeting, all weakness, inconfidence and unrest would fall from him and he would be the symbol of manly strength. When he did meet "E. C." at a children's party (he was eleven), he was impatient and aloof from the spectacle of childish games, ecstatic at her slightest gaze, but when he said goodbye to her at the tram "he stood listlessly at his place seemingly a watcher of the scene before him." His ecstasy and relief and gratitude for meeting in the real world the "insubstantial image his soul so constantly beheld" he released in the language of myth, and the poem "told only of the night and the balmy breeze and the maiden lustre of the moon."

Stephen was the first of twelve children. He was a long time making a confidante of any of his brothers and sisters; his distress at their undernourishment, their pale, childish joy in an existence bleak and debasing, made him shun them as much as possible. He was relieved but wary when he learned he would attend Belvedere College, the Jesuit Preparatory School. It was in these years that language as logic won for Stephen the coveted term competitions; apprehending intellectually was a process of his nature new and exciting to him, and it coordinated the culmination and concentration of sensible forms releasing his desire for the intelligible in discursive thought. But he was wary. Language and myth had not yet brought him self-knowledge, only acute self-awareness, and the essential spiritual power of the word which makes existence in a community possible was not yet his. He was still conceiving the Word in a mythic mode. Since he did not see himself in relation to a "thee", his subjectivity was as yet not to assert a "me". Consciousness ascends but in *pars pro toto.*

The cravings of his flesh, a growing intellectual conviction of his destiny, the squalor of his home life, the irresponsibility of his father, the unparalleled patience and faith of his mother (against which he chafed), the narrow religious character of his instruction, the mechanical pursuit of learning by his schoolmates, the squalor of his surroundings and the "dull phenomena of Dublin life" fretted his soul. His judgment was to exclude them from his existence and return in the off hours to his solitary pursuits. He spent his time in the company of "subversive writers whose gibes and violence of speech set up a ferment in his brain before they passed out into his crude writings." The moral law forbade the strange cravings of his flesh, his mythical thought warned him, but he silenced the warning and in secret he dealt with the mysterious growth of his body. At school he was a model of obedience and piety and diligence, but the intangible phantom of his mind mocked the voices of his father and his masters which urged him to be a gentleman and a good Catholic.

He was in the school play and for a brief moment, he experienced a freedom and fellowship; his parents attended with "E.C." So intense was his excitation at speaking to her afterwards that he fled into the dark streets to still the riot of his blood. He halted abruptly at the morgue. On the wall: a sign reading *Lotts*. The shame and secrecy of his fierce longings baffled him, and the effort to comprehend made him brood on the shame of his wounds. Judgment evaded him, but the conscience which might have alleviated his agony of soul exerted itself in a half hearted attempt to live with his family. Together they spent his competition money on food and entertainment, but it was useless to pretend a relationship he did not feel; he felt the first silent sundering of their lives. How could he be grateful as was his Mother to a God who would afflict him so cruelly and to a God who looked the other way at the dissolution and poverty of their household. He had tried briefly to understand the father and mother who had borne him, but a mounting "otherness" stifled his good intentions. He took refuge in "the intellectual imagination," hoping to absorb the cravings of his flesh, but it was short-lived and he returned to his wanderings. The pot of pink enamel paint gave out and the wainscot of his bedroom remained unfinished. He cared little that he was in mortal sin; he turned to appease the fierce longings of his heart. He returned to his wanderings, and in a nightmare he found release in fornication. "A young woman dressed in a long pink gown laid her hand on his arm to detain him and gaze into his face." The prostitute of his imagination took power over him, and his consciousness for the next six years is to be marked by that alternate ascent and descent in the creative act of his life born of the unconscious impotence to judge reality in and for itself by means of the coitional act of intellect and sense. The boy suffers the emotion of remorse in a traumatic retreat on the four last things: death, judgment, heaven and hell; heaven is not discussed. In an agonized reception of the Sacrament of Penance and an ecstatic reception of Holy Eucharist he makes a serious effort to amend his life. But the conviction that he was powerless to evict from himself a "besetting" sin, cooled his ardor.

> He named it with humility and shame and repented of it once more. It humiliated and shamed him to think that he would never be freed from it wholly, however holily he might live or whatever virtues or perfections he might attain. A restless feeling of guilt would always be present with him: he would confess and repent and be absolved, confess and repent again and be absolved again, fruitlessly. (*Por.* 177)

Hope, an alert emotion, which mirrors victory in its very face, was Stephen's heritage; it did not fit the perspective of his mythology, and thus he felt the first stirrings of despair. But his world was private, unassailable; his public image was cause for praise. He was invited to join the Jesuit order. Stephen's heart quickened at the call, but in afterthought he knew he would not accept it, for in reverie he imagined his terrible regret:

> What had come of the pride of his spirit which had always made him conceive himself as a being apart in every order? (*Por.* 187)

The last outpost of squalor and degradation comes when the Dedalus family moves once again, but his father will somehow send him to the university. In a rapture of anticipation of the freedom from boyhood he walks along the strand and in a moment of inspiration he beholds his destiny. He was born to create life out of life! With this knowledge his soul is born.

> He drew forth a phrase from his treasure and spoke it softly to himself:
>
> — A day of dappled seaborne clouds. —
>
> The phrase and the day and the scene harmonised in a chord. Words. Was it their colours? He allowed them to glow and fade, hue after hue: sunrise gold, the russet and green of apple orchards, azure of waves the greyfringed fleece of clouds. No, it was not their colours: it was the poise and balance of the period itself. Did he then love the rhythmic rise and fall of words better than their associations of legend and colour? Or was it that, being as weak of sight as he was shy of mind, he drew

> less pleasure from the reflection of the glowing sensible world through the prism of a language manycoloured and richly storied than from the contemplation of an inner world of individual emotions mirrored perfectly in a lucid supple periodic prose. (*Por.* 193)

The "intellectual imagination" has at least gained ascendancy in Stephen's consciousness, and through it he will create not "life out of life" as he so joyfully hoped, but discursively and brilliantly an esthetic theory which is his own potential blueprint for creation and Joyce's irreversible principles from which he made his works.

Stephen attends the university not with a show of that joy that preceded his going, but rather with a chafing discontent. His fellow students revile him, his instructors excepting only a few send him on a private journey to information; he does not distinguish himself; he cares less to adhere to a foolish waste of energy than to "await his Eucharist."

> He spent days and nights hammering noisily as he built a house of silence for himself wherein he might await his Eucharist, days and nights gathering the first fruits and every peace-offering and heaping them upon his altar whereon he prayed clamorously the burning token of satisfaction might descend.[18]

The landscape spoke to him; he created tiny epiphanic bits, but creation itself eluded him. He took to carrying an ashplant.

His mother deplores his reading, his irregular habits, his religious indifference, but since the recent birth of his soul, Stephen apprehends nets flung at him to keep him from flight: the net of religion, the net of nationality, the net of language. "I will fly by those nets," he tells Davin. He will from religion make a great novel; he will from nationality make another great novel, and the net of language he will use to release that mythic world in which the grave of his boyhood was spent. He will again be wary: his only weapons: silence, exile, cunning.

He is now apostate. "I will not serve that in which I no longer believe, whether it call itself my home, my fatherland or my church. . ." (*Por.* 291), he says to his friend Cranly. The echo of Cranly's quiet question, "Do you love your mother?" and Stephen's answer, "I don't know what your words mean," hovers around Stephen and his ashplant in the lonely shadow of a doomed god. Wotan with his ash spear that rules the world is preparing to leave Ireland for Paris as the *Portrait* ends.

It is only fair to mention, of course, that Joyce is quite careful not to betray the secret of the ashplant in *A Portrait.* He asks us to read the sequel, *Ulysses,* where the ash spear is shattered and Stephen becomes an artist.

Who is Wotan? Wotan is the southern form of the old Norse god, Odin, who like Zeus was the sky father, but there the resemblance ends.[19] Odin reigns in Norse mythology as a somber, aloof and solemn figure, in an awesome golden Valhalla where he broods upon the day of doom predicted by Erda, earth mother. On his shoulders perch two ravens who fly out each day through the world and bring him back news of all that men do. The name of one is Thought (Hugin) and of the other Memory (Munin), and while the other gods feast, Odin ponders on what Thought and Memory teach him. In his search for wisdom, he descends to the Well of Wisdom guarded by Mimer the Wise to beg for a draught of it, and when Mimir answers that he must pay for it with one of his eyes, he sacrifices his eye; he wins the knowledge of the Runes through mysterious suffering and passes his knowledge on to men to protect themselves; he wrests from the Giants, the enemies of gods and men, the skaldic mead which when tasted makes men poets. He is mankind's benefactor.

Odin is Wagner's Wotan in *The Ring of the Nibelung.* He is raised over the human world not as a giver of light but a shatterer of light, for he represents the "intelligent, moral talented people who devise and administer states and churches."[20] In *The Ring,* the world is waiting for Man to redeem it from the lame and cramped government of the gods. Man, then, is the hero of *The Ring* in the person of Siegfried who in the opera bearing his name destroys Wotan by breaking his shaft of power, the Sacred Ash Spear, with his father's sword "Nothung." Wagner's Siegfried is the happy young man of dauntless courage because no god has instructed him in unhappiness and fear. He knows no law but his own humor, "is a totally immoral person, a born anarchist, a born Buckoonin, an anticipation of the "overman" of Nietzsche. He is enormously strong, full of life and fun, dangerous and destructive to what he dislikes, and affectionate to what he likes; so it is fortunate that his likes and dislikes are sane and healthy."[21]

Siegfried is a "Freewiller of Necessity"; he does not act from conscience born of judgment, but from an instinct toward the good. He destroys Wotan to achieve Brynhild, Wotan's will, whom he ravishes, and together they face death fearlessly because they have consummated human love.

Joyce does not parody Wagner. He is seriously concerned for the genuine good of his own work to relocate those elements of *The Ring* which are false, because his own hero, Stephen Dedalus, suffers from Wotanism which depth psychology tells us has a special relation to the balance and crisis of consciousness.

> He (Wotan) receives the age-old wisdom of the Great Mother (Erda), the gift of prophecy, but in return has to sacrifice his right eye. Thus, with its ecstatic abandon and beserker frenzies of emotion, Wotanism, in its orgiastic as well as its mantic form, lacks the clear eye of the higher knowledge, which was lost through the "upper castration" performed by Erda.[22]

Stephen's Wotanism begins as early as the vision of his art which comes before him as a girl "whom magic had changed into the likeness of a strange and beautiful seabird":[23] that art was to be in human shape graceful, with proportion marked by the Irish Gift, holy, confident, and with the power of flight. Siegfried in Stephen is suggested by the Bird-Girl, to parallel the hero's conquest of the dragon, but Wotan who precedes Siegfried controls here in Joyce's use of Erda.

> He felt above him the vast indifferent dome and the calm processes of the heavenly bodies: and the earth beneath him, the earth that had borne him, had taken him to her breast.[24]

As Wotan, cohabitor with Erda, Stephen can create with a lowered artistic consciousness;[25] he has prophecy but its joy is dimmed by the foreshadowing of the doom he knows he must meet in the twilight of his godship. Wotan failed because he could not love and so does Stephen Dedalus, but the Siegfried who replaces the Wotan in Stephen does not gain Brynhild to consummate a human passion but to unite his own being; to make whole his consciousness; to illuminate that consciousness by honoring his own flesh as the rich instrument of his intellect thereby releasing a love of created being. "Nothung," Siegmund's sword, is Wagner's special name for it. It means "Needful".[26] When Stephen beholds the sword of love in *Circe,* which is the chandelier, he tries to prevent its descent on his shaft, by raising the ashplant to shatter the light. He falls as Wotan, he abandons the ashplant, and as is indicated in Chapter IX, p 145, it is put to a common human use. No longer does it rule the world; it is a walking stick. "Walk" is a recurring motif in both *Portrait* and *Ulysses.*

Mr. Ellmann in his discussion of "Nothung" assigns the mildest kind of superficial meaning to the esthetic moment in *Circe*.[27] First of all, he assumes that because Siegmund, Siegfried's father, names the sword "Nothung" in *The Valkyrie*, Joyce is simply transposing and rather wilfully at that because Ottocaro Weiss had miffed him a short time earlier at a performance of *The Valkyrie* by saying he preferred Wagner to Joyce's "Sirens", the music episode in *Ulysses*. But by Mr. Ellmann's own evidence in *James Joyce*, he has cited five other references that leave no question of Joyce's impatience with Wagner's *pars pro toto*. Finally, Mr. Ellmann has confused the externals of the scene in *Circe*. Why does Stephen raise his ashplant at all? Why the shattering of light, toppling of masonry? Why does he abandon the ashplant a moment later and in a berserk frenzy of emotion flee the musicroom? Mr. Ellmann says Stephen only knocks down the brothel lampshade. This is the wee amount of "light shattering" Stephen accomplished as Wotan, and once the shade is off, the light of Siegfried's sword, "Needful" shows a way. The Norse mythology strain recurring often in the *Portrait* and informing *Ulysses* is one aspect of its *integritas*. It is a means of conveying the crisis in Stephen's consciousness; it is the way in which Joyce creates "the uncreated conscience" and reveals its poetry. Stephen must renounce the old Wotan habit of sending only thought and memory to inform him of the hearts of men; the "intellectual imagination" must give way to the image-making power that functions not as intellect, but as a receptor through the flesh of the intellect's impregnation to beget creation. The union is accomplished through the energy of love.

Who is M'Intosh? He is a "tall lankylooking galoot" in a macintosh who turns up on page 108 in *Ulysses* as a mysterious mourner at Paddy Dignam's funeral in the Hades episode. He makes one other actual appearance about three o'clock in the afternoon as a "pedestrian in a brown macintosh, eating dry bread" who passes "swiftly and unscathed across the viceroy's path" (251). At the cemetery Bloom sees him from a distance, and what he says is not revealing at the time, but we must keep it in mind, for the identity was here in the beginning.

> Now who is that lankylooking galoot over there in the macintosh? Now who is he I'd like to know? Now, I'd give a trifle to know who he is. Always someone turns up you never dreamt of. A fellow could live on his lonesome all his life. Yes, he could. Still he'd have to get

> someone to sod him after he died though he could dig his own grave. We all do. Only man buries. No ants too. First thing strikes anybody. Bury the dead. Say Robinson Crusoe was true to life. Well then Friday buried him. Every Friday buries a Thursday if you come to look at it. (108)

Hynes, *Evening Telegraph* reporter, asks Bloom for the mystery man's name and goes away thinking his name is Macintosh (110). When the news item is printed, the man is listed at the end of the mourners as M'Intosh (632). But there is one other seeming error and that is Stephen Dedalus, B.A. listed next to his father as having attended the funeral. After all, M'Intosh was there, only his name is missing, but why if Stephen was not in that cemetery should he be listed?

Long before this newspaper listing, however, there are scattered shocks of awareness that Stephen might be the Macintosh. On the way to the cemetery Bloom spots Stephen in Irishtown on his way to either the strand or his Aunt Sara's in Strasburg Terrace. We know he goes to the Strand where the morning communion with himself takes place while the funeral procession journeys out to Prospects burial ground. At the cemetery, let us say that the chapel ceremonics and moving Paddy Dignam to his grave take about forty minutes. The mourners, then, would be standing at the graveside about 11:40. As Padriac Colum says, "Dublin is a small city, so small that one can walk from the center to the outskirts in twenty minutes."[28] The procession begins in southeast Dublin and makes a diagonal north across the city, past Eccles Street, Bloom's home, and out Phibsborough Road[29] to the cemetery which is a short distance beyond Circular Road. Stephen could walk to the cemetery in fifteen minutes at the most. Stephen's monolog could easily have been from eleven to eleven-thirty; he could have called in at his Aunt Sara's and borrowed a Goulding macintosh, or he could have been carrying it from school. The later is probably the better reasoning for it illuminates the color "brown" used in the *Nestor* episode. "Brown" is used fifty-five times in *Ulysses* with an earth connotation occurring most frequently. In *Nestor* Stephen knows he will return neither to school nor the Tower where he has been living with Mulligan and Haines. His "godship" is at an end; he will come to earth. Why then would he attend Paddy Dignam's funeral? And in disguise? The Wanderer, Wotan, often came among men cloaked and with the brim of his hat over his missing eye. This Wotan has to see how it is among men again, and in what context. The ritual, the last rites of the religion of his birth,[30] marks his own death as Wotan. The liturgy is painted with extraordinary lyric emphasis in "Hades". And the comedy of the weary Norse god attending a Catholic burial in disguise is lost unless M'Intosh is integral to *Ulysses* as a whole. In reality Stephen loves his father, too, and he has not seen him for several days. Finally, his mother was so recently buried; he may have glanced at her grave as if to say, "I am trying to do as you said." In *Circe,* Mrs. Dedalus does bring Stephen to the death of the god and to the birth of understanding.

But there are other proofs. Macintosh is said to eat dry bread at three in the afternoon; at one in the morning, Stephen finds "a few broken biscuits" in his pocket. Mr. Bloom examines Stephen's shoes in the *Aeolus* episode, "Been walking in muck somewhere." We know it rained a bit on the way to the funeral, that Bloom knew it would because his boots creaked; at the cemetery he looked down at his own shoes he had shined to attend this funeral with mild dismay; that it was muddy at the cemetery, then, and this rather than the strand is where the "muck" comes from. How careful Joyce was, however, to balance the plausibles (45). Wet sand and muddy cemetery. In *Circe* Bloom is accused of crimes that could be described as muck; he calls out, "No, no. Pig's feet. I was at a funeral" (463). In *Ithaca* the chair that symbolizes Stephen: ". . . its frame from top to seat and from seat to base being varnished dark brown" (690). The word "varnished" is revealing too in the sense of "exterior coating", "veneer", "front", "brown". But finally, and convincingly, "The man in the brown macintosh loves a lady who is dead" (327).[31] Stephen is the only one in *Ulysses* who answers to this description, and Joyce is speaking in the text.

At this point Bloom's early mysteriously emotional reaction to the man in the macintosh, "that lankylooking galoot," epiphanizes. "Now who is he I'd like to know? Now, I'd give a trifle to know who he is" has in it a proper urgency. Bloom is alertly curious about a stranger at the graveside: a burial, a foreshadowed birth in the future of Bloom and the man of mystery, his intellectual birthright; his ageless thought, Stephen Dedalus. "A fellow could live on his lonesome all his life," Bloom says, and this means that Bloom and Stephen, spirit and body could go their separate ways as they do. "Still he'd have to get someone to sod him after he died though he could dig his own grave" becomes an accurate description of what each of these men is doing. The twist is they will each die to the old life making the point of all this, their birth. "We all do," Bloom tells us, bury the dead in ourselves repeatedly. We all lack that conscience which sustains life in creative judgment. "Say Robinson Crusoe was true to life. Well, then Friday buried him. Every Friday buries a Thursday if you come to look at it." Bloom is Stephen's good man, Friday: he follows the lad to a brothel to be of service; he serves Stephen in the Musicroom; he sees to his money; he protects his feelings; he administers to the dying Wotan and is midwife to the birth of the artist, Stephen Dedalus, who was born on Thursday. "Thursday's child has far to go," Zoe tells him in the palm reading. Mr. Bloom, Stephen's good man Friday, the Flesh, serves whether it be at a birth or death. And, of course, it is Friday proper when all this comes to pass for Thursday's child and the burying Friday: Stephen and Mr. Bloom.

Joyce has carefully shrouded the first meeting of his antagonist and protagonist. We must understand they are bi-heroes before we reflect that they struggled against each other. Spatially, Stephen Dedalus cannot take up seven hundred or more pages as does Bloom, because the intellect does not occupy space. Joyce has managed to create the endless space of intellect through the techniques he used for Stephen.

Joyce's *mythos* is a creation through Homer and Chaplin. It is the narrative of two men becoming human and the spiritual account of the two humans becoming one person.[32] The new myth derives not from the mythological grand scale of either of the great myths, *i.e.*, not the classical heroic stature of Odysseus, but the essential human, intellectual and sensuous response to experience of Odysseus, the man; and not from the classical, heroic absurdities of the Chaplin canon, but from the romantic, sensual lyric Charlie, the man, who is a clown. There is a third element in Joyce's myth, Molly Bloom, who derives from Penelope in Homer, not drawn but distorted to classic scale and who alone possesses both an individual and an heroic nature on purely dimensional grounds. Joyce calls her *Weib* which means feminine essence, and he characterizes her: *Ich bin das fleisch das stets bejaht.* I am the flesh which always says "yes". It is Mephistopheles controverted: he says: *Ich bin der Geist, der stets verneint.*[33] I am the spirit that always says "no". Molly is to Bloom as Chaplin what the Flesh is to itself: intimate, appealing, rich voiced, beguiling, comforting, consoling, deceptive, revolting, heinous, unfaithful. Joyce says of her:

> . . . perfectly sane full amoral fertilisable untrustworthy engaging shrewd limited prudent indifferent. . . .[34]

Leopold Bloom, an advertising canvasser, whose habitual, final meditation before going to bed each night is to dream "of some one sole unique advertisement to cause passers to stop in wander," is himself a wanderer both by heritage and inclination. He is Jewish and at thirty-eight he has so far held and lost in the city of Dublin five jobs. His capital gains are minimal, his bank account low, but he does have a treasure that dwarfs material holdings; that is his wife, Molly Bloom, to whom he dedicates his act of existence. Molly Bloom of Spanish-Irish heritage has a Milesian flare but a Firbolg nature,[35] and she dedicates her life to indulging this nature. Her traditional memories are stunted into one major channel of promiscuity; her small world revolves around the gossip of intrigue, and her information is almost wholly intuitive which gives her an integrity among those she knows because she is herself. It is a self of utter abandon, a preconscious, unabashed natural state which depends wholly on a logic of personal feeling. She is gifted with a rich melodious voice which had wooed her Leopold in the beginning, and an ample body with which to sing. She sings not from a spiritual abundance as does the poet, but from a natural, lyrical sense. During her courtship she decided to marry her man Bloom because he told her the sun shone for her and called her his mountain flower.

Bloom's marriage to Molly was gay enough in the beginning: Molly's concerts; Bloom's masculine pursuit of her through the first years; two children Milly sixteen and Rudy who died in infancy. As the first male child of his love for Molly perished, so did his male pursuit, his masculine assertion, his headship, his progenitor role. But he did not admit this even to himself. The fundamental of his male nature sank to an unconscious level leaving the feminine to dominate his consciousness. His love for Molly became a pursuit in his thought life, and he worshipped her with an interior fever which inflamed his blood, stopped his speech, endued his action and motivated his analogous satisfactions, which were as diverse as they were unclean. His treasure is to him still greater than professional success, friendship, self fulfillment, ideologies of all kinds, faith. He is at thirty-eight, a man of many devices to get him through the day's human whorl, and he even has the wit and image intelligence to suffer Molly's betrayal with a kind of image equanimity. Molly, of course, is fundamentally amoral and suffers only the qualms of custom in her extra marital affairs. At present she is trifling with Blazes Boylan, a Dublin racetrack sharper who knows that Bloom knows and fully enjoys the knowledge. Bloom, however, wanders from Molly and home not because his business is so pressing, not because

Molly is having an affair, not because his daughter Milly is no longer at home, not because he loves the city of Dublin, not because he loves friends more than his wife. Like the Odysseus of old he has left home to fight a war over beauty: Troy fought over Helen; Bloom has left home to fight a private war between his conscious and his unconscious life over the beautiful which perished in the early years of his manhood (Rudy symbolizes this), and to get home, he must suffer as Odysseus suffered to maintain identity at all costs by coming to terms with his unconscious. Like the Chaplin of the movies Bloom exercises the act of his existence in a lyrical, romantic self-love under the guise of dame pursuit, bully pursuit, esteem pursuit, sensation pursuit, elegance pursuit, and in the long haul of his memory, a shadow falls between the potentiality and the act: Agendath Netaim. But Bloom hops over the shadow and goes gaily on bathing and lotioning his flesh, reaping the dwarf harvest of impotent seed. Alone and restless, mute and craving obscurely to adore, he is once removed from every reality of the objective world his senses might deliver to him. But he is sensate and observant; he is crafty (he's a Mason); he has a cunning at once noticing and noticeable, for everyone "knows" old Bloom, and he's good for a laugh, a tear, a sigh. Now with the advent of night after a full day of the nymph (Molly never leaves his thought), the finer instincts of compassion stir him, so in a hospital where a Mrs. Purefoy whom he knows only slightly is giving birth, he exerts this satisfying emotion and by an accident in being, he meets with Stephen Dedalus.

Stephen Dedalus is at the head of the table of medicoes who await the birth, dreaming outloud over the consciousness of the race as it is delivered to us through literary artists; and through the word, the sensuous man of many devices and the intellectual man of many tongues[36] have their first direct look at each other. Bloom did not know Stephen in his macintosh. It is ten o'clock; in the next four hours they will find through each other what each of them lacks. Bloom seeks the lost power of his manhood; Stephen seeks the lost power of his youth.[37] Each of these is symbolized by a son and a father, but each stands for something larger than an individual in their personal lives. The lost power of Stephen's youth, for instance, is many things which resolve into a whole after the encounter with the configuration of images presented to him in the musicroom at Bella's.

The Wotan characteristics in Stephen dramatize a more fundamental disorder of soul: *Non serviam*, the famous Satanic cry, endues his thought life with a night ritual of aggression against all established order. Essentially it is this unimaginative tough, straight, close grain in Stephen which must split and char to another form of ash before the glory of corporeal faculties will arise. Stephen's Christian origins give him the foreknowledge of his fall as the mythologic Wotan; his reverie is saturated with awareness of Lucifer's condition of rebellion:

> Allbright he falls, proud lightning of the intellect, *Lucifer, dico, qui nescit occasum.* (51)

Stephen knows his destiny and when the moment of Lucifer-Wotan renunciation comes, he is intellectually prepared but emotionally shocked into a coma of the heart. Joyce affects this by a sock in the jaw to Stephen which he well deserves, and the comic accident highlights the serious substance of Stephen's rebirth. He has spent a year away from Ireland studying in Paris without loving anyone there, and now, recalled to bury his mother, he approaches the second great spiritual crisis of his life. The captive poetic knowledge of his preconscious and the fettered love of his unconscious agitate with the buried mark of the beast a roiling motion of his soul toward flight. He goes with deliberate weariness and relished foreboding to *Circe.*

Mr. Bloom, man of marvel, is not so deliberate; he gravitates toward *Circe.* With his "moly" protection, no harm can befall him and his potato, the big panacea, will save him from all harm. He enters the musicroom and takes the limelight. He takes something else in this room of magic — all the shapes of his psychical deformities. He becomes the Flesh without an intellect. His intellect becomes Stephen Dedalus who has no flesh. Separate they are impotent: were they united, the creative power of intellect positing seed in the imagination of the Flesh would release the energy of love. In Stephen's case, Wotan is the ransom money; as Siegfried he will honor the memory of his father. In Bloom's case, his craving to adore would no longer be mute nor obscure. He would regain his manhood, and Molly would serve her husband. But all this depends on the ascent to consciousness; the achievement of judgment, the act of conscience. As we know, they conquer *Circe*; Bloom's intellect appears (however faintly, however comically), and Stephen learns the moment of his downfall as a god through his ashen, grave-returned mother.[38] In a rage he raises his ashplant, but the light he would have shattered becomes "Nothung". He abandons his ashplant and rushes into the night. In a nether world of "strengthless heads of the dead",[39]

Stephen makes humble efforts to love his accusers. He must understand before he can go home to his Father: he must renounce through love the black rite of his thought-life and its companions; the revulsion and bitterness for his family, friends, fellow countrymen. So, he burns the Dublin that he loathed and suffers the form of his black traffic to come before his mind in the shape of a Black Mass. Bloom in the meantime is chased by everyone in the book so he can outwit them by not doing the famous Chaplin corner. He stops suddenly and repulses the rabble with the talisman of his reclaimed manhood. Stephen, literally knocked out by the forces of hatred at his first attempt to love, has killed the priest who celebrated esthetic rites and the king whose ashplant was license. But the little man of "the flat spaugs and the walk," the man with the dark suit and the derby, the antic clown now marks his strides with the ashplant. This is one of the great comic moments in *Ulysses.* The clown as man receives his most important prop: known to every Chaplin fan as his cane, but in its new office the sign that he has risen from his paralytic couch and that through the miracle of redemption, he walks. That it is ash in Joyce rather than bamboo relocates its power. Bloom is now the "fallen aristocrat" turned beggar. Like Odysseus when he goes to Eumaeus, he must take whatever Stephen cares to give him for nourishment.

Bloom, the Flesh, brings Stephen round and leads him to nourishment (of sorts) in a cabshelter. They get acquainted. Stephen is slightly drunk, tired, bored with Bloom but tolerant, and to tolerate Bloom's new found judgment at this point requires a degree of charity. Although an ingratiating attitude informs his long tale to Stephen — Joyce calls it an "old" narrative — at times Bloom is effusively transported in his eagerness to establish his position as a man of ideals, as a champion of the good, as a man of compassion, as man of wisdom. But he would have Stephen know that when it comes to such things as the soul and a personal God, every man should hold his peace. Stephen's few rallies happen at these instances of views by the Flesh, and they come in the form of a rebuke by the intellect. But to maintain a growing harmony at any cost Bloom reworks for Stephen one of his key experiences of the day. He says he put the Irish Citizen in his place when he, Bloom, was accused of being Jewish and therefore an outsider, by, as he says, "letting fly", "your God was a jew like me." Fearful, however, that Stephen might take exception to his nationality, he quickly adds "in reality I'm not," and he is to deny his origins again before the night is done. But our little man is shrewd and nimble. No sooner does

Stephen reduce the above triumph to the reasonable position that all *secundem carnem* (627) is in the image of Christ because he is God, than Mr. Bloom dodges another way to clear the Jews of their unsavory name with humanity. All this brings him to the position that he is as good an Irishman as anyone in the country and deserves to have a voice in the reform he knows she needs. In the plans Stephen and his kind: poets, intellectuals, scholars, are to have the same chance as the peasants to earn their keep. "You belong to Ireland, the brain as well as the brawn . . . ." This brings Stephen into a short sally, "Ireland must be important because she belongs to me," on which Bloom trips. He cannot fathom "belongs to". Stephen rebukes him by demanding a change of subject. It now occurs to Bloom that his companion has a gifted singing voice and at once he is excited by mental plans to promote this boy on the Concert Stage. The more he casts his sideways glance at his young companion, the more Bloom congratulates himself on his extraordinary good fortune, and he begins to dream of their success together. There is a hand-picked assortment of jarvies and sailors in the cabshelter whose vulgar romantic talk and action at one time would have revolted Stephen Dedalus; he is, however, quiet, passive, allowing the work of magic to transform him. It is Bloom whose delicacy is revolted, and because he has talked his heart out for the moment, and he is faintly chagrined to subject his gifted companion to such crudity of mind and body, he suggests that they go to his home, the home of the Flesh, to speak further of these matters. "The only thing is to walk then you'll feel a different man," he says to Stephen, who accepts the offer, "Lean on me." The different man, of course, is that man, the gifted clown, Charlie; that man disguised as a beggar like his Homeric forbear, that man who found in the depths of his conscience the poetry of the "old man" which he is at present scaling off.

After an exhaustive penetration of the Intellect searching the mind of the Flesh and the Flesh aspiring to the structure of the intellect over a cup of Epp's Cocoa at Bloom's home, Stephen decides to go: "out of the house of bondage to the wilderness of inhabitation," but not before one last definition of himself as

> . . . a conscious rational animal proceeding syllogistically from the known to the unknown and a conscious rational reagent between a micro and a macrocosm ineluctably constructed upon the incertitude of the void. (682)

which enables Bloom to define himself

> as a competent keyless citizen he had proceeded energetically from the unknown to the known through the incertitude of the void. (682)

Their last solemn meditation is toward the light in Molly Bloom's bedroom during which Stephen quizzes Bloom on the possibility of creatures of other planets being morally redeemed by a redeemer. Bloom's answer is that if they existed, and if they were redeemed they would, like the creatures of earth, be "inalterably and inalienably attached to vanities, to vanities of vanities and all that is vanity" (684). And in gazing toward Molly they were silent:

> . . . each contemplating the other in both mirrors of the reciprocal flesh of theirhisnothis fellowfaces. (687)

The business of egress for Stephen from Bloom's nocturnal garden is not without labor. The gate lock is unused, must be turned with a key, must be prized loose, must reveal an aperture. Mr. Bloom does this. Stephen goes forth upon "the heaven born earth," or put metaphysically, Stephen's earthly instrument, his flesh, which was from all eternity designed as the perfect agent for his soul, is reborn. He has arisen; he can walk. The stranglehold of paralysis disappears more logically than Job's festering flesh, but the miracle is the same: Satan was given free reign, but he failed.

> Alone, what did Bloom hear?
>
> The double reverberation of retreating feet on the heavenborn earth, the double vibration of a jew's harp in the resonant lane. (689)

The soul journeys out of the flesh to create as Stephen must while Bloom stays at home to take care. Staying at home to take care is the proper function of body as body. From birth to death it is the heart of the soul's home. For the mind, the body as home provides nourishment, rest, comfort, garment. The wonderful comedy business Joyce has given to Bloom in the remaining moments of the book is brilliant Chaplin and magnificent Joyce. Who else but the Chaplin figure could bring off the ironic dream of manhood with which *Ulysses* ends, exhilarating above its tears? Who but Joyce could convince by the total vision of *Ulysses* that the dream is not after all ironic — that salvation lies in the poetry of conscience? Twentieth century mode is turning from desire toward need. It faces Joyce.

Conclusion

My claim for this study is that it examines and assesses for the first time since *Ulysses* was made in 1922, the brilliant *artistic synthesis* Joyce uses to communicate the space-time human image. His use of Chaplin in Bloom makes a whole thing of *Ulysses* by combining it with its original part, *A Portrait of the Artist as a Young Man.* The link between the two books is the vow to create the "uncreated conscience" of the race. Chaplin in Bloom illuminates who it is that makes the vow, what the "uncreated conscience" is, and the cinema form in the shape of its twentieth century hero creates those perspectives of mind and feeling necessary to experience Joyce's vision.

The critical anarchy that has for so long confused the sequelty of *Ulysses* to *A Portrait of the Artist as a Young Man* is a failure of the critical conscience to experience literature through intellect and feeling.[1] The first service of Chaplin in Bloom is to demonstrate with astonishing clarity the degree to which the sequel is dependent upon its precursor and the literality with which Joyce followed his esthetic principles. Joyce sought not to confound the mind but to enchant the heart. Those who are willing to take literally his critical precepts will know the extent of this enchantment, for they are the passage from one world to another in the Joyce works and the conditioning for his poetry. Those precepts, it is refreshing to recall, are not the truth because Stephen Dedalus of *Stephen Hero* says them nor yet because Stephen Dedalus is Joyce, but because what they contain conforms to the being of critical thought:

> The critic is he who is able, by means of the signs which the artist affords, to approach the temper which has made the work and to see what is well done therein and what it signifies. For him a song by Shakespeare which seems so free and living, as remote from any conscious purpose as rain that falls in a garden or as the lights of evening, discovers itself as the rhythmic speech of an emotion otherwise incommunicable, or at least not so fitly. But to approach the temper which has made art is an act of reverence before the performance of which many conventions must be first put off for certainly that inmost region will never yield its secret to one who is enmeshed with profanities.
> (S. H. 79)

Joyce makes it clear in *A Portrait* he is a mediator between the world of his dreams and the world of his experience. To insist that the fictional Stephen is not an artist or that Joyce is not Stephen because the accidents of biography are not the accidents of Joyce's fiction is to render not judgment but mere opinion based on alien esthetic. The primary function of criticism is to *judge* literature according to the artist's exemplar not according to the critic's rule. The essential activity in the Joyce canon is to see the way in which Joyce mediates between dream and experience and what the mediation signifies.

The temper making *Ulysses* is the same temper making *Stephen Hero* and *A Portrait;* the temper is Joyce the artist in his person and Stephen Dedalus in whom the temper is personified. Joyce makes; Stephen cannot make but he can reason his way to the beautiful. The principles Stephen establishes are the very ones being used to create him in *Stephen Hero* and *A Portrait,* the signs of which abound.

> For Stephen art was neither a copy nor an imitation of nature: the artistic process was a natural process. In all his talk about artistic per-

> fection it was impossible to detect an artificial accent. To talk about the perfection of one's art was not for him to talk about something agreed upon as sublime but in reality no more than a sublime convention but rather to talk about a veritably sublime process of one's nature which had a right to examination and open discussion. (S. H. 171)

The veritably sublime process of his own nature unfolded by the mature Joyce in *A Portrait* is transformed by art to the act of exercising existence on a creative level whether one's calling is to the making of art or the making of a creative existence. Stephen Dedalus becomes the symbol of the general creative act paralyzed in mythical thought. He it is who vows through logical conviction to create the "uncreated conscience" of his race. He is intellect striving to liberate for esthetic use his power of mythical apprehension. Joyce's sign that he is Stephen is the verisimilitude to human consciousness Stephen's act of exercising his existence bears. Side by side the intellectual strength, there is in Stephen a weakness of the flesh which has caused his paresis. He brings dishonor upon his flesh by bestiality and uncleanness which causes him to abandon the vessel of his creative potential. The outcome is he beholds the condition of the race through the transformation of his own condition by art to the universal malady of mankind in space-time: the non-being of judgment. He resolves to create the conscience of the race because his perception brings him to the knowledge of conscience not before created: the poetry of conscience.

The sequel to the vow taken is the keeping of the promise. *Ulysses* creates the uncreated conscience of the human race on earth. The only logical method consistent with the Stephen who lives in *A Portrait* is a continuation of the mytho-poetic nature of his creation. He is out of Joyce's spiritual action. How does Stephen solve his dilemma of artistic paralysis? The reclamation of flesh rejected? How does Stephen remain central to the struggle in *Ulysses* even though absent most of the time? Through a presence of his Flesh which now becomes a clown, for it has through folly paralyzed his creative act and mummed him into impotency. Joyce in the meantime sees the comedy in the sublime process of his nature, sees too the superior art of human comedy as a sane and joyful expression of his nature. Either poetic knowledge through Chaplin on the screen or the end of a search for the perfect symbol to signify his own and therefore Stephen's flesh results in Chaplin in Bloom. Signs afforded by Joyce that *Ulysses* is a sequel abound. The act of reverence the very young poet demands of the critic of art is precocious and true.

Joyce's signs weave a vast spiral of interconnecting ascents to his highest truth, the poetry of conscience. Chaplin in Bloom is the artistic synthesis of those symbols. He signifies not only the screen odyssey of modern man but the art form of cinema conveying in Joyce's works the ideogram of the place and condition of the poetry of conscience. The art of cinema illuminates form or soul through montage. Joyce's primary concern as an artist is with being and its existence. He was drawn to cinema as the inevitable divisive technique necessary to his depiction of the secret interior life of his own being and its personas, Stephen Dedalus and Leopold Bloom. The Chaplin figure in Bloom performs the miracle of analogy between the clown and human Flesh. Intellect conditioned and homeless in Stephen Dedalus and Flesh with a tenantless home in the Chaplin Figure in Bloom activates the essential human struggle to achieve the highest intelligibility of being: judgment. Chaplin in Bloom makes possible that penetration into the metaphysical interior of Joyce's work which operates beneath the language, the images, the real persons in their act of existence, their attitudes, relationships.[2] Chaplin in Bloom assigns meaning to metaphysical reality in Joyce.

This study of *Ulysses* is, therefore, a probing of the "truth of the being of the visible universe", Joyce so constantly beholds. To disengage the beauty of its form from the propriety of its matter is a metaphysical action of the spirit. This action does not reside as a special function of the intellect nor as a separated good of the flesh. It is quite of a piece with consciousness. The critic who looks at Joyce without the metaphysical consciousness will not be admitted to that inmost region of his art where poetry resides, for poetry and its prophetic knowledge is the secret Joyce yields to those who put off profanities.[3]

The syncretizing effect of Chaplin in Bloom is everywhere pervasive in *A Portrait* and *Ulysses.* Until this writing it has not been essential to know the significance of Stephen Dedalus' ashplant in *A Portrait.* In *Ulysses* Chaplin in Bloom, through the montage of intellectual cinema, shows Stephen to be a waning god who says, "My ashplant will float away." (50)

Before Chaplin in Bloom M'Intosh was a mystery thought by many to be a character from *Dubliners,* by Joyce's friends to be a grand hoax, for he was fond of asking, "Who is M'Intosh?" Chaplin in Bloom puts Stephen Dedalus in the necessary perspective by which we see that the liberating process from mythical thought makes him M'Intosh. Imbedded internal evidence from the text demonstrates conclusively Stephen's presence at Dignam's graveside. Stephen's M'Intosh sequence is analogical to his resting as poet to attend the rite of the religion of his birth. That he attends as Wotan is comedy. That he attends at all is portent of his liberation from bondage to mythical thought which esthetically freed knowledge will launch him as artist. What is important to see here, too, is Joyce's spiritual affinity with the religion of his birth. Fictionally he does enter the "city of the Church through the wicket of repentence" for in *Ulysses* Stephen does repent, burns the black crew of his corruption in the Black Mass of *Circe* and comes to a consciousness of his redeemable humanity.

Finally, the Chaplin figure in *Ulysses,* itself one of the great economies in literature, offers extended proof of Joyce's total artistic economy. *Ulysses* is no longer a debatable title allowing the reader freedom to include or ignore the Homeric parallels in his understanding of the work. At best this position contradicts Joyce's artistic integrity. When Ezra Pound in his enthusiastic essay on *Ulysses* in *Dial,* 1922, happened to say as part of a spontaneous accolade to the book that the parallels were private, he was taken literally. Here is his statement, much quoted and too widely accepted:

> Telemachus, Circe, the rest of the Odyssean company, the noisy cave of Aeolus gradually place themselves in the mind of the reader, rapidly or or less rapidly according as he is familiar or unfamiliar with Homer. These correspondences are part of Joyce's mediaevalism and are chiefly his own affair, a scaffold, a means of construction, justified by the result, and justifiable by it only. The result is a triumph in form, in balance, a main schema, with continuous inweaving and arabesque.[4]

Edmund Wilson writing on *Ulysses* in 1922 is convinced that "the major theme of the book is to be found in its parallel with the Odyssey,[5] but he complains that Homer and Homer alone has dictated the size and shape of *Ulysses.* Mr. Pound finds the Greek parallels tenuous and private; Mr. Wilson finds them a mistake.[6] After thirty-nine years many Joyce critics still accept this early unreflected opinion; even some of the fine scholars dismiss the Homeric parallels as Joyce's private delight.[7]

The Chaplin figure in Bloom presents the hero with a modern odyssey. The Chaplin myth and the Homer myth create Joyce's new metaphysical myth of Spirit returning to the home of the Flesh. The high comedy of the Chaplin myth through Joyce's technique of intellectual cinema locates an unmined vein of comedy in Homer. *Ulysses* is the comic image of space-time man. I have found the Schema Joyce used for making *Ulysses* invaluable in my study of the book. While Joyce deliberately withheld the Schema from extensive circulation and certainly publication during his life time, and it would seem without cause, it is easy to see the document is undispensable to illumination in *Ulysses*. My own first reading of the work, however, was without knowledge the Schema existed. What happened in that reading (eight years ago) was that Mr. Bloom materialized actually as a presence filling my mind and all the extra-mental environment with his existence on that day in Dublin, but the altogether disturbing sensation to me that translocated him and put him as it were "all over the world" was I knew him before, but I could not recall where or when. He presented himself a year ago at a Chaplin narrated re-run of *The Gold Rush*. In the meantime I had studied *Ulysses* with the Schema but without Bloom's identity. When the Chaplin figure in Bloom entered the Schema, the Schema was fully intelligible. Joyce's artistic wisdom probably accounts for his withholding the Schema. Perhaps he foresaw the need to realize Bloom before anything like a space-time image could be received. That his original signed Schema in his gift copy to Sylvia Beach is for the first time published in this volume devoted to Bloom's identity as the Chaplin figure is significant. Now the danger is past. In the foreground, Chaplin in Bloom confronts the modern world. The image of Odysseus is outlined by means of the successive ages that descend away from Bloom in the timeless space out of which he emerges.

The above segments in this conclusion are subsidiary to the great intelligibility made possible by the Chaplin figure in Bloom. That intelligibility is *Circe*, the place and condition of poetry in *Ulysses*. *Circe* is formed in the Thomistic doctrine of conscience which in turn cooperates with the patristic fathers, Basil and Damascene, in their theology of conscience.[8] Since St. Thomas properly can be said to extend Aristotle, his discussion includes the Aristotelian concept of man's faculty of moral judgment. Like the applied Aquinas in Stephen's esthetic principles, the moral precept upon which conscience is built in *Ulysses* is also applied Aquinas. No less than the operative esthetic, the Thomistic tract on conscience becomes an avenue to poetry.

Circe divides into three movements of the human spirit in the act of conscience: Witness; incite or bind; accuse, torment or rebuke. Bloom's stiff walk, a symbol of his paralysis, bears witness to his prostitution; Bloom's grandfather Lipoti Virag, a symbol of the Israelic race from which he springs, incites him to reject "the old man"; the "old man in Bloom" accuses him. But torment and rebuke come through Bella Cohen, Bloom's defection personified. As with the esthetic, St. Thomas on Conscience carries

Joyce up to a point. That point is the power of language in the service of discursive thought. This will deliver the bi-heroes, Bloom and Stephen to the place of poetry and condition them for the uncreated conscience. The uncreated conscience transcending *cum alio scientia,* knowledge applied to an individual case, is the act of *consciousness in ascent from the unconscious;* the act of intellect positing seed of its thought in the imagination of its flesh to beget judgment. Jacque Maritain speaking of St. Thomas's view of judgment has a poetic knowledge of the human faculty:

> In St. Thomas's view, in contrast to that of Descartes, judgment is not only an operation which takes place following simple apprehension and the formation of the concept; it is the completion, the consummation, the perfection, and the glory of the intellect and of intellection, just as the existence it affirms is the glory and perfection of being and of intelligibility.[9]

> The intelligibility with which judgment deals is more mysterious than that which notions or ideas convey to us; it is not expressed in a concept but in the very act of affirming or denying. It is the super-intelligibility, if I may put it so, of the act of existing itself, either possible or actually given.[10]

Joyce achieves the poetry of conscience through the act of Stephen's descent to Bloom; Bloom's ascent to Stephen: the cooperative, mysterious act of intellect and sense to beget judgment: the conformation through coupling soul with flesh. Stephen's judgment is artistic; Bloom's is domestic. A purified flesh is possible only through an intellect willing to live in it, listen to it, beget its creative thought through it. Imagination which is flesh never intellectualizes itself in the poetic morality of judgment. Joyce's uncreated conscience, its poetry, prophesies man's conscience will not be the simple ethics of doing good and avoiding evil, but that total continuing perfecting judgment begotten always and only by descent of intellect into flesh or sense, the act itself of affirming or denying. The act of existing in this ascending consciousness is less vulnerable to the privation of evil because awakened to the completion of good; less assailable to corruption through the flesh because quickened to the glory of consciousness. Joyce's morning knowledge in *Ulysses* is his gift of certitude to the twentieth century.

NOTES

All page numbers in parentheses within my text refer to the Random House edition of *Ulysses* unless otherwise indicated. I have checked all significant passages with the Sylvia Beach Copy of the First Edition at the University of Buffalo.

Schema

The Schema in the end cover is a reproduction of the famous original Joyce gave to Sylvia Beach in her gift copy of *Ulysses.* His handwritten message and name are in the right hand corner. Miss Beach's *Ulysses* is at the Lockwood Library, University of Buffalo, whose Board of Custodians has released the Schema for reprinting here for the first time. Mr. Peter Spielberg, Bibliographer of the Joyce Collection in Buffalo, noting publication of the schema in Marvin Magalaner's book where it is reproduced from the collection of H. K. Croessmann, considers the copy in the Croessmann collection "almost identical" with the signed Joyce Schema in Buffalo.

Chapter I.

1. Cf. Ernst Cassirer, *The Philosophy of Symbolic Forms,* trans. Ralph Manheim (New Haven: Yale University Press, 1955), II *(Mythical Thought)*, 36: "But there can be no doubt that the characteristic structure of certain basic mythical concepts is intelligible only if we consider that for mythical thinking and mythical 'experience' there is always a hovering between the world of dream and the world of objective reality." In Joyce's terms the world of dream is the inner world of potential analogy. Proportion through metaphor is achieved by the artist who mediates between the world of experience and the world of the images of experience which reside with intuitive notions. Cf. also Frederick D. Wilhelmsen, "The Philosopher and the Myth," *The Modern Schoolman,* XXXII (November 1954), 45: "Man grasps the subject of judgment in and through phantasms that are usually symbolic. Since phantasms are the stuff of symbolization and belong to the order of the body, the link between conscious intelligibility and myth must be the phantasm itself. Phantasm constructs in any one judgment both present the subject and symbolically re-present the predicate, which is the way in which the subject is seen in this act of knowing. The judgment is a unity, and what is *meant* — intended — of the subject is always the predicate. (They stand to one another as matter to form.) Thus the phantasm constructs, in this act of knowing, mean precisely what I intend (the term is used formally) them to mean. Nonetheless, although *this* meaning is given *this* phantasm in *this* judgment, the phantasm itself is the end product of a long history of construction. In previous acts of knowing the phantasm could, and probably did, mean something else. This prior meaning is latent within the phantasm; it pervades the phantasm, lying low, hovering beneath conscious intelligibility, mixing with all the subrational life of man. To speak technically, this prior, unarticulated meaning is the intelligible species existing *in habitu* — neither in act nor simply in potency. Thus a phantasm has been disengaged from the memory, a phantasm containing potentially a whole cluster of intelligible species. One of these species is illuminated by the agent intellect and thus actuates the intellect. The others are *there*, but they are not adverted to consciously. Hence in the judgment the explicit rationality of the predicate plays over and works through a large body of unarticulated knowledge." Mr. Wilhelmsen's philosophy of the psychology within poetic knowledge is helpful in spite of his denial that he is talking poetry (p. 42). The logical extension of his premise is the poet's mediation. Mythical thought liberated for poetic use is another way of viewing the reality M. Maritain discusses in "Poetic Experience," *The Review of Politics*, Vol. 6, No. 4 (October 1944), 387-402. See also Victor M. Hamm, *Language, Truth and Poetry* (Milwaukee: Marquette University Press, 1960) for philosophic examination of "poetry". Valuable bibliography.

2. Stuart Gilbert, ed., *Letters of James Joyce* (New York: Viking Press, 1957), p. 70.

3. *Ibid.*, p. 63.

4. Herbert Gorman, *James Joyce* (New York: Rinehart, 1948).

5. Richard Ellmann, *James Joyce* (New York: Oxford University Press, 1959).

6. Gilbert, *Letters.* Through correspondence with The Society of Authors I learn, however, that a new volume of letters is work in progress. Mr. Gilbert's volume while generally useful is marred by mistaken gentility. He has omitted at times Joyce's direct words in letters explaining in a footnote, "Unprinted here but easily imagined by adult readers." (170, 275). Imagining he is protecting Joyce and in mistaken loyalty, he has this note on omission of fact, "The names omitted are those of three of Joyce's friends, now living, and he certainly would not have wished them to be publicized in this context." At Cornell there is written evidence that Joyce requested his wife, Nora, to save letters written to her from Dublin. The omitted names above are mild compared to the degree of intimacy the 1909 letters contain. Joyce seems to have preferred extra-creative evidence of his life and works. It would seem he is the last artist who would tolerate omissions of any kind from either the works or the personal history documents.

7. Stanislaus Joyce, *My Brother's Keeper* (New York: Viking Press, 1958), p. 40 and *passim.* The new volume of letters should properly contain many from Joyce to Stanislaus. They reveal the truth of their relationship more accurately than either *Keeper* or Stanislaus' diary (also at Cornell), for Stanislaus has neither the skill nor the insight to be objective. The letters from James to him contain many quotations reflecting what he says and what James makes of what he says.

8. Notebook begun in 1904 and continued for at least ten years containing sketches of 33 persons and much material used verbatim by Joyce in *A Portrait* and *Ulysses.* Listed as No. 25, "Manuscripts," *The Cornell Joyce Collection, A Catalogue,* dissertation by Robert E. Scholes, June 1959.

9. Letter to Nora, August 29, 1904, Cornell Collection.

10. See Ellmann, p. 365.

11. *Exiles* (New York: Viking Press, 1951, p. 114. The scholastic definition of art, "the right reason about the thing to be made," is a way to understand the nature of Joyce's fictional repentence in *Ulysses.* The right reason about making the conscience of the race is his own particular conscience made universal through the poetry of conscience. The poetry of conscience cannot err, for poetry as connatural knowledge is transcendent truth.

12. Georges Borach, "Conversations with James Joyce," trans. Joseph Prescott, *College English,* XV (March, 1954), 326.

13. See *Republic,* III, 389, trans. Lane Cooper. Art as a lie has an ironic meaning in plato in the light of such passages as Republic III, 392: Socrates to Adeimantus. See also Jacques Maritain, *Creative Intuition in Art and Poetry* (New York: Pantheon Books, 1953), p. 87, n. 18, where he reasons that Plato, in the light of what he says in *Laws* has a larger design for *Republic* than its apparent subject.

14. Cassirer, p. 260: "On the one hand, the very lowest, most primitive mythical configuration proves to be a vehicle of meaning, for already it stands in the sign of that primordial division which raises the world of the sacred from the world of the profane and delimits the one from the other. But on the other hand, even the highest religious truth remains attached to sensuous existence, to the world of images as well as things. It must continuously immerse and submerge itself in this existence which its intelligible purpose strives to cast off and reject — because only in this existence does religious truth possess its expressive form and hence its concrete reality and efficacy. . . . Only when we turn from the mythical image world and the world of religious meaning to the sphere of art and artistic expression does the opposition which dominates the development of the religious consciousness appear to be in a sense appeased, if not negated."

15. *Stephen Hero,* eds. J. Slocum and H. Cahoon (New York: New Directions Press, 1955), p. 30.

16. Letter to Nora from Dublin, December 23, 1909, Cornell Collection.

17. Letter to Nora from Dublin, September 2, 1909, Cornell Collection.

18. Letter to Nora from Dublin, December 1, 1909, Cornell Collection.

19. Letter to Nora from Dublin, August 7, 1909, Cornell Collection.

20. *A Portrait of the Artist as a Young Man* (New York: Viking Press, 1925), p. 299.

21. See Ellmann, "The Backgrounds of Ulysses," Chapter XXII, p. 367, for various Irishmen in Bloom.

22. Arnold had no little effect on Joyce's world view. Critique within *Ulysses* of *Culture and Anarchy* is similar to Joyce's relocation of the elements in Wagner's vision in *Siegfried* (See my text Chp. 10, pp. 160-62). Arnold reasons beauty as sweetness and intelligence as light. Joyce sees the beautiful as the truth of being and subscribes to St. Thomas' definition, "*Pulcra sunt quae visa placent.*" Sweetness hardly covers esthetic apprehensions of all kinds. Joyce sees intelligence as the begettor of creative living through the phantasm born in the flesh. Arnold uproots the seed of spiritual anarchy through fusing the best of the two worlds: Hellenism, the Greek impulse to develope the whole man, and Hebraism, the Hebrew bent to develope the conscience of man. Joyce dissolves the spiritual paralysis of man through fusing two entities proper to man's nature: the intellect seeing the intelligible law in all things cooperates with the flesh, in which imagination operates, to perform an ascent to consciousness. Arnold's "free play of consciousness" becomes in Joyce an operative consciousness whose name

through poetry is conscience: judgment. Joyce's use of Arnold in *Circe* is parody. A major effect of the parody is the suggestion that Stephen Dedalus in his reach for self knowledge sees himself as a feeder of the "old man", Virag, who lives on grass. Drunk or sober, through the high sounding protest of all that precedes in Stephen's personal history, he is like an Arnold preaching sweetness and light whereas he should have been making art to reveal being and arranging the intelligible to illuminate it. Joyce's laws of creation are formed in the scholastic discipline. Arnold's laws for creative living are in no particular discipline, for he "distrusted rigid systems of thought." See *Culture and Anarchy*, ed. J. Dover Wilson (Cambridge: University Press, 1957), p. xxxv. Joyce's law is formed in the nature of man as he knows it to be with the help of St. Thomas and through the truth of poetry.

23. Harry Levin, *James Joyce* (Norfolk: New Directions Press, 1941), p. 87.

24. *Les Lauriers son coupés*, Dujardin's novel of 1887 from which Joyce claimed he derived the idea for the interior monologue. Richard Ellmann, p. 99, observes Joyce's fondness for the minor voice: "But Mangan was still unknown among the students, and Joyce insisted that he take his place among the literary saints. Five years later he was to make a more quixotic effort to bring Mangan to the notice of the Italians, and in later life he urged on the reputations of other obscure or forgotten writers like Svevo and Dujardin with the same zeal."

25. Marvin Magalaner and Richard Kain, *Joyce, The Man, the Work, The Reputation* (New York: New York University Press, 1956), p. 155.

26. Frank Budgen, *The Making of Ulysses* (London: Grayson, 1934), p. 108.

27. Arthur Knight, *The Liveliest Art* (New York: Mentor, 1957), p. 44.

28. Theodore Huff, *Charlie Chaplin* (New York: Henry Shuman, 1951), p. 44.

29. Contract for the Volta Theater in the Cornell Collection written in Italian.

30. Letter to Stanislaus, December 28, 1904, Cornell Collection.

31. Notebook, 1904-1914, Cornell Collection.

32. Ellmann, p. 624. Lucia's article, "Charlot", was consulted by Peter Cotes and Thelma Niklaus in the making of their book, *The Little Fellow*, The Life and Work of Charles Spencer Chaplin (New York: Philosophical Library, 1951), p. 157. Mr. Ellmann, p. 379, reads Bloom literally as "the decent man who, in his pacific way, combats narrowmindedness, the product of fear and cruelty," and, p. 384, "Joyce was not a propagandist for better treatment of minorities. The conception of the likable Jew attracted without overwhelming him. He decided to make Bloom amiable and even noble in a humdrum sort of way, but to save him from sentimentality by making him also somewhat absurd as a convert, a drifter, a cuckold. His remarks make clear that the two characteristics of the Jews which especially interested him were their chosen isolation, and the close family ties which were perhaps the result of it." But this is struggle to under-

stand Joyce's Bloom without Joyce's poetry. The meaning of Lucia's impersonation and her article escapes Mr. Ellmann.

33. See my text n. 4, p. 177.

34. See A. Walton Litz, *The Art of James Joyce* (London: Oxford University Press, 1961), p. 52: "It should be obvious from the passages cited in this chapter that Joyce, in revising *Ulysses*, ran the danger of placing disproportionate emphasis on the *schema* of the novel. The analogy between Bloom's adventures in the newspaper office and Ulysses' at the isle of Aeolus is a secondary aspect of the episode, and the various correspondences (Colour, Art, Organ) are less important than the dissection of Irish public life or the development of Bloom's character." Chaplin in Bloom illuminates the Schema as a space-time chart Joyce made for himself to establish psychic similarities between Odysseus and Charlie to make Bloom. (See Beach copy of Schema in end cover).

35. *Finnegans Wake*, pp. 185-6. Mr. Ellmann uses this passage from the *Wake* to introduce Chap. XXII, "The Backgrounds of Ulysses." The passage contains a typographical error which in itself is not unusual in printed matter. But this word is the epiphanic one in the passage: *squirtscreend*. In Mr. Ellmann's book the "s" is omitted within the word making *squirt* plus *creened* a meaningless term. *Squirt* and *screen* make excellent cinema sense.

36. Huff, p. 50.

37. James Agee, "Comedy's Greatest Era," *Life*, September 3, 1949. See also *Agee on Film* (New York: McDowell, Obolensky, 1958). See my text p. 15 for a discussion of Joyce's Letter to Nora telling her he cannot enter the social order except as a vagabond.

38. Gilbert, p. 53.

Chapter II.

1. *The Divine Comedy*, trans. Laurence Binyon (New York: Viking Press, 1947), p. 141, 11. 81-109.

2. *Ibid.*, p. 142, 11. 133-35.

3. Alfred Lord Tennyson, *Ulysses*, 11. 69-70.

4. Borach, 325.

5. Notebook on Dreams (1916) in Cornell Joyce Collection.

6. *Stephen Hero*, p. 77. This is a passage from Stephen's essay, "Art and Life", which he presents to the Literary and Historical Society at the University. Cf.

"Drama and Life", the essay Joyce read before the Literary and Historical Society of University College in 1900, *The Critical Writings of James Joyce,* eds. Ellsworth Mason and Richard Ellmann (New York: Viking Press, 1959), pp. 38-47. The real essay is transformed for *Stephen Hero* by disengaging the subtle soul of its image in real existence and giving it a new office. The paragraph just cited on p. 30 is an aspect of that soul.

7. Teilhard de Chardin, *The Phenomenon of Man* (New York: Harper, 1959), p. 226. This is one of the great new realities in modern thought by one of the most distinguished thinkers and scientists of the twentieth century. Through his insight as biologist and paleontologist, Chardin sets forth the way in which the Christian position is reconciled with the fact of evolution. Father Teilhard de Chardin, a Jesuit Priest [1881-1955], all of whose major works are posthumus, records the spiritual animation of his scientific work, *Phenomenon,* in a short philosophic treatise, *The Divine Milieu* (New York: Harper & Bro., 1960). Joyce was in Paris at the same time Chardin was attached to the Sorbonne. See my text, p. 115 for possible significance of their working at the same time.

8. S. H. Butcher and A. Lang, *The Odyssey of Homer* (London: Macmillan & Co., 1917), p. 150.

9. St. Thomas Aquinas, *Summa Theologica,* trans. Fathers of the English Dominican Province (New York: Benziger, 1947), I, q. 79, a. 13. In Intro. Pt. II of the present volume St. Thomas' doctrine on conscience and its relation to Joyce's poetry of conscience is discussed.

10. See Chardin, p. 263 for discussion of the gradual evolution of spirit from matter.

Chapter III.

1. Chardin, p. 217. Joyce wrote "Drama and Life", (see n. 6, Chp. II) when he was eighteen years old, twenty years before the possibility of coming into contact with the mind of Chardin. The similarity of their view is all the more striking when we compare the early Joyce with the general trend of Chardin's vision in its space-time sense: "Life we must accept as we see it before our eyes, men and women as we meet them in the real world, not as we apprehend them in the world of faery. The great human comedy in which each has share, gives limitless scope to the true artist, to-day as yesterday and as in years gone. The forms of things, as the earth's crust, are changed. The timbers of the ships of Tarshish are falling asunder or eaten by the wanton sea; time has broken into the fastnesses of the mighty; the gardens of Armida are become as treeless wilds. But the deathless passions, the human verities which so found expression then, are indeed deathless, in the heroic cycle, or in the scientific age, *Lohengrin,* the drama of which unfolds itself in a scene of seclusion, amid halflights, is not

an Antwerp legend but a world drama. *Ghosts,* the action of which passes in a common parlour, is of universal import — a deepset branch on the tree, Igdrasil, whose roots are struck in earth, but through whose higher leafage the stars of heaven are glowing and astir. It may be that many have nothing to do with such fable, or think that their wonted fare is all that is of need to them. But as we stand on the mountains today, looking before and after, pining for what is not, scarcely discerning afar the patches of open sky; when the spurs threaten, and the track is grown with briers, what does it avail that into our hands we have given us a clouded cane for an alpenstock, or that we have dainty silks to shield us against the eager, upland wind?" *Critical Writings,* p. 45.

2. *Charlie Chaplin* (New York: Henry Shuman, 1951), p. 35.

3. *Ibid.,* p. 27.

4. Gilbert Seldes, *Seven Lively Arts* (New York: Sagamore, 1957), p. 45. Seldes' gift copy to Joyce in 1924 now in "The Personal Library of James Joyce" at the University of Buffalo is uncut.

5. Robert Payne, *Great God Pan* (New York: Hermitage House, 1955), p. 146. This book contains many reports and some quotations from Chaplin gathered while Mr. Payne was writing the book.

6. In a letter to Nora, December 23, 1909, during the Volta Cinema venture, Joyce feels only the sadness of life: he speaks of his heart as quiet and sorrowful as he stares at the words he writes her; the letter confesses that his weaknesses are many, that he is sinful, jealous, selfish, generous, but not deceitful; that he is a child; that he needs protection from her from the storms of the world. In the next seven years he achieves a view about life's sadness; it becomes the comedy he envisions in his early essay, "Drama and Life": 'the great human comedy in which each has share.' *Critical Writings,* p. 45.

7. In Richard Wagner's opera, *Siegfried.*

8. See Random House *Ulysses,* pp. x-xiv.

9. Agee's brilliant criticism of *Monsieur Verdoux* in his posthumous work, *Agee on Film,* Vol. I, pp. 254, 288, 370 puts it properly in the Chaplin tradition, "to give his century the truest portrait of the upright citizen."

10. Huff, p. 84.

11. Seldes, p. 36.

12. Payne, p. 161.

13. *Ibid.,* p. 145.

14. *Ibid., p.* 144.

15. Seldes, p. 35.

16. Huff, p. 63.

17. *Ibid.*, p. 8. St. John Ervine writing in the *Observer*, September 20, 1925, explores Chaplin's art: "M. Bergson has defined laughter as the imposition of the mechanical upon the living. Mr. Chaplin illustrates the Bergsonian belief by his acting. The whole of his method consists in treating the absurd as if it were the commonplace. The more monstrous the fact becomes, the more determined Mr. Chaplin is to treat it as an ordinary event. He has other qualities. . . ." Among them, Mr. Ervine lists his nervous, disarming smile; the constant suggestion of the small boy timorously arming himself against authority and valiantly carrying out desperate enterprises with a sinking heart; his air of pathetic loneliness; the quickness with which he can silence a laughing crowd and compel it to be pitiful; his persistent humanity in grotesque circumstances. "His pathos does not dissolve the audience into tears; it is better than that sort of pathos. It is the sort that suddenly seizes the mind and alters direction compelling those who are bent on cruelty to be as bent on kindliness. . . . All the clowns of time have remembered this fact, that the longings of humanity can be expressed either in laughter or in sorrow, and have not forgotten that the guffaw is only another sort of sob."

18. *Ibid.*

19. Chaplin said this to Robert Payne when Mr. Payne was gathering material for *Great God Pan*. In an interview with George West in 1923 Chaplin said of Charlie, "He knows it so well that he can laugh at himself and pity himself a little." The "little" in the films is the time it takes to shrug, hop and go jauntily over the horizon.

20. Gilbert, *Letters*, p. 152. The question will naturally arise as to why Budgen paints Bloom as a tall, slender man with sensitive intellectual face and perfectly proper mien. Notes for the answer would be gathered under two headings: *Budgen sees Bloom as Joyce* and *Budgen does not see Bloom as Clown*. But what he made of this letter from Joyce it is hard to say. It would seem from the evidence of descriptive necessity in the *Making of Ulysses* that Mr. Budgen appreciates *Ulysses* more than he understands how to talk about it in words.

Chapter IV.

1. In Myron C. Nutting's studio in Paris. The drawing is printed in Richard Ellmann's *James Joyce*, Plate X between pp. 272-73.

2. *Stephen Hero*, p. 78.

3. *Ibid.*

4. Huff, p. 86.
5. Malcolm MacLennon, *A Pronouncing and Etymological Dictionary of the Gaelic Language* (Edinburgh: John Grant, 1925), p. 312.
6. The newsboys sing *We are the boys of Wexford* as Bloom dashes out. It is logical to suppose they continue to sing as they follow him.
7. Called a derby on p. 70.
8. *American Magazine* (November, 1918), 34.
9. Payne, p. 289.

Chapter V.

1. Ellmann, pp. 385-6. Mr. Ellmann locates many living people from whose personality and character Joyce drew accidents for his Bloom. Bloom is not a clown in Mr. Ellmann's view.
2. Sylvia Beach, *Shakespeare and Company* (New York: Harcourt, Brace & Co., 1959), p. 89.
3. The date with Boylan is at four in the afternoon.
4. *Ulysses,* pp. 260, 275.
5. See p. 18 of my text for contents of Joyce's letter to Nora from Dublin, August 7, 1909.
6. Agee, p. 9.
7. No doubt Joyce expected his readers to make the connection, but the difficulty was Chaplin did not gather an intellectual audience until after *Ulysses* made its reputation, In a letter to Stanislaus, November 19, 1904, Joyce shows a Bloom tendency when he cuts the letter short because Nora is trying on a new pair of drawers at the wardrobe.
8. Minnie Maddern Fiske [1865-1932], American actress cited by Eva Le Gallienne, *Six Plays by Hendrik Ibsen* (New York: Random, 1957), p. xxiii, as one of the actresses of genius who portrayed the great Ibsen heroines. Mrs. Fiske's Ibsen performances would make Joyce aware of her.
9. Arthur Knight, *The Liveliest Art* (New York: New American Library, 1957), p. 44.
10. Chardin, p. 257. The "Omega Point" is the point toward which humanity converges according to the evolutionary character of the world. It began in the

fullness of Alpha; it goes toward completion in Omega. Chardin's Omega Point could well be the intelligibility of Bloom's journey. See also Louis Gillet, *Claybook for James Joyce* (London: Willard-Schuman, 1958), p. 113.

11. Bloom's degree of self-knowledge is measured here by his awareness of the calypso enchantment cast upon him by "nymph". It has acted as a pillar of cloud making him invisible by day, and the inference is ironic, of course, and funny. Like the ancient Hebrews Bloom is one of God's chosen; they were hidden from the enemy by a pillar of cloud so they could progress to the promised land in safety; Bloom's pillar of cloud hides him from himself, his worst enemy. It is funny in the permissive buffoonry of the clown wherein guffaw is another form of sob. An added perspective comes in linking Bloom to Stephen who, "At times as he walked through the streets of Dublin he felt that he was really invisible." See p. 15 of my text.

12. Ellmann, p. 379, 382.

13. *Charlie Chaplin,* p. 57.

14. See Ernst Cassirer, *Language and Myth,* trans. Susanne K. Langer (New York: Harper & Bros., 1946), p. 92: "Here one is reminded forcefully of the principle which might be called the basic principle of verbal as well as mythic "metaphor" — the principle of *pars pro toto.* It is a familiar fact that all mythic thinking is governed and permeated by this principle. Whoever has brought any part of a whole into his power has thereby acquired power, in the magical sense, over the whole itself. What significance the part in question may have in the structure and coherence of the whole, what function fulfills, is relatively unimportant — the mere fact that it is or has been a part, that it has been connected with the whole, no matter how casually, is enough to lend it the full significance and power of that greater unity. For instance, to hold magical dominion over another's body one need only attain possession of his pared nails or cut-off hair, his spittle or his excrement; even his shadow, his reflection or his footprints serve the same purpose. The Pythagoreans still observe the injunction to smooth the bed soon after arising so that the imprint of the body, left upon the mattress could not be used to the owner's detriment. Most of what is known as "magic of analogy" springs from the same fundamental attitude; and the very nature of this magic shows that the concept in question is not one of mere analogy, but of a real identification." At this point in the novel Stephen's flesh is liberated; he has gone off with resounding footsteps on the heavenborn earth after an understanding with the Flesh. Mr. Bloom when he feels Boylan's form in his bed reasons discursively to the best solution concerning him. He gains power over him through mythical thought liberated: he not Boylan will master Molly.

15. The typescript for *Hades* at the University of Buffalo (VB4 in "An Annotated Catalogue of the James Joyce Manuscripts and Letters in the Lockwood Memorial Library of the University of Buffalo," Doctoral Dissertation, Peter Spiel-

berg, 1961, is dated 1918-1921 and contains the correction which results in the illuminative word; "Browbeaten" is crossed out and "chapfallen" is added:

chapfallen,
"Browbe?/ten Mr. Bloom, ^ drew behind a few paces so as not to overhear."

Joyce added Chaplin touches to both the typescript and galleysheets of *Ulysses*: *i.e.*, "stork legs" (65) appears in typescript but "stubbing his toes against the broken commode" was added to the sentence in the galley, for it does not appear in the handwritten manuscript at the Rosenbach Museum in Philadelphia. Mr. Bloom's clown flesh description, "You'll feel a different man." (644) is added to the typescript. "O please, Mr. Policeman, I'm lost in the wood." (59) is added to the galleysheet, for it is not in the Rosenbach Manuscript. "Sandow's exercises" (61) appears in the galleysheet probably as an extension of, "Well, I am here now.", the first use of the Chaplin, "I am here to-day." "Sandow's" is not in the Rosenbach Manuscript in this passage. "This is my body." and "in a womb of warmth," and "lemonyellow: his navel, bud of flesh: and saw . . ." (85) are all added to the galleysheet and missing from the Rosenbach manuscript. See A. Walton Litz, *The Art of James Joyce* (London: Oxford University Press, 1961) for a study of Joyce's artistic method of work. Mr. Litz traces from handwriting through to printed manuscript the essential evolution of *Ulysses* and *Finnegans Wake.*

Chapter VI.

1. Sergei Eisenstein, *Film Form* (New York: Harcourt, 1949), p. 35. See *Explorations* 8 (October 1957). This Ford Grant series of journals called "Studies in Culture and Communication" published at the University of Toronto, ed. by Edmund Carpenter and Marshall McLuhan devotes Number 8, the last issue, to "Exploring the Word". See Items 1-24, Mr. McLuhan's contribution, which are Joyce inspired.

2. *Ibid.* Sharaku, the Japanese Daumier, is an eighteenth century printmaker.

3. See *A Portrait of the Artist as a Young Man*, p. 258.

4. *Ibid.* Stephen Dedalus levels the "scullery-maid" charge against the Church; that the image surges up from Bloom as witness is one of the innumerable ways Joyce has of identifying Stephen with Bloom and with himself in so far as he is his own model for both characters.

5. *Finnegans Wake* is of course built on Irish myth. Artistic consciousness as rendered in *A Portrait* complexifies through *Ulysses* and achieves a *sensus plenior* in the *Wake.*

6. Aristotle, *De Anima,* ii. 1. 412 a 20-21.

7. St. Thomas, I, q. 76, a. 5.

8. Words in brackets mine.

Chapter VII.

1. Charles H. Taylor, Jr., "The Obstacles to Odysseus' Return: Identity and Consciousness in "The Odyssey," *Yale Review,* Vol. L, No. 4 (1961), 580.

2. See Claude Tresmontant, *Pierre Teilhard de Chardin* (Baltimore: Helicon Press, 1959) and Nicolas Corte, *Pierre Teilhard De Chardin* (New York: Macmillan, 1960), two studies valuable for their examination of Chardin's message in *Phenomenon of Man.*

3. "Black Maria" is used twice in the *Circe* scenario: 428, 475. Edison's "Black Maria", the world's first film studio, which he built near his West Orange laboratories in 1893 certainly comes to mind. As "paddywagon" in the International Film Market, it did deliver some trespassers to jail. Joyce was not unaware of the legal complications concerning film use nor of the vice of pirating. In a letter to Stanislaus, December 22, 1909 (Cornell Collection) he directs his brother to place a notice in the newspaper which will include an allusion to him (James) as the proprietor of an Edison & Americano enterprise, The Volta Cinematograph. Stanislaus is not to mention the American affiliation.

Chapter VIII.

1. *Symposium* (Discourse of Diotima), 205, trans. Jacques Maritain, *Creative Intuition in Art and Poetry* (New York: Pantheon Books, 1953), pp. 88-89.

2. *Ibid.,* p. 89.

3. *Stephen Hero,* p. 78. See *Intro.* I of my text for the Joyce esthetic principle governing artistic method.

4. When *Ulysses* was published in 1922, the Chaplin odyssey had reached its Ithaca in *The Kid* (1921). Chaplin reached world limelight by artistic merit at this point in his career. The adroitness of the epiphany here with its thin disguise of the name, "Charlie," spelled with an "ey" should have alerted readers of the first edition.

5. In the *Nestor* episode, (*U.* 35), Stephen describes God to Mr. Deasy as "a shout in the street." This is the poet's mythical thought in the process of liberation as the novel begins. Here in *Circe* Stephen suffers self knowledge; it leads him to illumination on the image of God in man and therefore to God Himself.

6. Plato's *mousike* originally meant an art of the Muses through *mousa,* a Muse. Joyce uses the two words as one to attract dependent images to the larger Platonic concept. For example: musicroom as the room in which Stephen Dedalus plays the pianola; musicroom as room of [*sic*] muses whose errors are never glorified; musicroom as music in a room of sick muses; musicroom as musi (muse) and *crom* (adj., Gael.) for *base* (in the moral sense) and *circle* (n. Gael). In the fullest sense the muse inspires the poet to create the poetry of conscience in this room.

7. Gr. *basilikos* (royal) and L. *gramen* (grass) and L. *-atus* (-ate as in potentate, official), whence official royal grasseater through the following action of the lawnmowers. Whoever feeds Virag grass aids and abets his cause which we come to see is not holy.

8. Zoe had said to Bloom just before they entered the musicroom, "Talk away till you're black in the face" (488). Now the being within him shows a coal-black throat.

9. A pun on pussy willow to establish metaphor in the Virag scene. He culminates in putrefaction after which he screws off his head.

Chapter IX.

1. Vernon J. Bourke, *Augustine's Quest for Wisdom* (Milwaukee: Bruce, 1944), p. 283. The quotation is from Augustine's *De Civitate Dei,* XXII, 24; II, 625-631.

2. *Portrait,* p. 255. See p. 23 of my text for Joyce's notebook entry under "Esthetic".

3. Neumann, p. 121.

4. *Stephen Hero,* p. 77.

5. *Portrait,* p. 243.

6. *Portrait,* p. 243.

7. *Portrait,* p. 245.

8. *Ibid.*, p. 248.

9. *Stephen Hero,* p. 80.

10. See James H. Robb, "Intelligere Intelligentibus est Esse," *An Etienne Gilson Tribute* (Milwaukee: Marquette University Press, 1961), pp. 209-227. Mr. Robb's revolutionary article demonstrates from St. Thomas' texts on the Agent Intellect in the *Summa Theologica* that the Thomistic extension of Aristotle's doctrine that man is a rational animal is properly that man is an incarnate spirit.

11. The Cornell Joyce Collection, Notebook 1904-1914 (Scholes No. 25).

12. *Portrait,* p. 196.

13. Listed as *Busy Day* and as *A Woman,* filmed in 1914.

14. *Ulysses* takes place Thursday, June 16, 1904. Stephen's answer foreshadows his symbolic birth. He will come to terms with his flesh: he will unite with Bloom. June 16, 1904 is the probable date Joyce fell in love with Nora Barnacle. See Ellmann, p. 162.

15. *Portrait,* p. 112.

16. Florry's line here is from Joyce's Notebook on his personal dreams and their interpretation (1916), Cornell Collection.

17. Chaplin's masterpiece of 1925. *The Gold Rush* is beyond Joyce's reach for *Ulysses* but prefaced by innumerable dances in other films.

18. Chaplin and the lamp girl. See p. 76 of my text.

19. Butcher and Lang, p. 170.

20. See Richard Kain, *Fabulous Voyager* (Chicago: University of Chicago Press, 1947), p. 289.

Chapter X.

1. German for womanicity.

2. See *The Two-Edged Sword* (Milwaukee: Bruce, 1955), Chp. VI and *passim.*

3. John L. McKenzie, S.J., "Myth and the Old Testament," *Catholic Biblical Quarterly,* XXI (1959) 281.

4. Cassirer, *Language and Myth,* p. 98.

5. See McKenzie, pp. 97-100.

6. Neumann, p. 10.

7. Ellmann, p. 390.

8. *A James Joyce Miscellany*, Second Series (Carbondale: Southern Illinois University, 1959), p. xvi. The forthcoming volume of letters from the Cornell Collection should remove doubt.

9. *Portrait*, p. 299.

10. *Stephen Hero*, p. 76.

11. Budgen, p. 107.

12. Cf. Wyndham Lewis, *Time and Western Man* (Boston, Beacon Press, 1957), Chp. XVI. See also Hugh Kenner, *Dublin's Joyce* (Bloomington: Indiana University Press, 1956), p. 109 for an extension of Mr. Lewis' insight that Stephen Dedalus is a prig. Mr. Kenner's conclusion is that Stephen is no artist at all and that Joyce's *Portrait* is ironic. See William T. Noon, S.J., *Joyce and Aquinas* (New Haven: Yale University Press, 1957), p. 22. Stephen Dedalus is "a putative artist"; it is but a short step for Father Noon to discard *A Portrait* altogether: "One might almost say that the two significant novels of Joyce (*Ulysses* and the *Wake*) are no more than an effort to put into practice the canons of art, static and contemplative, for which Stephen Dedalus is allowed to express a preference in the *Portrait* (p. 86). Kevin Sullivan, *Joyce Among the Jesuits* (New York: Columbia University Press,1958), p. 5, denies Joyce is Stephen Dedalus: "But, above all, this study should lay the ghost of Stephen Dedalus and preclude any further reading of *Stephen Hero* or the *Portrait* as either actual or "spiritual" autobiography. Mr. Sullivan refuses to take Joyce on his own terms, a peculiar paralysis of some Joyce scholars who like Mr. Sullivan have gathered valuable information but employ it to alien ends.

13. Hugh Kenner's astute analysis of much of Joyce's work in *Dublin's Joyce* is marred by his total rejection of Stephen Dedalus and his insistence that Joyce is irreversibly ironic in his *Portrait of the Artist.* The logical conclusion of such a position is that the lyric greatness of *A Portrait* must also go. To condemn Stephen Dedalus as an "aesthete" (p. 112) and yet to use his esthetic theory seriously as Mr. Kenner must to discuss Joyce's work is a contradiction. The chapter in question is 8, "The Portrait in Perspective".

14. *Language and Myth*, p. 98.

15. *De Anima*, ii. 11. 422b 18-19.

16. *Ibid*., 9. 421a 23-26.

17. *Summa Theologica*, I, q. 76, a. 5.

18. *Stephen Hero*, p. 30.

19. Edith Hamilton, *Mythology* (New York: Little Brown & Co., 1942), p. 308.

20. Bernard Shaw, *The Perfect Wagnerite* (London: Grant Richards, 1898), p. 32.

21. *Ibid.*, p. 48.
22. Neumann, pp. 379-80.
23. *Portrait,* p. 199.
24. *Ibid.*, p. 200.
25. See poetic experience and poetry, *Portrait,* pp. 254-63.
26. Ernest Newman, *Stories of the Great Operas* (New York: Garden City, 1930), p. 198.
27. Ellmann, p. 474.
28. Mary and Padriac Colum, *Our Friend James Joyce* (New York: Doubleday, 1958) p. 9.
29. See Kain, Chp. VIII and end cover map of Dublin.
30. Joyce was apostate when he died.
31. See John Henry Raleigh, "Who Was M'Intosh," *James Joyce Review,* 3, Nos. 1-2 (1959) 59-62. See also John O. Lyons, "The Man in the Macintosh," *A James Joyce Miscellany,* Second Series, ed. Marvin Magalaner, pp. 133-38. Both articles say M'Intosh is Mr. Duffy of "A Painful Case," *Dubliners.*
32. *Ulysses* takes place on one day; for Bloom and Stephen it is a separation from darkness or a wake of day.
33. The pun from Goethe's *Faust* makes Molly intelligible in comic terms as Mephistopheles is intelligible in tragic terms.
34. Gilbert, *Letters,* p. 170.
35. See Edmund Curtis, *A History of Ireland* (New York: Methuen, 1936), Chp. I for Milesian and Firbolg origin of the Celtic nation. See also *The Critical Writings of James Joyce,* p. 166 for Joyce's use of the terms.
36. "Art has the gift of tongues." This sentence is in Joyce's handwriting in Notebook 1904-1914, Cornell Collection.
37. Critics since Larbaud and Gilbert have insisted that Bloom seeks a son and Stephen a father. They base their contentions variously on Homer and Joyce. Odysseus' main search is a homeward route where first his wife and then his son will appease his heart. Odysseus, moreover, has not lost his son; he has lost his way home. Joyce admired the human traits in the *Odyssey;* as he told Georges Borach in 1917, "I am almost afraid to treat such a theme; it's overwhelming." The total humanity of the Homeric vision attracted him. The father motif in the *Odyssey* was only one of many that moved him.
38. See Shaw, p. 58. Erda, Wotan's mother, prophesies his downfall, and he confesses that he rejoices in his doom.

Conclusion

1. Cf. Levin, pp. 17, 19 and *passim*; W. Y. Tindall, *James Joyce* (New York: Scribner's, 1950), Chp. I and *passim*; Kain, Chps. I-IV; Kenner, Chp. 1; Kristian Smidt, *James Joyce and The Cultic Use of Fiction* (Oslo: Akademisk Forlag, 1955), Chp. III. This is a representative sampling of conscientious Joyce criticism where relationship between Joyce's two books exists indirectly. Sequelty is inferred. The interested Joyce reader will gain from the above critics' works if he goes to them with the established premise that *Ulysses* succeeds from *A Portrait of the Artist as a Young Man.* For direct statement on sequel and manuscript evidence see Litz, p. 2.

2. See Victor M. Hamm, "The Ontology of the Literary Work of Art: Roman Ingarden's "Das Literarische Kuntswerk," *The Critical Matrix* (1961), 171-209. A paraphrase of the Polish phenomenologist's treatise on the literary work of art heretofore untranslated and examined in detail by Mr. Hamm. For metaphysical reality in the literary work see p. 183 and *passim.*

3. Among the profanities: (1) Special pleading for minorities such as Jew or Catholic. Religion plays a vital role in Joyce's art, but he does not debate theological questions. He creates characters who are concerned with theology, but poetic knowledge shows Joyce their intellect and flesh. (2) Special pleading for the chasm that exists between the artist and society. Joyce is not concerned with manners, customs or attitude within eras: he is concerned with the unalterable laws governing the men and women that make up society. (3) Special pleading for the role of the artist. (4) Special pleading for his "post Christianity". Joyce does not plead for special views of reality. He creates the truth of the being of the visible world. To understand this, the critic must see *being.*

4. *Literary Essays of Ezra Pound,* ed. T. S. Eliot (Norfolk: New Directions, 1954), p. 406.

5. See Edmund Wilson's review of *Ulysses* in *New Republic,* XXVI, No. 396 (1922), 164. But there is this unconscious Chaplin description of Bloom: ". . . poor Bloom, with his generous impulses and his attempts to understand and master life, is the epic symbol of reasoning man, humiliated and ridiculous, yet extricating himself by cunning from the spirits which seek to destroy him;" Wilson's Chaplin criticism begins about 1925.

6. *Ibid.,* p. 165. In time Mr. Wilson was to correct early impressions and modify his position on the Homeric parallels. See "James Joyce," *Axel's Castle* (New York: Scribner's 1931), pp. 191-237.

7. See Litz, p. 21. "The many Homeric parallels not included in the final text of

Ulysses are significant, since they illustrate how much more important the Homeric background was for Joyce than it is to the reader. Invaluable to Joyce as a ready-made guide for the ordering of his material, the correspondences with the *Odyssey* do not provide a major level of meaning in the completed work. Ezra Pound was right in his early judgment of the Homeric framework:" Without the Chaplin myth it is difficult to grasp Joyce's method of establishing psychic similarities to create space-time man.

8. In *Summa Theologica,* I, q. 79, a. 13, St. Thomas quotes Jerome, Basil and Damascene to support his doctrine on conscience. For these definitions by the Fathers, turn to p. 100 in this book. Two of the insights pertain to Joyce's uncreated conscience, those of Basil and Damascene. St. Basil the Great, Bishop of Caesarea (329-379) in *Homilia in Principium Proverbiorum,* P.G. xxxi, 405, develops his thought on conscience in this mode: "For since we have in us a certain natural judgment (*judicium quoddam naturale*) by which we distinguish good from evil, it is necessary for us in choosing those things which are to be done, to judge rightly of these things, and like a judge who passes judgment on contraries with an equitable and extremely just mind, both to pursue virtue and to condemn vice." The verse continues . . . "and the counsels of the wicked are deceitful." *Ibid.,* 408: "Therefore, according to Solomon himself, 'The thoughts of the just are judgments.' One must act diligently so that within, in the secret forum of one's thoughts we make right judgments of things, and that we possess a mind like a scales which without any inclination weighs whatever is to be done. When any commandment and the vice opposed to it are presented to your judgment, yield the victory to the law of God rather than to sin. Is judgment to be made between an inordinate appetite for possessions and moderation? Pronounce judgment against covetousness of things not your own, give the stronger reckoning to virtue. Is there a conflict between disapprobation and gentleness? Inspire shame with disapprobation, and prefer gentleness . . . . . . Are deceit and simplicity, courage and timidity, prudence and foolishness, justice and injustice, modesty and immodesty, and, in short, any virtue to undergo judgment in the face of any vice? Then show the rectitude of your judgments in the hidden judgment of your soul, and holding the precept as a judge's counsel, show your hatred of evil, turning away from sin, and preferring the virtues. For if you act so that in every one of your actions those things which are better prevail, you will be blessed "In that day when the Lord will judge the secrets of men according to our Gospel, and their thoughts between themselves accusing or also defending one another" (*Rom.* II, 15,16); nor will you depart condemned on account of any inclination towards evil but you will be honored with the crowns of justice with which you have crowned virtue all the days of your life." Basil's mode is inspirational preaching illuminated by poetic knowledge in service to moral training. Joyce's mode as artist is making men and women who are in the act of ascending to the consciousness of "*judicium quoddam naturale,*" and who are achieving conscience. Basil perceives in the wholeness of mythical thought. Cf. St. Thomas,

I, q. 79, a. 13: "Wherefore, properly speaking, conscience denominates an act." Mythical thought names the object. Joyce perceives through mythical thought in service to his making.

St. John Damascene, Priest and Doctor of the Church, pronouncing on conscience three centuries after Basil, was born about 676 and died between 754 and 787. St. Thomas quotes largely from Damascene's *De Fide Orthodoxa,* IV, 22, (PG 94, 1197 seqq.): "On the Law of God and the Law of Sin": The good is whatever God wills. God is good and He is more sublime than any goodness; and likewise His will is good. For, finally, that which God wills is good. Now the law (*lex*) is that precept by which we learn this: that remaining in this precept we might be situated in the light, *John* I, 1, 7). The transgression of this precept is sin. . . . And so the law of God, mounting up our mind, draws it (the mind) to itself, stimulating our conscience, and this (our conscience) is called the law of our mind: so that the suggestion of the evil one, that is the law of sin, mounting up our fleshly members might not assault us through our mind. For, because we have freely broken the law of God *once,* through the admission of a suggestion by the most evil one, thereafter we have opened to him an access to us, we who have sold ourselves to him through sin. And through this it happens that our body is driven to this quickly and easily. For which reason that odor of sin and the *sense* (sense powers) which resides in the body, whether concupiscence of passion (*voluptas*) is called the law in the members of our flesh. And, therefore, the law of my mind, that is conscience takes pleasure in the law of God, or in His precept, and wills that (*Rom.* VII, 22, 23). But the law of sin, this is a suggestion, through that law, which is in my members, either through the body, and of that part of the mind which is expert in reasoning, is opposed to the law of my mind (*lex mentis meae*), that is, of conscience, and it captivates me (although I will and love the law of God and I am unwilling to sin and turn away from it) on account of an extraordinary mixture, and through the softness and ease of pleasure, as well as through the concupiscence of the body and as I said, the brute parts of the soul, it delights me and leads me on to serve sin. . . . For the Spirit aids our infirmity (*Ibid.,* 26) and gives strength to the law of our mind against that law which is in our members. . . . This is the same as if it were said, He teaches us what is to be said in prayer. From which it follows that the precepts of God cannot be fulfilled except through patience and prayer." (trans. James H. Robb). St. John Damascene unlike Basil does not perceive judgment as a total function of intellect and flesh, but rather a separated faculty independent of the flesh. His discussion confines itself, of course, to the flesh as evil. Basil's mode is poetic; John Damascene's mode in this discussion is moralistic. He seeks a purity away from the flesh which obscures our understanding of his meaning of conscience. Judgment is not possible without the flesh. Basil sees the good of the flesh; John Damascene, only its evil. Joyce's congenial reference to Johannes Damascenus (674) symbolizes Stephen Dedalus' previous misunderstanding of Irish paralysis.

9. Jacques Maritain, *Existence and the Existent* (New York: Doubleday, 1956), p. 26.
10. *Ibid.*, p. 28.

INDEX